INTO EXILE

RONALD SEGAL

INTO EXILE

McGRAW-HILL BOOK COMPANY, INC.
NEW YORK LONDON TORONTO

FIRST PUBLISHED 1963

© 1963 BY RONALD SEGAL

LIBRARY OF CONGRESS CATALOG CARD NO. 63-14559

PRINTED IN GREAT BRITAIN

CONTENTS

FOR MY MOTHER

CHAPTER ONE

CHILDHOOD

Up the slope of Lion's Head that faces the Atlantic climbs the suburb of Fresnaye, protected by an occasional shift of air from the flat heat of the sea front in summer and lifted in the winter from the damp that settles by the sea. Not long ago, at the beginning of the century, it was one huge private estate, which succumbed to the swelling demand for land overlooking the sea and only four miles from the centre of the city. Then, as the price of land in the fashionable suburbs rose, the Fresnaye plots grew smaller, gardens were severed and sold, and the rich – caught between the desire to pick profits seemingly over-ripe and a longing for the status and seclusion of space – moved inland into the shadow of the mountain, to Kenilworth and Constantia. Meanwhile, Woodstock, the closest inland suburb to the city, degenerated into factory and slum. A whole social history of Cape Town could be written round the development of these four suburbs; part of it is contained in the definition of *chutspa*, the Hebrew for 'cheek', that gained currency during my last years at school – a Jew who moved from Woodstock to Kenilworth without first going to Fresnaye. Constantia remained too Gentile for the joke, submitting only with the noisiest reluctance to those Jews whose wealth could sporadically be made to compensate for their connections. Jews never attacked Constantia head-on; they laid stealthy and individual siege to it, after the most careful calculation of the cost.

During the war, when the anti-Semitism of the Nationalist Opposition in Parliament bayed to the call of Mr Eric Louw – now South Africa's Minister of External Affairs – a group of Jewish businessmen asked my father to participate in the purchase of a large Constantia estate then up for sale. My father was Chairman of the Cape Jewish Board of Deputies at the time, and conscious of the genteel grumble against the movement of Jews to Constantia – they were accused of a concerted effort to annex the area – advised against it. For the person he was and the position he held, he was right, I suppose. Murmuring against Jewish infiltration anywhere would only have excited me to the anger of busy promotion. Much of the division between my father and myself later followed these turns. The estate was eventually sold to a Gentile concern, which broke it up into building plots and netted over twenty times the cost price.

I was born at No. 6, Avenue Disandt – all the roads in Fresnaye have French names – in a house that had been called Clonbrook by its builder and which kept its distant name because my parents liked it. It is a lop-sided house, single-storeyed from the road through a passage bearing sitting-room, study, dining-room, kitchen, maid's room and my sister's bedroom, and then – over the lounge and my parents' bedroom – sprouting another storey for the rooms that my two brothers, the white nanny and I variously occupied. The bedrooms opened out into a small veranda, edged by the mauve bougainvillea that climbed from the garden below, overlooking the sea and the suburb that tumbled towards it.

From what age is a child conscious of class? Babies seem to know about money, that it is something to be held fast in the fist and slipped under the pillow; but the sureness of knowing that there is as much of it as one wants, and that having as much as one wants distinguishes from others – how soon do a child's eyes open to that? My earliest memories are of our being rich and, at the same time, of there being something insecure about it, as if the money was there only for as long as I could clutch it in my pocket. Even more persuasive than the large house, and the garden with the two trees in lilac flood at the bottom of the lawn, were the servants, three Coloured, one African, and – above all – the white nurse. In a country where class followed so closely the contours of colour, the possession of a white servant, however young or incompetent she might be, promoted one to membership of a small and shrinking aristocracy. That such possession, indeed, should have been possible at all was a product of the Poor White problem that persisted until the boom days of the second world war and the industrial expansion that succeeded it.

The Anglo-Boer War of 1899–1902 had left the Afrikaner countryside in the northern provinces a smouldering waste, with whites forced either into tenant status on the larger farms or to the towns, where only certain forms of work preserved their dignity. Ever since the introduction of slaves to the Cape in 1658, one year after the first free burgers arrived, manual labour had been a non-white caste mark, degrading and defining, earning over the years the title of 'Kaffir work'. To such forms of employment, with their corresponding deeps of pay, no white would descend; squalor, starvation and a constant clamour for loans, animals and land, were preferable to sinking once and for all under the surface of colour.

The devastation of the countryside, conducted at Kitchener's insistence to starve the Boer guerrillas into surrender, only accelerated an existing drift. In 1716, an official of the Dutch East India Company had complained: 'Every common or ordinary European becomes a gentleman and prefers to be served rather than to serve … the majority of the farmers are not farmers in the real sense of the word, but plantation-owners, and many of them consider it a shame to work with their own hands.' Yet plantation-owners were precisely what only a fraction of the Afrikaners could become.

By the middle of the nineteenth century, the frontiers had been fixed, and the land-hungry could no longer feed themselves by seizing another stretch of the horizon. Farms which began as huge tracts of grazing land, hundreds of square miles sometimes, were split by Roman–Dutch inheritance laws into holdings uneconomically small, often absurdly distant from one another. Yet the smallholders continued to use the wasteful and primitive methods that they had learnt on far larger units, until the little land they had lay exhausted and barren. And this process was speeded by sporadic droughts, pestilence and mineral discoveries that boosted land prices by prospecting and speculation. The Boer General, Deneys Reitz, wrote of these 'poor burgers': 'Our Commando had of late been receiving reinforcements of inferior quality, mostly poor whites from the *burger-erven*, the slum quarters of Pretoria, a poverty-stricken class that had drifted in from the country districts after the great rinderpest epidemic of 1896 – they had become debased by town life, and had so little stomach for fighting that their presence among us was a source of weakness rather than strength.'

A first product of rural poverty was the sprouting of the share-cropper class, families forced off their land to work on farms in return for a share of crops or cattle. Farm labour by wage had already become 'Kaffir work', the preserve of cheap and manageable black labour; and competition soon forced the cropper's share under harsher landlords from two-thirds to a mere one-half, increasing rural poverty still further. The one escape seemed to lie in the towns, and especially the mining areas; but blacks did all the unskilled labour on the gold and diamond fields, at forbiddingly low rates of pay, while artisans from Britain and elsewhere in Europe monopolized skilled labour.

In the Western Cape, the Coloured artisans practised their skills with a discipline and adaptability new to the impoverished rural Afrikaner, who found himself in a business world alien in language and habit and concerned much less with white prestige than with profits. A Ministry of Agriculture estimate in 1917 claimed that more than 105,000 people, or over 8% of the total white population, were living in poverty, while nearly a third of these had fallen into a condition of 'absolute poverty'. By the late 1920s, the Carnegie Poor White Commission judged the number of 'very poor' as somewhere between 220,000 and 300,000, or from 12% to 16% of the white population. And during the severe depression of 1930–1, the proportion climbed to one in five, a frightening figure for a group distinguished – according to the Commission – by conservatism and isolationism, apathy and fatalism, ignorance and indolence and irresponsibility, a lack alike of self-reliance and self-respect.

Though the vast majority of these people continued to consider themselves superior to the non-whites with whom they were increasingly forced to compete for work, it became clear by the early 1920s that economic equality between black and white would inevitably lead to social and political equality as well. The Nationalist-Labour Coalition of 1924 acted with speed, sacrificing – as all its successors have done – the logic of economics to the lunacies of colour. The 'civilized labour policy' guaranteed to the unskilled white worker, mainly in the public services, protected jobs at rates of pay related not to his productivity but to his needs as a 'civilized' person.

In the Prime Minister's Circular No. 5 of 1924, 'civilized labour' was defined as that 'rendered by persons whose standard of living conforms to the standard generally recognized as tolerable from the European standpoint', and 'uncivilized labour' as that 'rendered by persons whose aim is restricted to the bare requirements of the necessities of life as understood amongst barbarous and undeveloped peoples'. Underneath all this cultural cosmetic, of course, the distinction was – as it has remained ever since – starkly racial, providing occupations and wages to whites whose social conduct would degrade a slum and refusing them to blacks of the highest educational status or intellectual level. As Sheila Patterson wrote in *The Last Trek*, 'under these conditions "Kaffir work" becomes acceptable so long as it was not done for Kaffir wages or side by side with Kaffirs.' Between 1921 and 1928, the number of white labourers employed on the railways soared from 4,705 to 15,878, all earning 'civilized' wages of 3s. to 5s. a day with free housing or a housing allowance provided. Naturally, this programme was expensive and wasteful; the replacement of 1,361 'uncivilized' labourers by 'civilized' ones cost £73,508 by the beginning of 1926. But the money was considered well enough spent if it only preserved South Africa's ruling complexion; and all the fingers of government – manipulation of the

customs tariff, the choice of tenders by its departments, direct
subsidies to amenable concerns – were busily employed in
persuading private business to adopt the policy and so contribute to meeting its cost.

I cannot remember that any of my nurses possessed the dis-
tinctive marks of civilization, except perhaps for a proper
acquisitiveness. Two were dismissed for parading in my
mother's clothes so unimaginatively late that my mother got
home before they did, and one absconded with almost the
entire linen cupboard. I remember Greta, a young German
girl, because I kicked her in the shins and fell into a sorrow
afterwards; and I will remember Nellie, an Afrikaner at the
outer edge of twenty, all my life.

Nellie must have been among the last who was born into,
and clambered out of, the Poor White problem; by the time she
left us, at the beginning of the war, white poverty clung only to
the constitutionally irretrievable and a few of the very old. Yet
white poverty still crusts the outlook, like soil in the potato
skin, of many Afrikaners today, a legacy of the degradation
they endured and are so fearful of having to endure again.
Nellie's bearing to colour was rigid, lest a sudden sag should
blur the distinctions of service and return her to a state where
white and black were levelled by economic competition. In the
presence of my parents, she preserved towards our four non-
white servants a quiet assumption of command, breaking out
into shrill abuse or high complaint as soon as my parents were
out of sight and hearing.

Towards my brother Maurice – seven years older than I –
and myself, she was by turns boisterous and blind, ignoring all
but what she felt was absolutely required of her for days on
end and then unaccountably taking complete charge with a
breezy brutality. I remember once, when Maurice, who must
have been eleven or twelve years old at the time, tried to stop
her from slapping me, that she deposited him on the bed,
threw an eiderdown on top of him and then sat firmly on his
head. Her strength was a source of constant dismay to us, and I
early discovered the imprudence of physical disagreement.

Instead, on what I felt to be issues of principle, I conducted sullen campaigns of passive resistance before which she sometimes retreated in puzzled distaste. But her temper was hot and unpredictable, and more often than not she would batter me into a temporary surrender. I loathed her, and passionately pitied the men with whom she so laboriously corresponded each night after putting me to bed. When I expressed this audibly on one occasion, however, I received such a slap that I resolved in future to reserve my compassion for myself.

As the youngest child, I was extravagantly spoiled by my family, but I could never get my parents to believe that Nellie was conducting a reign of terror in their absence. I suppose I must have given a very inadequate picture of persecution; I was certainly uncowed, and my irresistible demands for deference must have persuaded my mother that any discipline I was getting behind her back, where she could not flinch into forbidding it, was probably deserved and productive. I was beginning to think that Nellie was for ever inescapable when my parents returned home inconveniently one night to find her, securely wrapped in my mother's perfume and fur, entertaining one of her friends. Her departure was swift, and all the more celebrated because I was considered too old to need a successor.

Towards my parents Nellie was always equivocal, carefully observing the obedience of her employment but suggesting in her manner to them that she was, after all, white as well – a sort of consort in hegemony – and that there were all sorts of things she would never dream of doing and would regard as a studied insult if asked of her. She somehow managed in addition to imply for me – I cannot think that she tried this on my parents, or she would not have stayed for so long – an obscure superiority to my background, because we were Jews in a country finally hers. I doubt that she ever said anything remotely direct to me, but my mind at that time would have caught and held all the burs it brushed against.

Throughout the 'thirties, Afrikaner nationalism increasingly made use of anti-Semitism to whip the 'volk' towards the

dominion of the future. One of my first political memories is
of pamphlets – they were pink and stridently printed – distributed outside the shops of my father and other prominent
Jewish businessmen by members of the Nazi Greyshirt movement, calling upon the public to boycott foreign businesses,
especially those owned by Jews, and support national-minded
or Afrikaner commerce. Nor was this agitation a thread of the
lunatic fringe. *Die Burger*, Cape Town's Afrikaans daily and
then the mouthpiece of the Nationalist Party leadership, regularly attacked British–Jewish capitalism as the scourge of the
'volk' and invented Hoggenheimer, a bloated figure with
grotesquely Semitic features, with a fat cigar and diamond
rings covering his fatter fingers, as the cartoon accompaniment
to its editorial shrieks. The leader of the Nationalist Party himself, Dr D. F. Malan, had leapt into parliament from the editor-
ship of the paper, and the traffic between Keerom Street, where
Die Burger had its offices, and the Opposition benches in the
House of Assembly nearby, was known to be heavy.

It is not surprising that I should have felt the wealth of my
family as something ambiguous, a stage to stand on, but only
for as long as I could feel it there solidly under my feet. Its
existence was constantly under attack. And so I have grown up,
having to spend money in order to know that I had it, periodically appalled by my extravagance and alternating splurges
with sudden spasms of saving.

The insecurity of South Africa's one hundred thousand-odd
Jewish community has made it perhaps the most vital and at
the same time ignominious in the Diaspora. It has thrown up a
hugely disproportionate percentage of those whites involved
in revolutionary politics, while its public surface is frozen into
a conformity of silence towards apartheid, unbroken even by
those government measures which concern its moral traditions
most closely. Against the Group Areas Act of 1950 – which
empowers the Nationalist government to herd into residential
and even commercial ghettoes different races – organized
South African Jewry in its secular form, as the Board of
Deputies, has made no public protest, sent no deputation of

intercession to the government. When, in 1956, the government hurled through parliament the Native Laws Amendment Act, by which the Minister of Native Affairs was empowered to ban 'mixed' religious services, the Catholic and Protestant religious communities – except for the Dutch Reformed Church, which made its own covert representations – protested publicly and vigorously, many of their leaders threatening to disobey the law as soon as it was put into operation. Yet the synagogues stayed silent, as though any squabble over the freedom of worship was foreign alike to their future and to their past. One of the two Chief Rabbis, it is true, wrote an article criticizing the Act, but he did so in the communal press and emphatically in his 'personal' capacity.

I have often asked the community – in print and from public platform – how it regards itself. For if South African Jewry is a race, as the immigration forms produced by the Department of the Interior proclaim it to be, it should denounce laws of specific race discrimination. And if it is only a religious community, how can it watch in silence any assault upon the right of men to worship as they please? Moral escape might conceivably be found for a community so diffuse and disorganized that no one could reasonably claim for it a significant voice. But South African Jewry is perhaps the most organic and organized community outside of Israel itself, with a Board of Deputies to which almost every communal activity is affiliated. It has its own press and a tradition of legislative lobbying on matters specifically affecting Jewish interests, a Zionist Federation to which the bulk of the community contributes time and money – the *per capita* contribution of South African Jewry to Zionist funds is the highest in the world – and a religious solidarity only brushed by the movements of reform and suffering less from apathy than most of its counterparts in the Diaspora.

It is easy enough to understand, of course, without excusing, the silence of the community. Organized Jewry in South Africa will not clash with the government for precisely the same reason that it has produced so energetic a Zionism.

Caught between the ever-present threat of Afrikaner persecution and the ever-growing possibility of black revolution, it regards its stay in South Africa as temporary, to be secured by sedulously avoiding any provocation of the authorities. Throughout the 'thirties, the most strenuous efforts at acquiring immigration permits for Jewish refugees from Nazi Germany yielded the most meagre results; and when the Hertzog–Smuts government grudgingly agreed to one small shipload, Dr Hendrik Verwoerd, then Professor of Applied Psychology at the University of Stellenbosch and now Prime Minister, accompanied five fellow professors in a deputation to the government to persuade it to change its mind. Even General Smuts, whose reputation as a friend of the Jews has somewhat more substantial backing in fact than his reputation as either a statesman or a philosopher, felt strongly that wide-scale immigration would provide his enemies in Keerom Street with bludgeons to batter him.

South African Jewry cannot forget the experience of the 'thirties; the constant threat that the neo-Nazi element within Afrikanerdom would whip up anti-Semitism into popular violence has left scabs on the group consciousness which no number of current reassurances can peel. And in their scepticism over this at least, South African Jews are right. The preservation of white solidarity under pressure from increasingly clamorous non-white unity has covered Nationalist politics with a thin crust of amiability. Cabinet Ministers visit Israel or attend local receptions and ceremonies, while the Afrikaans press pays proper attention to a national struggle that it claims merely mirrors its own. And, in return, leaders of the Jewish community present occasional tokens of gratitude to members of the government. Yet the antagonism persists, a seething under the surface, requiring only the right opportunity to bubble to the top. When, a few years ago, two Jewish members of the parliamentary opposition attacked forced farm labour in the Eastern Transvaal, the back-benchers of the government hissed and spluttered with anti-Semitic speeches and interjections. And when, in November 1961, Israel supported a resolution for sanctions against South Africa in the United Nations Political Committee, Nationalist politicians and newspapers, with the hot participation of the Prime Minister himself, flourished complaints and threats at the country's whole Jewish population. The Board of Deputies protests the insignificance of such incidents rather too much. Perhaps it knows that severe economic difficulties might deflect the racial hysteria of the Nationalist Party from the non-whites, who cannot credibly be blamed for manipulating the economy in order to destroy Afrikanerdom, towards a white community that can.

From the moment that I began to look at South Africa through political lenses, it seemed to me that the only survival possible for Jewry there depended upon the shaping of a non-racial society. In calling upon Jews as Jews, as I have done despite my family's stiff disapproval, to back the non-white revolutionary movements, I have not pretended that such an alliance would earn the special tolerance of gratitude. An anti-white terror would hardly take breath to discriminate. I have only maintained that racialism, as we have learned by now to platitudinize about freedom, is indivisible. There may, perhaps, be no real future for whites anywhere in Africa. The South African Jew who genuinely believes that, would be well advised to begin his latter-day dispersion at once. I have never believed it. I believe that there is a future for all races in South Africa, but only through the most concerted efforts by all South Africans to keep the techniques of revolution as non-racial as are, at the moment, its objectives. In a society of race rule, Jewry must logically be menaced by racial repression and racial resistance alike. Only a South Africa finally blind to race can give to Jewry the security that it pretends to itself it is purchasing by its silence.

Am I still a Jew? If Jewry is an acknowledgment, then of course I am. My childhood was bounded by Jewish horizons, and trying to escape from them would be like trying to slip over the edge of the world. Yet, if Jewry is a commitment, then I ceased to be a Jew as I crept out of my childhood. As far back as I can remember, the religion had no meaning for me at all, although I went dutifully to synagogue and either edged my way into conversation with my neighbours or bored myself with the bits of translation that I could understand. I studied Hebrew with listless dislike, but since I usually managed to mislead my private tutor into Jewish history, where the glitter of the kings and the blood of the martyrs provided some excitement, I reconciled myself to the requisite one hour a week. My tutor must have been extremely easy to mislead, for I can reach into the attic of my mind and bring down whole armfuls of facts and anecdotes on life under the kings and in the Diaspora. But I can read Hebrew only with the greatest difficulty and write it not at all. Not understanding the prayers, I found the praying even more distasteful than I might otherwise have done and, in spasmodic protest, demanded proper reasons for what I regarded as my enslavement.

The explanations, which supposed that I should behave in the same way that Jewish children had done for thousands of years, seemed to me eloquently irrelevant. I had never given much thought to God, but when I did, I quickly convinced myself that he was unlikely to find all that noisy praying in a foreign language very congenial. The ritual that ringed me about either bored or infuriated me. While the candles were being lit and the prayers pealed over the silver cup of wine every Friday night, I would ache to sit down and start talking, and prohibitions against mixing milk and meat produced an obsession in me to smear my steaks with butter. I drew the attention of my parents to their interminable inconsistencies – that they would eat in restaurants where the meat had not been properly killed or cooked, and would ride and write on the Sabbath while refusing to smoke or play rummy for pennies with me. My whole family was Orthodox, however, despite their temperamental inconsistencies, and roundly condemned all movements of reform. We dutifully trooped to synagogue on the High Festivals and celebrated them afterwards in style, at dinners to which anything from thirty relatives and guests would sit down. The Day of Atone-

ment was approached with awe and observed with rigorous
fasting.

My home itself was a hearth of Jewry, and my whole childhood seems now to have passed at its flames. My grandfather had
emigrated from Lithuania at the end of the last century, staying
in Cape Town for a short while and then moving on to the
German governed territory of South West Africa. After opening a general store in Lüderitz, he had summoned his family, of
which my mother was the eldest child, to join him. Although
he himself was casual and sometimes buccaneering about the
faith, his wife was not; she objected to his appetite for spring-
bok, which he could hardly have been expected to trap and kill
by carefully slitting its throat. Eventually she withdrew to
Cape Town, where she could rigorously control her kitchen,
and my grandfather, on his regular visits, distracted the traffic
by his tempestuous driving. Meanwhile, my mother, together
with the younger of her two brothers, who died during the
great flu epidemic of 1917, embodied their racial loyalties in a
passionate Zionism.

My father had emigrated from a town Polish and Russian by
turns, as a boy of nine, to push a way alone through the commercial undergrowth of Cape Town. Meeting my mother at a
town hall dance at the end of the first world war, he had
snatched her away from a man who helped to console himself
by becoming in time one of the country's biggest dealers
in hide, and within a few months married her. My grandfather, who by then had spread himself over farms, shops and
property in Mariental, the karakul district of South West
Africa, believed that his son-in-law should find his own way
to a similar success. Backed with capital by a shrewd entre-
preneur, my father and two other businessmen joined their
three shops into Ackermans, which speedily multiplied its
branches throughout the country and scooped up much of the
working-class trade. By the time I was born, therefore, on the
14th of July, 1932, my parents were rich enough to travel
widely and devote much of their time to communal concerns.

Although my father had been an active Zionist as a young

man, status and temperament during the 'thirties turned him to the South African situation of Jewry, while my mother only intensified her allegiance to the establishment of a Jewish state. To our home in Fresnaye their friends and associates would come, in a ceaseless flow, to gossip and argue and plan under the deepening sky – world leaders of Zionism whom my mother had met at congresses in Switzerland, Jewish members of parliament involved with my father's work on the Board of Deputies, and business associates who wandered foot-loose through the conversation until they realized that they were being subtly, if assiduously indoctrinated, when they would all at once lapse into deep contemplation of their hands and search feverishly behind their eyes for a polite door by which to leave. Similar talk still goes on in similar homes in South Africa – small square rooms of conversation sealed off from the cries of Africa in the street outside – but it cannot be the same. For then Hitler was in the shadows of the driveway, and the house stood with all its rooms lit, as though watching for the first stone to crash through the windows. I do not try to excuse the tended hedges – there was African anguish and anger on the other side of them, though muted still behind the backs of the police and only very seldom heard on our patch of nervous lawn – but Nazism had forced a way into our lives, admitting at the same time part of the real world around us. It is easy enough to complain that we were seeing it all obliquely, only as Jews; but I can understand how difficult it was in the 'thirties for my parents to see it in any other way.

Although I was sent to bed when allowing me to stay up any longer seemed likely to court social calamity, I was left to talk as much as I liked for as long as I stayed. And by all accounts, I talked with few pauses for breath.

I was, inevitably, disliked with passion by most of my relatives and those friends of my parents who took me at all seriously. To an uncle who berated me for spending the sixpence he had given me entirely on sweets, I contemptuously replied: 'Well, what did you expect me to do? Invest it in property?' He has regarded me ever since as some sort of intricate explosive, to be kept at a distance; when I spent an evening with him at his son's home in Johannesburg three years ago, he sat on the edge of his chair the whole time and looked at me under anxiously half-closed eyes as though he expected me to blow up at any moment. The number of my mother's relationships that I am reputed to have damaged beyond repair strikes me as improbable; I remember well only the debris that resulted from my congratulating one of my mother's more comfortable friends on having two of everything – 'Two cars, two houses, two necklaces, two rings and two chins.'

I suppose that I could have gained the notice that I did as a child only in a society enveloped by leisure as by some warm protective lap. My mother's friends spent their afternoons at each other's houses playing bridge and scratching about in the lives of those of their acquaintances who were not there at the time; in the evening they were joined by their husbands at dinner parties, trips to the cinema, or further conversation over cards; and, to provide distraction, there were auction sales and random drives around the peninsula for the entertainment of visiting celebrities. One woman friend of the family's summed up those days with an unconscious irony that can only be described as heroic. Pestered by my mother to involve herself in work of some sort – we were in the early days of the war, and those who did not busy themselves in raising money for refugees were serving intermittently at canteens for servicemen – she moaned on the bed where she was being energetically massaged: 'Oh, I have thought about it, you know I have, constantly. But one gets so involved – Tuesdays and Thursdays are bridge, and Mondays and Fridays my massage, and on Wednesdays John expects me to entertain his friends, and on the week-ends John's at home and I can't run around – when can I find the time?' Nor was this anything like as inane as it sounded. Leisure so intense had become a fever in order to be morally endured at all – there was no lying back and closing of the eyes, only a hectic panting after pleasure, cards and dinner parties and teas in town and shopping, interminable shopping for drawers already difficult to close, drives which kept the

body moving but never for a moment lit the mind, visiting
where the visitors were as reluctant as the visited, but buoyed
up by the same sense of fulfilling some necessary purpose,
something done and expected to be done.

I don't suppose there can ever again be a social regime quite
like it, so fatuous and easily futile; the war jolted it first, the
reek from Buchenwald and Auschwitz sent it reeling, and the
collisions of colour since the Nationalist victory in 1948 have
hurled it helpless and blindly clutching to the ground. The
houses still stand in their careful gardens, the dinner parties
survive, though seldom the bridge in the afternoons, but the
servants in the kitchens are a presence now, sharp eyes staring
at one's back while one bends over the food, a laden air before
the sky cracks wide. There is nothing feverish about the leisure
now – only a silent grinding together of nerves hidden and
revealed in a set series of social twitches. They take pills now,
to make them sleep and to keep them awake, or the older ones,
my mother's friends, travel rather more often to Europe and
for longer stays, or spend much of the year in quiet houses
ninety miles away along the coast, while the still tenacious send
money abroad so that their children at least should not suddenly be reduced to what they – how long ago? – once were
themselves. And it all seems so pointless, so ludicrously,
lamentably a waste; an end like the beginning surely soon, with
only the degradation of success in between.

Staring at the typewriter keys I can see again No. 6 Avenue
Disandt in pulsations of colour – mauve bougainvillea clamber-
ing up the side of the house to my bedroom window, from an
opulence of white magnolia floating just beyond the wide red
veranda, with the groomed green lawn in front and the rush of
trees and houses down to the interminable blue of the sea below. And, in the kitchen, Page from Bechuanaland, and an
unending succession of Coloured maids and cooks, and Philip
the Coloured driver in his white coat standing in front of the
waiting car on the driveway, and Nellie, infinitely white,
sitting upstairs over a magazine, with my parents white and all
their friends white and I white in the lounge below. White

children in South Africa seem to accept the implications of race as they grow to distinguish shapes and smells and sounds, so that, almost as they begin to speak, they tighten their voices to colour. It is an awareness that seeps irresistibly into the mind, displacing whatever indifference might – in so very few homes – have been carefully cultivated, seeping continuously, as though the air itself contained some ubiquitous mist, which left large stains behind wherever it settled. Even Philip, who had been the driver since before I was born and who would play with me for hours in the garden and even listen gravely to my extravagant talk, was an object rather than a personality, a prop for the bicycle he was teaching me to ride, a shoulder to climb on when I wanted to pick figs off our tree, most often just a pair of brown hands on the steering-wheel of the car. His children would visit him, every now and then, to play with careful self-effacement in the yard; and, when they did, they always produced a sudden shock in me. I never thought of him as having any children; he was the Coloured 'boy', ageless, whose condition and function alike were contradicted by the equality of children.

I remember still the horror I felt when Page, the African 'house-boy', complained to me that I wet the lavatory floor each night. Couldn't Master Ronald be more careful? He had the whole house to clean, and Master Ronald should try and make it easier for him. It was not the effrontery of it that offended me; I had suddenly been brought up short before his humanity, and a humanity looming all the larger for appearing in an area of my life that I considered so exclusively my own. It was as though he had slapped me suddenly across the face. I can see myself standing there – a child, just five years old, staring up at that tall, thin, large-eyed black man – in a stupor of shame. Scrupulously I avoided him for several days, until I could speak to him again in that blind brushing past which had defined him so securely before. However cold that mosaic floor of the lavatory felt to my feet and however strong the warm backwash of my bed, I saw to it that I should not be called careless again. I would never again give him cause to

push his way into my life. But while I said it over and over to
myself, I knew that having pushed his way once, he was there,
a person, human beyond hiding.

The depersonalization that is the objective and accomplishment of the colour bar has been sufficiently remarked by men
like Trevor Huddleston and Michael Scott; for the Christian it
must be accounted blasphemy. But for those who know no god,
for whom life itself has a value immeasurable and unique, it is
equally anathema, a kind of ultimate ugliness. It is precisely
this which makes race rule in South Africa the execration it is –
the refusal to give life a value in itself, to acknowledge humanity. White supremacy not merely subjects, it finds it necessary to
mutilate first. Before it can feel secure in controlling men, it
must make them into objects. It must deface to endure.

The Afrikaner policeman who beats an African woman in a
sudden explosion of hatred recognizes her humanity. It is an
attempt to subdue life that merely admits it. The real brutality
is not cruel, it is merely blind. It is the easy unconsciousness of
command, in the kitchens and gardens, the factories and mines,
where for so long the non-whites have been impersonal limbs,
noticed only in their service, never possessing an existence outside of the needs which they momentarily satisfy. Even now,
when the African presence has come to be felt as a great gathering danger, a crouching to spring, most whites do not think of
hungry and enraged men and women, but of hunger and rage,
not of people in rebellion, but of rebellion itself.

There were interruptions in the happiness that I remember
my childhood to have been – Page by the lavatory floor, Nellie
pinching me in pique, the scream as I saw a mottled green face
on the curtains in the dark, a frenzy of rage at my brother
Maurice's miserable teasing of me, when I flung half the books
in the library at him long after he had swaggered jeering from
the room. I even remember once having started to run away in
protest at my mother's absences from home for those mysterious meetings of women Zionists. I packed a suitcase with
shirts – I clearly did not anticipate a change of trousers and
socks – and got halfway down the stairs. There I was met by a

lawyer friend of my parents. We sat down on the stairs to discuss my decision.

'Why?' he asked.

'Because that terrible woman is never here.'

'What terrible woman?'

'My mother, of course.'

He looked very disapproving, and then suddenly smiled; I felt a quick flush of triumph.

'She's always running off to meetings,' I said, 'and this will teach her a lesson.'

'Where will you go?' he asked.

'To the top of the road,' I said, forlornly.

But I didn't after all. My mother joined us on the stairs and said she was sorry, and that she did not enjoy the meetings and would much rather stay at home with me, but that she had to go to them because they were helping to find a home for the Jews persecuted by Hitler. I studied the explanation, felt that I had made my point satisfactorily – the top of the road was a long way off, I had never seen it – and agreed to be carried back to my room. I demanded and got a luxury of love. When my mother or father, in a twitch of irritation, complained of my reputation as the most spoiled child in the country, I was silently proud I mattered for myself, beyond my family. Other people spoke about me. And I directed myself to finding occasion for them to speak more.

One night I walked into the lounge and surveyed the four women playing bridge there.

'Good God,' I cried, 'your ages must amount to simply thousands.'

I was carried off to bed with a deep glow of satisfaction at the laughter I had heard. Only once did I feel ashamed. I was saying how beautiful I thought somebody was. And an old friend of my mother's took me on her knee and asked me whether I did not think that she was beautiful too. 'No,' I said. 'I think you are the ugliest woman I have ever seen.' She burst into tears. I was horrified. I had not meant to hurt her. I had meant her to laugh. But no one was laughing.

I was seven years old when war was declared. The Jewish community, severed by the sea from the atrocities of Europe, suddenly found itself hanging, for survival itself, from the ledge of British resistance. If Britain collapsed, so would South Africa, and the home-trained storm-troopers would march across our lawns, through our houses, pushing us into trucks and driving us off in the night to the concentration camps. I remember the day that Paris fell to the Germans. We were clustered round the radio, and for the first time fear for myself, not a nebulous foreboding but a clutch cold at my stomach, seized me as I heard the news and watched the faces round me. This, I remember feeling with astonishment, was happening to me, not to them. And then, suddenly, I felt a rising of rage, as I have felt so often since at any encounter with what seemed to me unfair. It was unfair that our lives could be shattered by sounds from the wireless, that we could not close and lock the front door to voices so far away on the other side of the sea. I wanted to fling myself kicking, beating with my fists, but there was nothing to fling myself against.

In the House of Assembly, the Nationalist opposition, to the raucous cries of Eric Louw, brayed their hatred of the Jews. I used to go with my father or a friend of the family's to hear the debates and sit there silently raging at Eric Louw, as sallow-voiced he jeered at the Jews in flight from the fall of France, ready there as everywhere to profit from their country of adoption till danger appeared, when they packed their possessions and left. My loathing of white rule in South Africa today requires little reinforcement. Yet somewhere running through it must be the memory of those debates in parliament, of those figures on the opposition benches, sullenly rejoicing at the fury unleashed by Hitler against Europe's Jews and consoling their powerlessness with the prospect of the fury that they would unleash one day soon against their own.

At the beginning of the war, the elder of my brothers, Cyril, immediately volunteered. My father did so as well soon afterwards, but received a letter from Smuts asking him to remain behind and continue running what had become a large commercial concern. In August 1940, my sister Hannah was placed on a ship to the United States. Germany seemed to be winning, and the possibility of Jewry's extinction in South Africa a consequent matter of time. One member of the family at least, my parents felt, should have the chance of survival if Britain fell. In 1943, as soon as he reached 18, Maurice volunteered as well. I became the only child, and the love with which I had been lavished turned all at once to frenzy.

CHAPTER TWO

SCHOOLING

ON the other side of the Kloof Road, which bucks and rears its
way around Lion's Head to Camps Bay and the Twelve
Apostles, the houses and gardens of Fresnaye disappear into
Sea Point, the most populous of Cape Town's suburbs by the
sea. Here the huge post-war blocks of flats, drearily similar,
shoulder their way towards the sea, or squat in smug serenity
along the Beach Road, to provide countless small balconies on
to the spray and crash of the Atlantic below. Here, seeking
their private views of the sea, come those whose incomes cannot yet cover the upkeep of gardens and a careful display of
rooms, and those who have grown too tired or too lonely to
care for such elaboration any longer – the couples whose
children have married and settled in homes of their own, and
the children who have married and left the homes of their
parents on the way to their own. Along the Beach Road, the
elderly walk in the evening, taking a little exercise before a film
or the game of cards in the lounge; and, during the day, the
younger women bring their children to the beaches and lie in
the soaking sun. Yet only on a Sunday somehow, when Cape
Town comes to stroll along the Beach Road, or at moments in
the evening, when the brash coffee-bars are noisy with cinema-
goers, does Sea Point seem to twitch its limbs and show itself
still alive. For the rest, it is listless, fluorescent-lit, a community
that glitters like a pile of cold-cream jars in a chemist's shop
window. The sun and the sea should wash it to the sparkle of
salt; instead, they seem to drain its colours thin, like the
street-lights lining the whole length of the beach front.

Silent all the while another community exists in Sea Point,
concealed in the bellies of the flats, the African house-boys and

Coloured maids, scrubbing and polishing, sweeping and cook-
ing, behind the curtains and beyond all but the sound of the
sea. Very few of these other men and women have rooms in
the blocks themselves. It would be too expensive, even if it
were legal; and, as it is, the government has laid down a limit
to the number of non-whites permitted to lodge on the
premises. And how, under apartheid, should it be different?
For if all the servants employed in the flats were to live there,
each block would have its own compact subversion, a visible
gnawing at the foundations of white sufficiency.

Early in the morning the trains and trackless trams bring the
servants from the African 'locations' and Coloured slums to
Sea Point, to work from half past seven and before that, until
eight and often ten o'clock at night, for a wage that sometimes
falls below £8 and seldom rises above £12 a month. And here
in the flats, miles away from the kind open squalor that is the
poisonous profusion of Cape Town's slums, they serve out
their captivity – so many daylight life sentences – between the
barbed wire of the sea and the high walls of the streets. For if
they are released from the floors and the furniture and the
kitchen for a few hours in the afternoons, they have nowhere
to go. They are forbidden even the sea only a few footsteps
from the flats; there is no café which they might visit, no room
of their own in which to rest. And so they stand and talk to each
other in the backyards of the flats, and some of the blacks who
are bold sometimes stroll for a while in the streets. But it is
only those who are bold, or angry and careless, who stay for
any time in the streets. For the streets of Sea Point must appear
as white as the living-rooms in the buildings that line them; and
there are police in small black pick-up vans to see that this is
so, to peer at passes for a stamp or a signature that is not there,
and to carry the suddenly criminal to the courts, often to prison,
sometimes to distant farm jails for months and even years.

> There is the pick-up van.
> Now, what have we done to you, Pick-up Van?!
> All around us are pick-up vans.
> Now, what have we done to you, Pick-up Van?!

It is a song sung by Africans in the townships of the Reef, among the shanties of Cato Manor outside Durban, and surely sometimes under the breath in Sea Point, where the pick-up vans patrol within the sounding of the sea.

I have long felt that if I were an African, I would find Sea Point more than I could bear. Here to be held a captive, by beaches and rocks that gleam and roar before a sea that stretches endlessly away, is captivity with a taunt in the very opening of the eyes. To me Sea Point is cruel as not even the farm-jails of Bethal or the mine-compounds on the Free State Goldfields are cruel. It is a lattice on hell.

At that end of the suburb which merges along the coast into Bantry Bay, the Cape Town Tramway Company a hundred years ago settled some of its Coloured employees into a thin row of houses which subsequently became known as Tramway Road. Descendants of the original inhabitants still live there, with others who snatched at any house to fall vacant – a thin line of Coloured families stretching the width of a single street, from the Main Road to a church on the corner of Kloof Road and the frilled skirts of Fresnaye.

In the early summer of 1959, a Coloured man was found hanging from a tree in the bush at Bakoven, just beyond Camps Bay. Aged 58, Frederick Johannes Mitchell had been, on all evidence, happily married for 35 years; he had 5 children and 11 grandchildren. Pinned on his clothing was a note. 'Group Areas is the cause of my doing away with my life. My property will be taken from me. I have struggled to get it paid off, and I know that I will never get my money back that I paid for it.' And when journalists questioned his wife, she sobbed to them: 'My husband had no other reason for doing what he did. He was an honourable man. He never drank, he was very religious.' One week later, on November 14th, another Coloured, Joseph Bougaardt, aged 55, was found hanging from a tree in Camps Bay. And the inquest concluded that he, too, had committed suicide because of the Group Areas Act.

The Group Areas Act of 1950 is aimed at reducing the whole non-white population of South Africa to a regimented, right-less cheap labour force, not only strictly separated on all but labourer level from the whites, but carefully divided among themselves, Indian from Coloured, Coloured from African, and African from African in artificial tribal zones. Tormented by the threatening potential of non-white unity, the government provided in the Act for the compulsory establishment of separate residential and commercial areas for whatever separate ethnic groups it proclaimed, so creating a pattern of ghettoes across the country to destroy whatever non-white commerce and industry still existed and split up the resultant proletariat into easily manageable pieces.

The zoning declarations made to date promise the uprooting of hundreds of thousands – perhaps even millions – of people when the Act gets into its stride; those areas which have so far been racially 'adjusted' already involve many thousands in forced removals and economic devastation. The whole Indian merchant class, small in number but constituting the only real non-white bourgeoisie, will wither in its coerced isolation; for it is to be torn from its homes and businesses among the other communities and flung down on undeveloped land far from the thoroughfares of commerce. With its central area still finally unzoned, the city of Durban – where the bulk of the Indian merchant class lives, and almost half the country's total Indian population – is to endure a racial resettlement under the Act that will cost some £20,000,000 and displace more than 165,000 people. Zoning of the city centre is likely to cost as much again and more, and will drag thousands of businessmen down to financial ruin. Much less dramatic, and for that very reason, perhaps, so much more pitiable, are zoning declarations in small towns up and down the country, where a handful of Indian trading families, with the relatives they support, are to be hurled from the shops and houses that they have held for generations, to stare starvation helplessly in the face of the bare veld which they have been offered instead. There are Indian traders in the town of Lydenburg in the Transvaal who carried many of the white farmers in the area on credit through the depression years of the early 'thirties; their recompense is the

B

approval with which their expulsion from their houses and shops, to undeveloped land some miles away from the town, has been greeted by those whom they once helped to save.

It is difficult to believe that a government calling itself Christian and claiming some share in the inheritance of Western culture should prepare so openly for the destruction of a people; its spiritual predecessor, the Germany of the Nazis, pretended less to established sanctity. The truth, of course, is that the Nationalist government, like almost all white South Africa, does not believe that it is oppressive when it manipulates the lives of its non-white subjects. Oppression presupposes a moral relation, and the whites do not judge the non-whites morally at all. Where no rights are admitted, no oppression can be confessed.

And so Mr Tom Naude, as Minister of the Interior, heading the department responsible for the administration of the Group Areas Act and himself enjoying a reputation as one of the more moderate members of the Nationalist government, could get up in parliament in April 1960, and complain that far too many South African Indians were businessmen. There was no reason, he said, why some of them should not leave their shops and do manual work. He was growing tired of their attitude. They were for ever seeking interviews, but never offered any proposals to facilitate administration of the Act. The Group Areas Board had been far too lenient with them, and the position could not continue as it was. 'The Indians should not think that they are the only people with a right to trade in South Africa,' he felt it necessary to add. That a Nationalist Cabinet Minister, even one of the more moderate, should feel disturbed about the leniency with which race persecution was being pursued ought not to surprise anybody: but that he should actually expect the race so persecuted to expedite its ruin reveals a degree of self-deception that cannot be considered sane.

The Indians have lived in South Africa for one hundred years. It is their country, by their presence and acknowledgment, as India is no more than a distant embarkation point. Yet Dr Verwoerd, the Prime Minister, in speaking of them

three years ago in parliament, swept away in two brusque
sentences the mosques and schools and social centres that they
had with inexhaustible hope and endurance built over the
years; denied them their professions, and trades, and liveli-
hoods. 'In my opinion the Indians are not our problem in the
first place, but the problem of those who are so anxious to take
the care of the Indians on their shoulders. If other people are
worried about the Indians, let them take the Indians back there,
where they would have better opportunities of employment.'
It did not surprise me when, on my way into exile, I heard in
Bechuanaland that someone had shot Dr Verwoerd; it surprised me only to hear that it had not been an Indian.

The anguish of the Group Areas Act is peculiarly Indian, but
its edge will gash all but the whites themselves. The Coloured
have been in the towns and cities of the Cape for as long as the
whites, helping to swell them from road-halts to industrial
centres by their skills and resilience. And, inevitably, a wide
racial blurring has taken place in the poorer working-class
areas. There are many streets, especially in Cape Town, where
Coloured and white have lived together as neighbours since
houses were first built there. But now whole communities are
to be moved, as zoning declarations under the Act pelt upon
the province, striking above all the Cape Peninsula, where
some 400,000 Coloured and 350,000 whites live together,
occasionally still just a common wall away from one another.
Churches, schools, shops, clubs, cafés and playgrounds must be
abandoned, together with thousands of homes. Whites in the
town of Paarl, thirty-six miles from Cape Town, will possess
one bank of the Berg River, where nearly all of the town at the
moment stands, while the Coloured are to settle on the other
side, leaving their properties derelict behind them—for there
are nowhere enough whites in the area to occupy them – while
they attempt hopelessly to build sufficient housing for the
homeless. Though a backlog of 10,000 houses already exists
within the city of Cape Town alone, thousands of people are
still to be thrust from their homes, to add themselves to those
already crowded into some of the most squalid slums in the

world. Nobody knows, of course, what all this will cost, least of all those who concocted and now administer the law. And the calculation cannot be made in money alone.

Frederick Johannes Mitchell, Coloured, aged 58, with a wife and 5 children, hanged himself that day in 1959 because Tramway Road had suddenly been zoned for white occupation, because he knew that within weeks he would lose the home he had lived in almost all his life, as well as much of the capital he had collected over so many careful years to invest in it. His wife, his five children and his eleven grandchildren will suffer without him the savageries of a law that he himself found one way to escape.

At the beginning of 1939, six months after I had turned five, I was sent – despite a concentrated protest campaign that encompassed nearly every technique of resistance outside of violence – to school at King's Road, just the other side of Tramway Road from Avenue Disandt. The existence of a Coloured neighbourhood, only a few hundred yards from my home and so near to my school, excited me. Philip took the car through it sometimes on the way to school or home again, hooting away the children, barefooted and frayed, who played or just sat in the middle of the road. And it made me feel my superiority, all the reassurances of wealth. We might be menaced as Jews in a South Africa at war, but we had money meanwhile, and money, I decided, was the difference between Tramway Road and Avenue Disandt. I jumped up and down on the wide back seat of the Chrysler and thought, this is what I have and they haven't. I have the gleam on the green paint, and a garden to play in, and my own pine trees for the kernels I collect in my jar. And then, sometimes, there entered my delight a sudden discernment. I was better than the Coloureds because we were the same. If they were not also people, it would not matter that they were different. I began to study Philip's features – I wondered what colour his blood was underneath the skin – to test and to demand his liking for me.

Soon Tramway Road will disappear, if it has not done so already, that Sea Point may be white, without even a thin line of Coloured houses to mark its edge. Perhaps its name will be changed, that the very memory of it may the more easily fade. Perhaps the speculators will build blocks of flats where the houses now stand – it must be a desirable area now, and one will be able to catch something of the sea from the balconies – and then surely the Coloured will return to the road, to the kitchens and the floors of the flats, a black Sea Point running like some subterraneous river below the white.

School disconcerted me by merging my identity. I took an immediate loathing to the brown uniform which I had to wear and to all the other brown uniforms which surrounded me, hemming me in until I felt that I was permanently stuck in a brown lift between brown floors. I recall making some pointed comments at home about brown jackets and Greyshirts, but my parents could hardly clash with compulsory education, even if they had wanted to, and I am sure they thought that school would do me no end of good.

I do not remember those first few months, or the five or six years that followed them, as peculiarly cruel – I soon found school tedious rather than scalding, and placidly endured the lessons till I heard the final bell and could run down the steps to the car waiting to take me home. I learnt that I made friends with enormous difficulty. Despite all evidence to the contrary, I am shy and delicately approach other people, unless I feel assured that the way is clear, when – I confess – I rather storm them instead. Perhaps I have always been so greedy for fame because it would make all the necessary approaches for me, searching out and isolating the rebuffs in my absence.

With the rest of the children in my classes, I seemed to myself to have nothing in common. I wanted to talk and I wanted them to listen; and perhaps, if I had had anything to say which would have interested them, they might have deferred, with some necessary limitations, to my demands. As it was, there were far too many of them who wanted to talk as well and wanted me to listen and, as though this were not disquieting enough, found my interests even less absorbing than I found theirs. We attempted various concessions, but they were all so

drearily unsuccessful as to set my mind against the strategy of
compromise for the rest of my life. I lost an extravagant number of marbles before I permitted myself to accept that I did
not have the fingers for them, so that I gave up playing just as
my popularity was beginning to soar. I suppose I realized then,
in a flush of cynicism that has ever since been quick to fly to
my face, that money was a source of considerable power and
so was probably worth much more than anything it bought.
I learnt a number of its drawbacks later, but my immediate
reaction was to plan on how most easily I could become a
millionaire. I announced to my family that I had settled upon
a specific ambition at last and invited their co-operation. Un-
happily even then I was alternating periods of diligent saving –
when I would scrub my half-crowns till they shone and then
put them under my pillow for security at night – with hectic
spending sprees, when I bought large presents for myself, and
little ones for my parents, in order to deflect any comment. My
motives were therefore seriously questioned; but I refused to
defend my sincerity, and taking advantage of the opening
offered me instead, I extracted the promise of a ping-pong set
and so confirmed the worst suspicions of my cunning. My
mother had already decided on such evidence that I had more
than enough imagination to become a writer, while my father
simply hoped that I would escape becoming any one of the
number of things I threatened to be.

Not long afterwards, my habit of scattering half-crowns
under my pillow nearly turned the wits of my sister-in-law
once and for all. My parents had gone to Hermanus, a small
town along the coast a hundred miles from the city, to celebrate their silver wedding, and after a week invited my sister-
in-law – my eldest brother was with the army somewhere – and
myself to join them. Despite my shrill cries of protest, I was
thought too young to have a room to myself and so was
forced to share one with Doreen. On the first night, she suddenly awoke to hear the muffled clinking of silver and, sitting
bolt upright in her bed, addressed herself to finding the burglar
in the dark without allowing him to know that she knew he was

there. After discovering half a dozen shapes and sinking under the bed-clothes in the belief that she would rather lose her money than have her silence suddenly enforced, she lay there – for two throbbing hours, she later with bitterness maintained – listening to the regular chinking of my half-crowns as I turned my head on the pillow. At about four in the morning, she fell asleep, to wake up and haggardly watch me removing my money from under the pillow to my pockets.

I did not openly rebel against the attitudes and assumptions of my age group. I just never grew into that camaraderie that sends out its first shoots at school and develops later into the trunk of white supremacy. Whites are born and schooled and salaried to rule together, and clear – under all the tensions and distractions – there gleams that one ultimate recognition. For me school became a recognition only of difference, and the expectation of disillusionment. I did not like those I found myself among; and I hoped profoundly that I would never become a part of them, even at the very moment that I prayed one day I would. I found myself more and more recoiling from the personality of the playground, and with it all the habits of thought and speech which animated it.

Matching the division between myself and my fellows was the difference between my own interests and the extraordinary subjects that I found I was expected to study. My appetite for romance was huge. To the confusion of my family, I devoured *Gone with the Wind* at the age of eight – though of course I swallowed whole the bits that the book was bought to taste – and then graduated to a biography of Disraeli, which confirmed my yearnings for spectacle and sudden success, and pledged me to politics as a clearly profitable career. But arithmetic I found dull, and the study of Afrikaans a tedious insult. I could not picture myself in a career that required intimacy with the multiplication tables, and the thought of ever arousing a crowded assembly to its feet with my eloquence in Afrikaans was too rich for even as greedy an imagination as mine comfortably to digest. I did well enough in arithmetic because my conceit would not allow me to appear incapable of an accomplishment

quite so generally shared, and I ground my teeth over the
seven-times table. But Afrikaans I resisted with cold disgust, as
the language of the Greyshirts and the Hoggenheimer cartoons
and the shrill innumerable Nellies whom I hoped that I had put
behind me for ever. It even became a source of quiet pride that
I should get the highest marks in the class for almost every
other subject, and the lowest – the results of the retarded not
excepted – in Afrikaans. I regularly slipped from the first or
second place to fifth or sixth on my Afrikaans mark alone, and
once hurtled to thirteenth on an Afrikaans examination in
which I scored 28%. All argument was useless against what had
become an obsession, until I was warned that I would have to
pass in Afrikaans in order to pass any further standards, when
I submerged the feet of my principles and applied myself to
getting as little over the 40% demanded as I reasonably could. I
even learnt by heart an Afrikaans composition on 'A Day by the
Sea', which I served up with the necessary garnish all the way
to my Senior Certificate. Since examiners in the language
seemed to show a generic fondness for holidays and celebrations as the subject of composition, I was able to make of my
'Day by the Sea' an invaluable event, suitable to birthdays,
picnics, trips into the country – though this required a little
imaginative adjustment – and sudden encounters with a variety
of animals.

The study of South African history was less a bore than a
debauchery. I knew that I was gobbling down one distortion
after the other, but I swallowed them greedily. Even frontier
clashes were exciting when sandwiched in between arithmetic
and Afrikaans recitation. I have forgotten nearly all the dates I
used so readily to reel off, but not the blatant propaganda –
those interminable 'Kaffir Wars', dressed as defensive stands
against packs of marauding savages, those interminable settler
wrongs, fed by officious missionaries and callous administra-
tions, and those interminable trekkers, rolling civilization and
Christianity, like so many creaking works of art in shining
frames, through the night of Africa.

Every year on the 16th of December, the Afrikaners celebrate the Day of the Covenant, the anniversary of the Battle of Blood River when, in 1838, the trekkers under Pretorius avenged the murder of Piet Retief by Dingaan and, fortified by their vow to repay victory by consecrating the day to God, broke the back of Zulu power for generations. This is the Passover of the Afrikaners, the day of jubilant rededication to their past and the spirit of the new South Africa, when the leaders exhort their trekker-dressed disciples to prepare for another Blood River. The trek is not history, it is a religion, the Old Testament of Afrikanerdom to which the Gospels have not yet been added. In it are the Commandments, rather different from the Decalogue, and the distinctions, above all the distinctions, between black and white, missionary and trekker, English and Afrikaner, the chosen and the discarded of God. Here are the years of bondage, the flight, the wandering in the wilderness, the battles and the brief possession, the dispersion and the final threatened fulfilment. And in the history lessons up and down the country, in city and small farm school alike, are the Bible readings, the teaching of the Scriptures to the young.

The religion, of course, has its temple, in a squat grey monument carrying at its centre a cenotaph with the inscription, illumined by the sunlight at a certain time of the day: 'We for you, South Africa.' The *Year Book and Guide to Southern Africa* describes it invitingly.

The history of the Great Trek 1834–8 is depicted in the magnificent Italian marble frieze which surrounds the Hero's Hall. In the crypt may be seen the symbolic cenotaph (the altar of sacrifice) as well as the eternal flame of civilization in a colourful niche of red marble. The central figure at the entrance is a Voortrekker woman shielding her two children from the dangers of barbarism – one of Anton van Wouw's outstanding bronzes. Granite figures (three times life size) of prominent leaders of the Great Trek, add rugged grace to the four corners of this massive masonry encircled in a laager of ox wagons – typical of the defences employed during that period.

The Monument was completed in 1949 at a cost of approximately £300,000. It is closed on Tuesdays and Sunday mornings.

When the monument was completed, the celebrations were attended by a quarter of a million people, many of them dressed in trekker costume and some bearing beards that they had grown especially for the occasion. Dr Malan, Prime Minister at the time, intoned in his speech a hymn to the spirit of Afrikanerdom. 'Back to your people; back to the highest ideals of your people; back to the pledge which has been entrusted to you for safekeeping; back to the altar of the people on which you must lay your sacrifice; back to the sanctity and inviolability of family life; back to the Christian way of life; back to the Christian faith; back to your Church; back to your God.' Back, back, back. Backs to the wall, backs to Africa and the world. By Blood River in Natal every year on the 16th of December, the cry rings out, and the old with their crumpled faces and the young with their starched mouths – how many were at school the same time as I? – turn back to the flame, to the cenotaph, back to the past.

Upon white English-speaking children, the trek taught in this form of racial ecstasy has varying effects. Almost all of them grow up with a vision of the African as predatory, treacherous and cruel, ready with his numberless naked hordes to sweep down upon white South Africa and bear it off into savagery. He is untaught and unteachable, behind his eyes always the darkness of Africa, waiting to entrap and then for ever to engulf. Between black and white there can never be peace, only a temporary truce, while each side watches the other uneasily for any signs of weakness. The Afrikaners, whipped back to the past by their politicians and their clergymen whenever they show a sudden inclination to stray, retain the vision brightly all their lives. The English lose sight of it in the traffic jams and summer sales of the cities; they prefer the quiet impersonality of service, the African's assegai changed to a white coat or apron. But the vision survives all the same in the deeps of the mind, and any serious riot brings it shooting to the surface.

It is the treatment given to the English in the history books that produces in the minds of English-speaking South Africans the whirls and eddies of submission and revolt. The attacks upon their missionaries, whose liberal agitations their acquired vision of the African makes mischievous and repugnant, they transform into an embarrassed impatience with their own Church. To many of them, priests like Scott, Huddleston and Reeves are no less anathema than they are to an Afrikanerdom traditionally plagued by the subversives of the Anglican communion; to most of them, the Church preserves its comforting place in their lives while it condones their prejudices, and abdicates its authority the moment that it conflicts; to only a few does the history of clerical assaults upon the colour bar provide the substance of guidance and of pride.

The mass revolt of the English is an imperial one, an obsession with the Crown that is almost Jacobite and that shows itself in an obdurate attachment to the flag and the anthem, whatever is legislated in Cape Town or threatened in Pretoria. To the attacks in the history books on the tyranny of English governors, the greed of English capital and the arrogance of English generals, the English – descended, above all in their bastion of Natal, react with a passion of pride in their imperial connection. It might be comic were it not every bit as predatory and a great deal more cold-blooded in its manifestations than the race hysteria of Afrikanerdom. When the 'kaffir was fixing the coolie' during the Durban riots of 1949, there were outbursts of white jubilation in the streets. Doubtless those who rejoiced while Africans made furious by frustration burnt Indian families alive in their homes, had sunk to a level of individual degeneracy that it would be extravagant to hold against the whole community. But the appeals of the Durban City Council for more sweeping racial declarations in the city than even the government Group Areas Board was willing at the time to allow, must commit the community as far as it can ever be committed by the actions of its elected representatives.

It is a singular savagery that can outbid even the assaults of a
Nationalist government upon a stricken and defenceless people.
Of course, there are rational and courageous opponents of
white supremacy among the English-descended in South
Africa, just as there are rational and courageous Afrikaners to
whom the policy seems evil and deranged. But nowhere in
South Africa have I encountered a loathing of colour so intense
as that displayed towards the Indians by most white citizens of
Natal. I have been accused often enough of intolerance myself.
I know that there have been times when I wanted nothing so
much as to ship the proudly English of the province to a strip
of ice in the Antarctic, where they might enjoy the gleaming
white of their surroundings without having to devastate a
people in order to do so. Durban is, of course, no longer a
citadel of empire. That it should mournfully hanker still to be
so is surely one of the stains that the imperial idea will have
left in its passage through history.

Afrikanerdom has watched with increasing impatience the
rebellions against its authority in the minds of its own imperial
subjects. Its schools in the period following its defeat in the
Boer War successfully resisted all Milner's attempts to anglicize
the conquered republics, and this success profoundly impressed
it, not only with the power of schooling, but even more with
the dangers of ever permitting such power to be exercised in
the pursuit of any objective but its own. In 1948 a group of
prominent Afrikaners organized into the Institute for Christian
National Education, and containing in their number the present Minister of Finance and the present Superintendent-
General of Education in the Cape, proposed a new educational
policy for South Africa that amounted to a ruthless and perpetual policing of the mind. Sponsored by the influential
Federation of Afrikaans Cultural Societies, the Institute not
only proposed the extension of Christian National Education
to all schooling in the country, it also defined the objectives
and programme of such education with a precision that permitted no doubt over the degree of indoctrination intended.
Christianity was defined as 'the creeds of the three Afrikaner

Churches', and Nationalism as 'the love of one's own, especially one's own language, history and culture'. A brisk paging
through the Institute's policy statement would have made it
sufficiently clear that this indoctrination was not meant for
Afrikaners alone, but for the English-speaking and the non-
whites as well; the years of power since 1948 have confirmed
this plan in each new stair laid by the government downwards
to the abyss of the Christian National State.

Article 6 (i)

The spirit of all teaching must be Christian-nationalist; in
no subject may anti-Christian or non-Christian or anti-
nationalist or non-nationalist propaganda be made.

Article 6 (vi)

History should be seen as the fulfilment of God's plan for
humanity ... God has enjoined on each nation its individual task in the fulfilment of His purpose. Young
people can only undertake the national task fruitfully if
they acquire a true vision of the origin of the nation and of
the direction of the national heritage. Next to the mother
tongue the history of the Fatherland is the best channel for
cultivating the love of one's own which is nationalism.

Article 8 (iii)

The parents *in community* (*not as individuals*) must establish,
maintain and control schools which will foster their own
view of life, they must appoint the teachers and keep a
watch on the teaching.

Article 14

It is the Afrikaners' sacred duty to see that the Coloureds
are brought up Christian-national. Only when he is
Christianized can the Coloured be truly happy; and he will
then be proof against foreign ideologies which give him
an illusion of happiness but leave him in the long run
unsatisfied and unhappy. He must also be nationalist. The

welfare and happiness of the Coloured lies in his understanding that he belongs to a separate racial group (hence
apartheid is necessary in education) and in his being proud
of it.

The architects of apartheid have been accused often enough
of inconsistency, of instituting a society in which there are
separate seats in public buses, separate benches in public parks,
separate entrances and separate counters in public buildings,
but mixing in the kitchens, the nurseries and the shops. The
criticism is irrelevant. For apartheid never intended, even in
its bizarre academic heresies, a separation of white and black
into two horizontal societies. It divides those who order from
those who obey; it is a line between the above and the below.
The injunctions on the buses and buildings are not signs of
separation, but symbols of status. They advertise the relationship in house and factory. This is traditional segregation, as
Smuts practised and developed it. The originality of apartheid
is that it requires not only obedience – Smuts could be short
with the recalcitrant – but contentment, a harmony of rule in
which every grade of society gives assiduous thanks for being
what it is and nothing else. While the minds of Afrikaner
children are being mutilated into believing beyond question
in their national task to rule over the Fatherland, millions of
Coloured, Indian and African children must be taught that they
were born, and are always unprotestingly to remain, the servants of the chosen servants of God. And, in between, the
English-speaking whites, segregated in their special schools,
will learn to enjoy the status of the *beta plus*, surrendering all
claim to final command in return for their minor share-holding
in white supremacy.

Article 8 (i)

There should be at least two kinds of primary and secondary schools: one for the children of Afrikaans-speaking
parents, with only Afrikaans as medium, and the other for
children of English-speaking parents, with only English

as medium. In each there should be the right relationship
between home, school, church and state.

Under the dual-stream policy of Botha and Smuts after
Union in 1910, parallel-medium schooling was encouraged for
whites as a stimulus to the mingling of children across the language line. With the accession to power, however, of the
Nationalist Party, Language Ordinances established compulsory single-medium education up to Standard VIII or two
years before matriculation in the two Provinces of the Transvaal and the Orange Free State. Every white child is taught
in the language which his school principal or – on appeal –
the Director of Education judges that he knows best, not in the
particular language that his parents may desire for him. In the
Cape Province, still far too often thought of as the cradle instead of the coffin of the country's liberalism, single-medium
schooling has also been made compulsory to Standard VIII.
The parents may change the language-medium of their child
in secondary school if they can obtain a written statement from
the principal, countersigned by an Inspector of the Education
Department, that the child is capable of benefiting from instruction in another language. But the ultimate decision rests
with the officials of the Education Department, so that any
escape over the barbed wire depends entirely upon the capri-
ciousness of its guards. Even Natal is in the process of being
brought to heel, and – despite vociferous protests by the
Executive Council of the Province and a series of passionate
mass meetings – a noisy proponent of Christian National
Education has been appointed Provincial Deputy Director of
Education.

With separation accomplished throughout most of the country, the Department of Education is applying itself to the minds
in its care. School library censorship in the Transvaal forbids
teachers to lend or give to children any books that are not
specifically named in the official guide; and the official guide
presents a picture of Afrikaans literature, hardly fifty years old,
as equal in both significance and bulk to an English literature

that has flourished for five centuries. Far less quietly, courses in civics and race relations teach the virtues of a disciplined and all-white trade union movement, while providing appropriate instruction in the conduct essential to whites in their dealings with Africans. The Institute for Christian National Education was direct enough in the statement of its objectives:

> Our Afrikaans schools must not merely be mother tongue schools; they must be places where our children will be *saturated* with the Christian and National spiritual cultural stuff of our nation.

It should be no source of astonishment, therefore, now that the preachers are in power, if the practice follows so closely upon the preaching. What was once a propaganda pamphlet has been hoisted into law. The Orange Free State Language Ordinance of 1954 muffled none of its drums.

> It shall be the general policy of the Administrator to recognize, reveal and cultivate the Christian principle in education, and to maintain the national outlook, in order to develop in pupils a Christian philosophy of the world and life, to inculcate a healthy sentiment of undivided love for and loyalty to the common Fatherland, and to cultivate an esteem for the traditions, language and culture of all sections of the people.

It is not in the field of white schooling, however, that Christian National Education has caused the greatest devastation to date. Article 15 in the Charter of the Institute dealt with the education of Africans.

> Native education should be based on the principles of trusteeship, non-equality and segregation; its aim should be to inculcate the white man's view of life, especially that of the Boer nation, which is the senior trustee.

A mere year later, with the Nationalists in power and one of the Institute's Directors, the late Dr E. G. Jansen M.P., appointed Minister of Native Affairs, a special government Commission on Bantu Education was appointed to accomplish, among other things –

> The formulation of the principles and aims of education for *Natives as an independent race,* in which their past and present, their inherent racial qualities, their *distinctive characteristics and aptitudes* and their needs under ever-changing social conditions are taken into consideration.

The Commission did its work exceedingly well, and its report concocted a form of schooling for Africans that promised to keep industrialist and housewife happy with 'the principles of trusteeship, non-equality and segregation' for many years to come. English and Afrikaans were to be taught

Paragraph 924

> in such a way that the Bantu child will be able to find its way in European communities, to follow oral or written *instructions,* and to carry on a simple conversation with Europeans about his *work* and other subjects of common interest.

Paragraph 932 (c)

> Your Commission recommends that handwork in the first four years of school should aim at the establishment of the habit of doing manual work.

In Paragraph 759, the Commission objected to Bantu schools of 'a Western type' as out of harmony with existing Bantu social institutions. Instead, it proposed, with both eyes fixed on the ever-increasing numbers of unnecessary black wives and children in the cities,

> that special steps should be taken in the Reserves to facilitate and encourage the evolution of a progressive, modern and self-respecting Bantu order of life. Cosmopolitan areas in industrial centres where people of many languages and customs are herded together provide particularly difficult conditions for the orderly and progressive development of Bantu culture.

Any doubt that Bantu education was aimed at creating a migratory male labour force, content with its condition and trained only as far as required by necessary employment, was soon dispelled by the Bantu Education Act of 1953 and its amendments in 1954 and 1956. The government made it a crime to run a school for Africans without registration and refused to register schools of whose teaching it disapproved. Missionary schools, some with traditions a century old and more, were closed or permitted to survive only with crippled curricula. Teachers were dismissed for displaying the slightest reluctance to promote the new education, and the more vociferous banned from gatherings or banished from their homes. Teaching in the vernacular was enforced, and one recent calculation[1] has set direct instruction in English and Afrikaans at six hours and forty minutes a year.

The government bought lavish space in foreign newspapers to proclaim the vastly increased attendances at Bantu schools. It made no mention of the results. For under its regime, the number of matriculants each year, with those granted 'exemption', or a standard high enough for entering a university, had shown a dramatic overall decline.

Year	Entries	Total Passes	Exemptions	Passes as % of entries
1953	547	259	90	47·3
1954	523	234	127	44·7
1955	595	230	110	38·7
1956	768	354	164	46·1
1957	745	292	135	39·2
1958	660	248	113	37·6
1959	630	118	38	18·6
1960	716	128	28	17·9

In 1953, addressing parliament during a debate on Bantu Education, Dr Verwoerd, then Minister of Native Affairs, was frank. 'When I have control of Native education I will reform it so that the Natives will be taught from childhood to realize that equality with Europeans is not for them ... People who believe in equality are not desirable teachers for Natives ...

[1] Marion Friedman in *The Spectator*, 23.2.62.

When my department controls Native education it will know for what class of higher education a Native is fitted and whether he will have a chance in life to use his knowledge.'

From King's Road, I went to Sea Point Boys' Junior School, where the years seem to have glided past in a haze of easy submission. I emerged from the wrappings of my home five mornings a week, satisfied to endure if not enjoy the five hours before I was able to return. School was an exertion before the long laziness of the afternoon, a book or the beach, and at last the excitement of the dinner table at night. Unhappiness would be failure, and I was fearful above all else of failing. The subjects, except for Afrikaans, were distracting enough to speed the time, and I would often hear the final bell with a small explosion of surprise, leaping from my desk as the teacher nodded his head and bounding down the steps to the car. I found no friends. At King's Road I had made the effort and failed, and I saw no reason why I should risk my self-assurance again. I persuaded myself that the boys in my class belonged to the school, and would seem as out of place in my home as one of the desks.

I took elocution with a forceful woman, small and slight and broad-foreheaded beneath a fringe of straight and heavy black hair, who coaxed and berated me into winning medals at the annual Eistedfodds. On to the low stage of the Banqueting Hall I would go and carefully enunciate Milne's set piece –

> Jonathan Jo
> Has a mouth like an 'O'
> And a wheelbarrow full of surprises.
> If you ask for a bat,
> Or something like that,
> He has got it, whatever the size is.

I remember that poem particularly, because I longed to go to the lavatory all the time I was reciting it. My feelings must have shown in my face, if in a carefully transmuted form, since I was awarded full marks for expression.

It was early in Junior School that I discovered the fascination

of the stage, with its display and applause. The Standard Two
class performed the play at the annual prize-giving, and I was
chosen to star in it, as an old woman persecuted by a ruthless
Victorian landlord. As the curtains parted, I was discovered,
my head bound in a handkerchief, with a shawl, the colours
and texture of a tea-cosy, reaching round my shoulders to my
feet.

'Oh, woe is me. Alas! Alack! Nowhere to go but over the
hill to the workhouse!' I was saved in the end by the ministra-
tions of a boy scout, who in between pestered me with acid
drops. I was a huge success, and my choice as the female lead
in any school play irrevocably confirmed.

Soon afterwards, however, I first encountered the vanity of
success. I acquired a passion for the cinema, and would sneak
into the local 'Odeon' or 'Marine' when I was supposed to be at
the beach. Happily, my parents were too involved in communal work to notice my pallor, or they would have investi-
gated the singular effects of the sun on my skin. For two or
three afternoons a week – or more often, when the change of
film allowed – I indulged my appetite for spectacle and excitement. And then I came second in the Pot O' Gold Competition.

The 'Odeon', throwing itself into war work with belated
energy, held a competition to collect comforts for the soldiers.
Entrants would be awarded various points for different donations – one for a pencil, three for chewing gum, five for a
magazine, ten for a packet of cigarettes – and whoever collected the largest number of points would win a ticket admitting him and one other, free, twice a week, for six months,
to the 'Odeon'. The second prize was a free ticket for three
months, and the third prize a case of Scotch whisky. I was not
interested in the whisky. I had no conscious longing to comfort the soldiers. But I craved for the free ticket. My passion
for the cinema was expensive.

For weeks I assembled pencils, magazines, chewing gum,
cigarettes, socks – I got twenty points, I seem to remember, for
a pair of socks, regardless of colour. I recruited my most remote relations into knitting socks, levied a magazine tax on

visitors to the house, and pestered the neighbours for several streets around – they regarded my pleas for cigarettes with suspicion – till I was able to deliver three crates of comforts to the 'Odeon'.

The 'Odeon' was a first-release cinema, and it was seldom that it showed the same film for more than a week. But on the day that I was presented with my three month free ticket second prize – I still wonder today how I was beaten for first – *How Green Was My Valley* was screened. It took Cape Town by storm. Week after week, month after month, it played to crowded houses, in two of which, each week, I would be sitting together with someone who had earned, or bought at a discount, my hospitality. The ticket was not transferable – I was soon known to the doormen and all the usherettes – and I never found the courage to stay away. I must have seen *How Green Was My Valley* twenty-six times. I knew everyone's part off by heart. I couldn't sleep at night. At last, just before my ticket lapsed, the film gave place to another. I didn't care. I had lost my passion for the cinema, and it was months before I went again.

It was with Standard Six, and my entrance into the High School, that my life seemed to swerve all at once out of control. I can't believe that I shall ever be as unhappy, and helpless, again as I was for the five years that followed. If there is a part of me today that never unclenches itself to take, and so never gives, it is a part of me petrified by the action of those years. I sometimes catch myself in a moment of overwhelming misery, not knowing why, and then suddenly I know that I have been back emotionally to that time, when I would hide in the school lavatory and cry till my heart was exhausted.

I almost escaped going to the High School altogether. My mother, grudgingly persuaded that she was incapable of anything but spoiling me, and wanting a rather less lurid education for me than a government school could produce, set off with me for Grahamstown to interview the headmaster of a well-known public school. He welcomed us warmly, and the pen was poised for my enrolment when he mentioned casually that although I was Jewish, I would have to attend chapel, of course. My mother stared at him, explained that that was impossible, of course, and swept me from the room. We returned to Cape Town.

At Sea Point Boys' High, I was glaringly the richest boy. Gentile children of similar economic background went to Diocesan College, the Anglican public school, where Jews were discouraged. Some Jews went all the same, including the two sons of my father's partner, though usually after an irresistible contribution to building funds. My parents, however, regarded Diocesan College with distaste. It would be a degradation to buy a place for me there. The other schools, where the sons of rich Jews went, were either too far away from Sea Point – my mother's one skirmish with boarding-school was to be her last – or inescapably Christian in complexion. I had been happy enough at the Junior School. There seemed no reason why I should be any less happy at the High.

My class teacher in Standard Six, a formidably thin-lipped, lined and sallow-faced Afrikaner woman, took a shrill dislike to me from the moment I first answered to my name. What it was that angered her – for she was somehow always angry with me – I was never able to discover. Half the class was Jewish, so that it could hardly have been my Jewishness, unless she seized on me as a representative Semite. The staff, I soon realized, was uncomfortably aware of my background; the gym master had married a counter assistant at Ackermans, and two other teachers found occasion to talk of the share market to me, in the hope, I supposed, that my father helped to manipulate it. Perhaps it was the combination of Jewishness and money that excited her. Elocution had ironed the South African accent from my voice, high-pitched already, and she must have considered me extravagant. Doubtless too, she found me immoderately bumptious and set herself to drain off some of my self-confidence. She displayed a tireless and inventive energy. There was hardly a lesson in which she missed a chance to shrink me – her mimicry was sharp, and it was difficult to blame the class for laughing – and sometimes she would order me to stand while she directed herself to a long scrutiny of my conceit. On two occasions she made me hold a suitcase of books over my head for half an hour. And stimulated by her example, a small group of boys in the class would search me out at break and continue the taunting.

Had I been any less arrogant – or fearful – less eager for acclaim, had my family not lapped me with so much reassurance, I would have found these new attentions less cruel. As it was, they seemed to me motiveless, yet malignant, and the injustice I felt was greater than the ridicule itself. I had never been prepared for such a reception. My whole life before had denied it. It wasn't fair.

For a while I considered asking my parents to take me away, but then I would have had to explain. And that would have meant disclosing the humiliation. I could not do that. I did not want them to believe that I was any less regarded at school than at home. And my spirit reared in rage. No one would force me to leave. I would not be bullied.

I will carry the marks of that year, like the white patches left on the skin when the scabs have peeled off, for as long as I live. Fifteen years later, when a gang of political thugs was menacing me and members of my family in consequence of my call to boycott Nationalist goods, I lost my careful hold on myself only once. I was sitting in my office typing letters, my revolver within reach, when the telephone rang. I picked up the receiver, expecting to hear the usual crackle of half-coherent abuse, and suddenly I started to shake. It was the voice of my Standard Six teacher, shouting at me. Did I know the Natives? Did I know that they were savages, content if left to themselves, but cruel and terrible if aroused? Would I take the blame for the blood that I would cause to flow? I closed my eyes. I was running over the same long beach with the unseen feet following faster behind me, and the sea ahead. I felt the chair shift suddenly under me and my heart pounding. And then I heard her voice again, and saw the phone, and, without saying a word, replaced the receiver.

Ever since that first year at High School, I have hated bullies

– not loathed or despised them, in an intellectual shrinking, but hated them, with a hot instantaneous rush of my blood to seize and stop them. I do not know how many motives make up my own vendetta against racial rule. But not the least of them, I am sure, is my hatred of bullies, of those who beat down others with the power of their place.

Of all the emotions that my Standard Six teacher aroused in me, this was the strongest, with the one wry result that she could hardly have wanted – my rebellion against the privilege of race.

In Standard Six too, began my long skirmish with gymnastics, from which I invariably emerged battered and ashamed. There are boys who can jump on to their hands and then stroll upside down for hours. I could never get my legs to rise beyond the horizontal without losing my balance altogether and toppling over on my back. I enjoyed exercise, for I had and have a physical conceit – I still stretch springs for a few minutes every day – but my clumsiness when required to balance myself was bizarre. I had a reasonable horror of breaking my neck, and shrank from diving over a box on to my unprotected head, the contents of which I invested with some value. I used to ache with envy of the three boys who had distant deficiencies and sat on the platform of the hall, reading books, while the rest of us flung ourselves over various obstacles, arching and circling, to land on our feet, or, as with me, on our faces or backs. There was one especially fat boy in my class who was even less graceful and more terrified than I, and for him I soon acquired a lavish protectiveness.

My awe, of course, was directed to the best gymnast in the class, who could rise and wheel and plunge through the air, smooth and effortless like a gull at sea. He was good without being brilliant at his work – I don't think I could have accepted brilliance there as well – and inevitably the leader of the class throughout our years at school. I flushed under his occasional notice and would slide into daydreaming of the awe he would one day return. We became friends, though never close ones, and I saw him only once after we had left school. He was sight-seeing in Cambridge with his wife, and I literally ran into him on my way to the library. We exchanged a few startled inquiries and parted in embarrassment. He had grown plump, and I sat for the rest of the afternoon on the lawn by the river, sulking over the hungers of my childhood and the flashes of beauty now unmysterious and melancholic in my remembrance.

High School was not all misery, of course. With a shake of surprise I often found myself glad I had not given up and gone, and there was some joy in just being left alone. I fell in love with Latin, though I continued coldly to loathe Afrikaans. This had a bewildering effect on one of my teachers, a man of strong emotions who took me for both languages. Wildly he fluctuated between his delight at my proficiency in one of the subjects, and fury at my stumbling in the other. He could not believe that anyone might naturally be so quick in Latin and so clumsy in Afrikaans. I must have made him lose his temper more often than any other boy in the class, for Afrikaans was his home language, and my clumsiness smacked of contempt. Eventually, I think, he decided that I was odd rather than wilful, that my mind had a limp for which it would be cruel to blame me. For he continued to lavish his attention on me in Latin classes, but began assiduously to ignore me during Afrikaans.

I reached my deepest enjoyment in the English lessons, which it required some effort for me to see as work at all. No one in the class could write an essay, recite a poem or argue an interpretation of a text more fluently than I, and so I could conceal in this stark superiority for a while the loneliness and the humiliation of the daily break, when I would set off on my own, only sometimes to escape the organized teasing of those in my class or, as though by inevitable inheritance, successive conscripts to Standard Six.

From Standard Seven to the end of my schooling, I had as my English master a skilled artisan of language, whom it was a discipline merely to watch at work with words. From him I learnt to exercise my own aptitude, which gradually, grudgingly lost the flabbiness of ease. But I never liked him. He used language like acid, to burn his dominion into our minds. Periodically he would seize on one of the class and subject him to a soliloquy of measured cuts, like a public whipping. There was nothing ill-willed in it, as in the taunting by my teacher in Standard Six, just a display of talent, the tasting of power. He had hardly begun when the class would start to laugh in rising hysteria, enjoying the ridicule of the victim all the more in its fear for itself. My facility in English usually secured me from the lashing, though I remember one occasion – after I had written an essay without any verbs in a bout of impressionism – when he conducted a public post-mortem on my style and held up one pretension after another to the scrutiny of the class. I was furious, all the more since I recognized the justice of his assault. His assaults on others overwhelmingly embarrassed me. I wanted to extricate myself from these anguished exhibitions, and I usually sat looking fixedly at my desk until they were over.

Every now and then I would soothe my excited conscience by envisaging what would happen if I suddenly intervened. My visions were invariably discouraging. Once, after a peculiarly painful session in the playground, when I had been mimicked and joyously jostled by a group of older boys who had taken exception to my accent, I resolved to enjoy the persecutions of others in the English lesson. But I didn't. I soundly despised the rest of the class for laughing, and surrendered instead to the condolences of self-pity. The victims at least had the solidarity of each other. I wondered whether it would help if I was to antagonize the English teacher just so far as to share moderately in the common persecution. But I knew it would make no difference.

Under the supervision of the English master were the Dramatic Society, the school *Chronicle*, and the annual magazine. Continuing my flirtation with the stage, I played the comic female lead in two productions. The first, a thundering mystery called *The Bat*, required me to wear a pink kimono and two large oranges, one of which slipped – I have never understood how it remained unremarked – down to my stomach, while the other clung to my neck. I got flu before the end of the run in subconscious self-protection. The second, a war-time farce the very name of which I have forgotten, was significant for having audibly puzzled my grandmother at one of the performances in her search for my face beneath the make-up. It established me, by its success, as a popular figure in the playground, but soon faded in the school mind and returned me to a ridicule all the harsher for having been so happily interrupted.

I worked on the *Chronicle* as Assistant Literary Editor, but withdrew altogether when, in the following year, the Printing Editor was elected the Chief Editor instead of me. I had reason enough to sulk – the succession was by well-established precedent in the literary line, and I was the natural heir – but I reconciled myself to my popular defeat by resigning as the Assistant Chief Editor and refusing to contribute to the paper. It was my first experiment with boycott, and not a successful one. That year's *Chronicle* was no worse than the one which I had helped to produce, and my only consolation lay in its not being any better. I wrote for the school magazine that year a poem about the sphinx, smiling mysteriously by the Nile, in admiration I suppose of its self-sufficient impenetrability.

To the Debating Society, under fluctuating supervision and in patent despair, I devoted myself, to be elected at last its Chairman. I discovered that I could hold an audience even when it was hostile to me, that it did not matter in the rapids of my voice how high or how odd was my accent. It gave the first real boost to my assurance since I had entered High School, and later encouraged me to risk the microphone when I reached university.

In between I studied for my bar mitzvah and sang in the synagogue choir, seduced less, I confess, by the pleasure of singing – the ritual remained enigmatic and irritating – than by the payment I received for rehearsals. I cannot remember how much we were paid – I know it was a sliding scale – but I clearly thought it insufficient, since I was constantly agitating for a rise. Eventually, strident with the sanctity of labour, I led a deputation to the Cantor, who only restrained his temper, I suspect, from regard for my father. He rejected our demands, and I called a strike, confident in my knowledge that the Day of Atonement, the high-point of the religious year, was only a few weeks away. The choir practice was cancelled when all but the Rabbi's son and the adults stayed away, and talks were hastily called. After a tense ten minutes of impassioned rebuke, the Cantor agreed to meet our demands halfway, and we accepted his terms.

My bar mitzvah came and left me with £300, though not before a passionate family argument over whether the money I would receive was mine to spend as I pleased. My parents provokingly maintained that it was their own friends, after all, who would be giving me the presents, and that I should, in consequence, take their advice, depositing the money in the post office, where it would slowly increase. I replied that the money would certainly come from their friends, but that there would have to be a bar mitzvah first. And there would not be one if I refused to sing my portion of the law in the synagogue. I had acquired an appetite for antiques and disputed the advantages of a fixed $2\frac{1}{2}\%$ interest rate a year. If I invested the money in Georgian silver, I claimed, I would double my assets in no time, and not be suddenly impoverished if the post office failed. With a backward glance at our shared insecurities, I also reminded them that assets should in part be portable. There was no telling when we might not have to live off the proceeds of a snuff-box.

I suspect that this was the one argument which carried any weight, and in the end we cheerfully compromised. I would put my money in the post office and withdraw it as I found a recognizable bargain. I certainly bought several pieces of silver, though none of them was recognizably a bargain. The prices of antiques rocketed with post-war liquidity, but my collection, partly sold in the predatory days of publishing, was never worth more than I paid for it. My grandfather, who had contributed one-third of the capital outlay, provided the most incisive commentary. One evening I led him up to my bedroom, where my treasures were carefully displayed on black velvet in my

bookcase. For a few minutes he stood staring at the antiques –
a few snuff-boxes, the glitter of my Georgian tea-set, the cluster
of colour around my spoons. I waited for his admiration.

'Curiosities,' he muttered, shrugging his shoulders, 'curiosities.' And he walked from the room.

The one who had awoken and fed my appetite for collecting,
I still think of with wonder. Archie Shacksnovis had set off
in fifth century Athens, moved magnanimously through the
Renaissance, and ended up in Regency England. A Rhodes
scholar, he had played rugby and rowed for Oxford, written
passable poetry and shone with steady brilliance in his law
studies. Returning to South Africa he had sped to supremacy at
the bar, with hardly a hiatus between his success as a junior
counsel and his opulence as a silk. With his mounting income – he
acted for many of the mining companies – he more and more
indulged his magnificent taste. He collected first editions, old
silver, pictures, Chinese porcelain and jades, snuff-boxes and
vinaigrettes in gold and painted enamel. He advised artists
and helped them lavishly, contributed to *Voorslag*, Roy Camp-
bell's magazine of dissent, became one of the country's top
sports commentators, entertained joyously and conversed with
anyone on anything. He liked the best foods and the best wines
and began to surrender himself without reticence to both. He
grew thick, seemed shorter than he was, and started to gamble
wildly on horses. The more he earned the more he spent, and
gradually he borrowed till, at the end, his debts constantly
threatened to engulf him. I was studying at Cambridge when he
died. I heard that his collection had been sold to meet the
demands on his estate, and had still not sufficed.

My solicitor in Cape Town once told me of his own professional experience with Archie. He had briefed him for an
important case, and Archie had flown down from Johannesburg for a week-end of consultation. All Saturday morning he
had walked around the city, visiting art dealers and bookshops,
and in the afternoon had gone to the races, where he had lost
the entire figure on his brief. That night he had entertained
some of his friends at the city's foremost restaurant, and had

retreated to bed beyond four on Sunday morning. After a late lunch, he had then taken up his brief, and smoking continuously, without interruption for dinner, had produced by midnight a brilliantly argued opinion, which it would have taken the average silk at least a week to prepare. On Monday morning he had returned by the early plane to Johannesburg, and the case itself was settled out of court soon afterwards to the solicitor's staggered satisfaction.

I met Archie when I was eleven, early in 1944. He had had a heart attack, and, in sudden response to a suggestion from my mother some months before, arrived to convalesce with us at the Cape. He fascinated me, and I became his passionate disciple. He treated me as an equal in taste and talent, discussing my future with me as though I was certain to get whatever I wanted by our joint exertions. He took me buying with him, placing the purchases in period with an abundance of story, so that a first edition novel by Henry James, a Georgian silver wine label, or an early Africana oil painting, became invested for me with the movement and colour of a whole far age. He started my own collection with three eighteenth-century Irish silver spoons, and during the rest of his life, in sudden spurts of generosity, gave me presents, one of them – a pair of hand-painted Chinese tiles – from the core of his own collection. In the coming years, when he visited Cape Town, or I went to stay with him in Johannesburg, we would talk together till the early morning – of everything from Ming porcelain to the career of Rufus Isaacs – and he would listen and encourage while I found words for my most extravagant desires. He became my substitute for friendship with boys of my own age. I took to smoking his expensive imported cigarettes; and, at the age of fifteen, I even went to the races with him, winning £20 on what must have been one of his own few fortunate excursions. Later, my brother Maurice married his daughter Ruth – they were to be divorced shortly before his death – and I gradually grew away from him, perhaps because I felt that I was having to share him at last with the rest of my family. Near the end of his life, I saw him hardly at all. But he

was always part of my mind, and whatever richness my school-
days had, like the colours deep in polished silver, lay in my
experience of him.

From time to time during those years there reached me from
a muffled distance sounds of the rising racial clash. One night,
in August 1946, Dr Elen Hellman, an old friend of the family's
and a prominent member of the South African Institute of
Race Relations, brought Margaret Ballinger, the African representative for Cape Eastern in the House of Assembly, to
dinner. It was a tense evening, for Africans had been killed by
the police in Johannesburg a few hours before. I stared in
astonishment at the talk. I had discovered for the first time the
existence of an organized African resistance.

Nothing so startles anyone who has watched the course of the
racial struggle in South Africa as the reputation for shrewd
enlightenment enjoyed abroad by the huge mining concerns.
In 1890, the average monthly wage of an African miner was
£3 3s., and from that year onwards the mining companies
exerted themselves to effect reductions in their labour costs.
By 1903 the average wage had fallen to £2 14s. a month, where
it remained, with minute adjustments, for decades. Even though
the price of gold rose by 97% between 1931 and 1940, African
wages increased by only 8% during the same period.

In 1943 the Smuts government appointed the Lansdowne
Commission to investigate wages and other conditions of employment for African miners on the Witwatersrand. The
African miner, it was established, got 2s. for each eight-hour
underground shift (an average of £2 19s. 6d. a month), and
1s. 9d. (£2 14s. 2d. a month) if he was a surface worker, while
the monthly value of food and accommodation provided by the
mines was estimated at £2 16s. 4d. a head. As a result of the
Commission's recommendations, underground workers received an additional 5d. a shift, to a total of 2s. 5d., and surface
workers an extra 4d., to a total of 2s. 1d. The recommendation
for a 3d. cost of living allowance was ignored. The average pay
for underground miners, therefore, became £3 8s. a month,
with payments in kind adding a further £1 10s. The value of

money had plummeted since 1890, yet African wages were little more in 1943 than they had been 53 years before. Today, after a rise of 3d. a shift in the minimum underground wage between 1943 and 1952, and another of 4d. in 1953, the basic wage for the underground miner is 3s. a shift, while the surface worker earns only 2s. 3d.

In 1946 African bitterness broke briefly through the cold concrete of the mining compounds. Through May and June, the African Mineworkers' Union made approaches to the Chamber of Mines for a rise in wages, but it met with threats as the only response. On the 4th of August leaders of the African miners assembled and agreed upon strike action. Eight days later, on the 12th of August, some 75,000 miners stopped work. Several thousand deserted their compounds and marched to Johannesburg, demanding their passes and the right to return to their homes. The Chamber of Mines rubbed its eyes in momentary bewilderment, and then called on the Smuts government for help. Police were ordered to baton – and, if necessary, to shoot – the strikers back to their compounds. Thirteen men were killed, hundreds admitted to hospital. But the strike survived. Workers at different mines all over the Reef refused to go down the shafts till they received the pledge of a rise in their wages to 10s. a shift – the extravagant demand of 1s. 4d. an hour. When they were forced, at rifle point, down the shafts, they sat in the tunnels underground and refused to move, until the police drove them up again to the surface, 'stope by stope and level by level' as the *Rand Daily Mail* dispassionately described it. All known supporters of the African Mineworkers' Union were discharged, hundreds were arrested, and the homes of suspected subversives throughout the country searched by police. The strike was over. Mine owners clanged closed the gates of the compounds and resolved to permit no further disturbances within the concrete walls. Since 1946 numerous attempts have been made by the African political movements and trade unions to organize the miners. All have failed. Few murmurs of disaffection escape the constant vigilance of those employed by the mining companies to listen, observe and report. And when Harry Oppenheimer talks in London of his reputation for liberalism, he doubtless recognizes how fortunate it is that his African miners do not form part of his audience.

In 1946, too, the country was convulsed by a new attempt to solve the Indian problem. Eighty-six years before, the first Indians had migrated to Natal as indentured labourers for the sugar plantations, on the understanding that they would receive citizenship rights on the completion of their contracts. But as their numbers rose with successive waves of immigration, so did the fright with which the whites regarded them. From 1883 onwards special taxes were levied on them and laws passed to curtail their freedom of trade and travel, while the Orange Free State banned them altogether. Yet they continued to build their homes and schools and shops, and even evolved a small but dynamic merchant class which competed with whites for trade and property. This was a development that white South Africans, and especially the English-speaking citizens of Natal, who felt themselves the most menaced, could not be expected to permit.

In 1943 the Smuts government, at war with the Axis powers, passed the Trading and Occupation of Land (Transvaal and Natal) Restriction Act, which prohibited the sale of any more land by whites to Indians in Natal, and pegged Indian trade in the Transvaal, for a period of three years. Then, in March 1946, Smuts introduced the Asiatic Land Tenure and Indian Representation Bill to make the principal provisions of the lapsed 'Indian Pegging' Act permanent. Indians in the Transvaal and Natal could purchase property from whites in special 'exempted areas' alone, while in compensation they were offered three white members in the House of Assembly and one in the Senate, elected on a separate communal roll, to represent them.

The Nationalist Party and the Natal-centred, jubilantly English Dominion Party joined voices to denounce the franchise provisions of the Bill as threatening the survival of white supremacy. Only the Native Representatives and a few in the

C

governing United Party itself protested against the patent race discrimination in the measure. But among these last was Jan Hofmeyr, Minister of Finance, protege of Smuts and his gen-eally accepted successor.

I had for years heard Hofmeyr spoken of as the liberal hope of the country, the one man with influence and vision enough to swerve white South Africa from its course. I went to hear him speak in the Assembly on the Bill and was stirred, as were many others, by his strong denunciation. Gradually I had acquired a distaste for the doctrine of white supremacy, and suddenly I hated it. Like the whole country, I waited excitedly to see how Hofmeyr would vote. If he went into the lobby against Smuts on so critical a measure, a split in the govern-ment seemed inevitable and with it at last the creation, under his leadership, of a significant liberal force. He voted for the Bill.

The Indian community rejected the new law with disgust. In an unprecedented display of unanimity, not one of the thirty thousand Indians entitled to register for the communal voters' roll did so. The three seats in the Assembly and the one in the Senate remained vacant, till the Nationalist government in 1949 repealed the franchise provisions of the Act. The restrictions on property purchase were welcomed by the new regime, which built on their foundations the structure of the 1950 Group Areas Act.

Two thousand Indians went to prison in a passive resistance campaign during 1946, while India itself recalled its High Commissioner from South Africa and severed all trade between the two countries. In December the United Nations General Assembly debated a complaint by the government of India against the Act, and – despite the objections of Smuts that the issue concerned South Africa alone – resolved by 24 votes to 19, with 6 abstentions, that the treatment of Indians in South Africa should conform to the provisions of the Charter. It was the first of many defeats that South African governments would recalcitrantly suffer at the U.N.

Smuts, of course, the philosopher-statesman, admired im-

perial Britain, and consistently showed himself accommodating
to British capital. Spokesmen for the Chamber of Mines were
often at his ear, suggesting and advising. English-language
newspapers, spokesmen for the mines and secondary industry,
despised and regularly denounced the Nationalist opposition.
Almost all English-speaking South Africans, loyal to the
British connection, remembered with disgust the Nazi sympathies of those who led resurgent Afrikanerdom in parliament.
To the Jews a Nationalist victory was unthinkable. Nazism had
been defeated in the war, and the concentration camps of
Europe were being dismantled. That power should fall into the
hands of such ravenous anti-Semites as Eric Louw seemed to
them the material of nightmare. And non-white South Africa
itself, prohibited from all but a small peripheral participation,
watched the struggle for parliamentary power with helpless
horror. The Coloured knew that the defeat of Smuts would
evict them from their squatting rights in the backyards of
South Africa, to the regimented rightlessness of the Africans
and Indians. And the Africans and the Indians, already suffering the predatory trusteeship of Smuts, viewed the chances of
Nationalist victory with despair.

In May 1948 white South Africa, with a few thousand Coloured in train, trooped to the polls. The United Party of Smuts
had emerged from the 1943 general election with a massive
majority, which it seemed that no normal electoral swing could
dangerously reduce. On election night I sat with my family
listening to the results in the urban constituencies as they
blared from the radio. When we went to bed, well after midnight, the United Party enjoyed an intimidating lead, though a
few constituencies on the urban edges, particularly in the
Transvaal, had crumbled to the Nationalists. The day after the
election, in the late afternoon, my parents were flying to
Johannesburg for a conference of the South African Jewish
Board of Deputies. On the plane with them was Senator Conroy, Minister of Lands in the Smuts administration. Ermelo,
the constituency neighbouring Standerton, the seat of Smuts
himself, had just fallen to the Nationalists. 'Ek is bang vir die

Oubaas,'[1] Conroy said. By the time the plane landed in Johannesburg, the defeat of Smuts in his own constituency had been announced, and everyone knew, though the United Party still had a majority of the proclaimed results, that the Nationalists had won the election.

While the Afrikaner countryside celebrated its triumph, the largely English-speaking cities held their breath in stunned disbelief. The Nationalist Party, with a popular vote of just over 400,000, had 70 seats in a House of 153, but its ally, the Afrikaner Party, with just over 40,000 votes, had won 9 seats, to provide an overall majority of 5. The United Party, with its swollen urban majorities, had polled almost 525,000 votes, but won only 65 seats, while the Labour Party, with some 27,000 votes, had 6. The 3 Native Representatives increased the opposition strength to 74. The Jewish community panicked, and some even made hurried preparations to leave. A few who had acknowledged their Jewishness furtively, if at all, were suddenly fervent Zionists. But soon it became clear that the Nationalists were not, after all, so greatly to be feared. The mining houses continued to make vast profits, even vaster ones when the exploitation of the Orange Free State goldfields began. Industry faltered and then bounded forward again. Ministers made soothing noises to the Jewish community, and continued to permit the transfer of Zionist funds to Israel. The government applied itself to dealing with the non-whites. Why, after all, were the new rulers to be feared? The primary object of any white administration was the control of non-white discontent. The Nationalists might stimulate more resistance by their gratuitously savage laws than the leaders of the United Party had done, but they were even more ruthless in protecting the structure of white supremacy. For the moment, English-speaking white South Africa heaved a sigh of relief.

[1] 'I am scared for the old chief.' 'Oubaas' was the title by which Smuts was commonly known among his followers. A blend of affection and awe, it literally means 'old master'.

CHAPTER THREE

UNIVERSITIES

UNLIKE my brothers and sister, I had never gone abroad as a child, trailing my parents on trips to Switzerland, France or Italy and then returning to busy long sojourns in London. I had been taken to London as a baby, spending my whole six months outside of Africa in a state of semi-consciousness, and then been cut off by the war from following precedent. With peace, a trip abroad was dangled as the reward of a first-class matriculation; and that ambiguous accomplishment – my pass in Afrikaans was an object lesson in clairvoyance and the interminable efficacy of 'A Day by the Sea' – added the proper element of piquancy.

I do not think I shall ever experience again the awe with which I climbed into the aeroplane for London. English-speaking South Africa, of either Testament, has always been colonial, with London as its cultural capital; and travelling overseas is not merely an escape from the tedium of an outpost society, but a pilgrimage to the shops and to the theatres of the West End – in that order. On the ledge of the world where they conduct their profitable commerce, the English-speaking 'Europeans' – the very name they give themselves sounds their sense of exile – sigh for an end to business hours, some intermission from the hot red earth they see all around their feet, from life among strange peoples whose complaints and demands are so disconcerting, from the tensions and threats so oppressively requiring response. Going abroad is 'getting away from it all', to the tranquillity of their own language spoken in its own streets, or the distraction of other languages which carry no stirrings in their deeps and may therefore in safety be ignored. So many would like to leave the ledge altogether, for the smooth highways of home; but then commerce is nowhere so profitable as on the ledge, and the sun is lucid there as the sound of the sea, and a garden stretches in hot colours to the front gate, and there is a servant for the kitchen and a servant for the car and a servant for the flowers and the carpets. Since Sharpeville and their sudden sharp sight of the drop to the rocks below, English-speaking South Africans have surveyed their ledge rather more disconsolately than usual and shot a few guarded glances at the flat lands of home. Some have even clambered off the ledge at last and have settled in England, surrendering their gardens and their servants and the respect in the bank manager's eye. But it is too great a wrench for most, and they hold what they have on the ledge, keeping their eyes carefully turned from the direction of the drop and sighing over the irresistible comforts of exile.

That day I left by aeroplane for London, halfway through my sixteenth year, I, too, felt that I was leaving exile for an undiscovered home. The irony is sharp, for now I am in London again, inescapably in exile. And home is only a longing for life on that ledge, for the clashes of peoples and colours, the anguish of struggle there and the joy that make all else somehow dreary and deserted, like a city street at half past three in the morning. It is difficult for me to remember just why it was, as I fumbled with my seat-belt, that I felt the gaping excitement of going home. Somewhere was the feeling that at last I was climbing over the garden gate into the street outside, that ambition was my only real home and that ambition was there in the street, with the crowds and the clatter and the stride of recognition. London was the scramble of Disraeli, on bruised knees and elbows to the top of the stairs, the landing of talent. And somewhere too was the escape, from the littleness that life in South Africa seemed so insurmountably to be. If one was going to be famous, only London could bestow an acknowledgment that mattered; in the authority of romance, the Lord Mayor of London appeared bulkier than the Prime Minister of South Africa. Entering London was entering history; the titles one earned there glowed with the glamour of those who had possessed and endowed them. And if after all one was to fail, and I was only too aware of the terror that lurked for me in failure, London provided deeper hiding-places than Cape Town, far more comforts of rationalization and distraction. It was unthinkable that I should fail, of course, but it was always well to make provision for it.

My parents had supplied me with a list of their friends in London who were likely to endure me, and I had a handful of relatives for protection and nostalgia. In between visiting as much of my family acquaintance as I could and tramping from one historical foot-print to another, I was to try and insinuate myself into Oxford for a degree in English. Inevitably, it was on the family acquaintance that I found myself increasingly dependent. Too many books had led me to think of London as a succession of boxes, each squarely within the next and the centre recognizable from the last outside. Instead, I found only a vast diffusion, an irregular spread, but tight, like spilt milk on a polished table-top. For a while, wandering from one line in the guide-book to another seemed contact of a kind with the city. But after two weeks I realized that I was no nearer London than one is near the sea in a small rowing-boat, and I clutched at the family acquaintance.

There is a freemasonry about Zionism that hurdles language and class. Jews who meet each other at conferences or on ships and find themselves clinging to the same vision of a Jewish State quickly exchange friends and addresses and load each other with indeterminate invitations. Most of my family friends in London were emotional entries of this sort, and most of them offered me as a result little more than I had run from in South Africa. They were all generous and warm – that they should have put up with my noisy dissent at all argues well enough their loyalty and kindness – but the harbours that they offered were Levantine, and less a part of London to me than the colonial Cape. One of the few with a purely peripheral interest in Zionism and more a business associate of my parents than an emotional ally was a middle-aged manufacturer of forceful ugliness and a double-bass voice. Given to chain-smoking, and gin-rummy for dizzying stakes, he fascinated me both as an original, which he clearly considered himself to me, and as the archetype of big business abroad, with his escape from the choppy drabness all around him on the raft of his expense account. He had no awe of his accumulated capital, and when his appetite required, dipped into it with a commentary on the inexhaustible richness of life for the instruction of his adult children. He had divorced his wife many years before, and though she was still alive, this fact was assiduously avoided. In a world of cheaply printed paper coupons, his table was lush, with butter in blocks and smug slices of meat. I was delighted and appalled.

I had never measured money before, except as it affected my personal relationship to others.

Colour is so compulsive in South Africa; the sharpest liberalism often cuts the colour bar without ever reaching the economic glint underneath. Yet here was a society, uniformly bleached, in which the possession of money divided some from others as bleakly, if not as brutally, as a thin stretch of skin in South Africa. For my frequent host, there was no interminable queuing, waiting at bus-stops in the rain, no hoarding for a Sunday lunch. And money was more than pleasure, it was power. His poorer friends deferred to his success as his children deferred to his control over their incomes; and he accepted the deference not with pride, which might have been more generously endured, but with an avaricious cynicism. His worst suspicions about other people were consistently confirmed, and every confirmation demanded further proof. I cannot believe that he was peculiarly unhappy, though many people excused their surrender to him by pretending pity; he was greedy without guilt, and ambitious without charity, and he drew even from his restlessness a profound satisfaction. I have met his commercial counterparts in innumerable forms wherever I have lived, but I have never encountered another with his huge and honest appetite for power.

I was vigorously attracted before becoming far more vigorously repelled; it was so difficult at first not to enjoy and even a little to envy his unencumbered cynicism. Here, after all, was the obvious way to climb, and I visited for a few effortless days my six-year-old ambition to become a millionaire. But the power he exerted seemed so sterile, as though he commanded a high sand hill in the Sahara. There was something so finally pointless about the money he spent and the effort he made to heap up sufficient to spend; it was like getting perpetually drunk. Had I seen him as an original, I think that the marks he left on my mind would soon enough have faded. But only his frankness was his own, his basic lack of guile; the cynicism with which he laid his motivation bare, highlighted the drapery in which his associates covered their own. Culpable he was, but much less so than those about him, whose desire for money was far more demanding and destructive for being raised to a level of piety. He, at least, was brazenly a materialist. So many others whom I now remember having met and heard were idealists self-travestied, their money their religion. It is they who seem to me the ultimately vicious; they practise the black mass of humanism.

I decided that I did not want to be a millionaire. I became a socialist. I still am. It seems to me intolerable that money should be power, if only through the unequal stripping of restraints. It has never mattered to me in itself that money should enable an escape from queues and ration cards and a whole life spent in one room; what matters surely is that some people cannot escape, because they do not have the money. I have no guilty and embarrassed dislike of the rich. Wealth seems to me the subject of compassion, not because it corrupts – which it so often does – or misleads – which it does even more; but because it is ultimately useless, a kind of interminable self-sacrifice. I cannot guess at the annual income of the richest man in Southern Africa. But I am sure that he cannot spend all he earns, that there are only so many restraints he can escape at only so much expenditure. For beyond a certain point, one does not escape restraints by spending money, one begins to accumulate them, till one is back to where one started, frenziedly attempting to escape, like a squirrel in a water-wheel cage. Yet, in order that escape for him may become finally impossible, other men must be restrained, in the sterile concrete compounds of the goldfields, in the eight-hour shifts underground – six thousand, even ten thousand feet down in the stale, dusty heat – for the three shillings saved towards the buying of a blanket against the cold.

All this is primitive, of course, and no longer part of a society civilized to affluence. Here in Britain there are no slums – well, hardly any by South African standards. And the skyscape is a reassurance of television aerials. Yet every release from restraint that is enjoyed by only a few creates new restraints for the many left behind. I cannot think any society desirable which grants to some and denies to others on the basis of vast disparities in wealth. I do not seek a uniform state; conformity frightens and revolts me. And it seems to me that socialism must struggle against conformity if it is not to degrade below the level that it wants society to surmount. Yet it is a hollow humanism that must bind individuality to economic inequalities. An individual is not such because his income permits him to dine and dress at greater expense than others. Quite the contrary, it seems to me that economic discrepancy creates far greater conformity than it destroys. I have always found the rich drably the same; with mysterious exceptions, their personalities are the money which they make and spend like so many automata. And the poor in the main wear their poverty like some inner uniform, as similar in their own acquisitiveness as the rich are in theirs. Such people are not free. The rich are tied to their expense accounts and the poor to the easy glamour of their television sets as tightly as the African is tied to his passbook and his shanty-town. Much more tightly, perhaps, for the African beats at bullet and bludgeon to escape.

The African experience – of slave ships and brandy bartering, the gun and the whip – has swollen through centuries of wrong and deceit to a wild longing for freedom. That this longing has been twisted or altogether betrayed by many of those who claimed to be satisfying it, has intensified rather than diminished the longing itself. And the longing knows no frontier, but extends to contain the continent. I have always played socialism by touch. If I hadn't, I would probably have joined the Communist Party years ago, and ended up by flagellating myself in the propaganda pamphlets of Moral Re-Armament. The socialism of trade union bosses and the parliamentary left in the affluent society fills me with dismay, and I can see why British radicalism is tired and distraught. But out of Africa, I have long had faith, a new form of socialism can come, a real economic democracy founded and flourishing in freedom. It is paramountly for this reason that I lift my chin and say, 'I am an African.' Running down through all the gravel and rock, that is my pipe.

After a few weeks in London, I travelled up to Oxford for an interview with the Senior Tutor at Balliol and a view of the spires that had stretched their imaginary shapes for so long across my ambition. I was astounded. I had imagined the university sprawled along a river bank, with the town, noiseless and small, nosing one side. Instead, I was run over by the city I found, tossed into the endless grey drizzle around by the roar of the streets, and the busy shouldering crowds. At least the grey air was Gothic; and fortifying myself with a gulp of recollected reading – Shelley after all, I decided, had squatter's rights before Nuffield – I set off to see the Senior Tutor of what I had already begun to consider my college. Armed with an introduction from its Visitor, Viscount Samuel – of all my family's acquaintances, the one that I made with the greatest initial timidity and subsequent delight – I believed that I would be required to do no more than be inventively glib, produce a few details and sign a few forms. The Tutor, however, turned out to be far more muted, if no less astounding, than the city. Having learnt that I was sixteen, he gently suggested that I should wait two years before trying to enter the university, muffling the impact of his refusal in references to the bulge of ex-service students still blocking the limited accommodation and the age at which English matriculants traditionally turned themselves into undergraduates. I was incredulous and insistent. He remained polite and even kind. I could, he explained,

write the college extrance examination if I wanted a bash; he
spoke as though it were a stone wall, but I quickly licked up
the comfort he permitted himself to spill and returned to London convinced that I would batter my way into Oxford yet
with a little resolute effort.

A tutor was engaged, an ironic Anglo-Catholic who was
hilarious on the habits of several well-known contemporary
writers he knew, and I began with fitful conscientiousness to
prepare for the examination a few weeks away. Doubtless the
whole adventure was ridiculous – I hardly knew enough French
to identify my aunt's pen with propriety, and the French paper
I wrote must have provided the examiners with unaccustomed
delight – but I had not given up believing in the infallibility of
my luck, having long since recognized that most of my successes bore only a bastard relationship to brain. In the event, of
course, I failed to talk the selection committee over – I give
thanks that I shall never quite know how deplorably – and
I hurriedly applied for admission to the University of Cape
Town instead.

Arid as the exercise is, I often find myself wondering whether
I would ever have involved myself in politics, on any but the
most casual level, if I had got into Oxford. The three and a
half years that I spent at the University of Cape Town were
much more than a platform apprenticeship; the memory of
them would fill me with a horror of racialism even if the last
seven years had not provided me with more than sufficient
cause.

I intricately remember the first day I attended classes. It was
several weeks after they had begun, since I had only returned
from England at the beginning of April, and none of my few
former school-friends at the university were taking the same
subjects as I. I had met no one in the English class and was prepared for a protracted isolation. But as soon as the lecturer had
left the room, I found myself sucked into a whirlwind of argument on modern poetry, gradually subsiding to leave only
three strident participants – a young white girl, a thin angular
Coloured man with astonishingly green eyes and an energetic

forefinger, and myself. Finding ourselves rapidly abandoned by our audience, and with the morning free of any other classes, we transferred our argument to the union and stretched it from morning tea to lunch, leaving poetry for education and then, irresistibly, education for politics. I found myself thinking with disquiet, as the argument staked claims to more and more ground, 'She knows a great deal, much more than I thought. And he knows more than either of us! He hasn't read as widely, but he has read much more deeply, and he has thought about it all with much more courage and honesty.' It was a blow from which my sturdy racial benevolence reeled and would soon fall once and for all flat on its face.

We became fast friends, the young girl, the Coloured man with the green eyes, and myself, though we had all three of us to scramble over countless habits of impatience and distrust in order to do so.

Leah lived in Woodstock, the brimming backyard of the city, where factory and slum were steadily suffocating the few roads running up the mountain-side in which Coloured and white still lived in neighbouring homes. Her parents had come from Russia as adults, too late for easy assimilation, and years of economic struggle – from which they had not long escaped when first I met them – had held them back from the smug cultural digestion of the Jewish middle class. Though all four children were going or had gone to university – one sister was lecturing there – Yiddish was still spoken sporadically in the home, from affection, security, pride and occasional necessity, for Leah's grandmother never admitted to enough English (despite her sudden signs of knowledge when she overheard herself discussed) for more than the simplest exchange of greetings. Under her quiet government, the kitchen withstood all attempts at emancipation; and when her descendants, carelessly or in a fury of defiance, dug their meat knives into the butter, she would fly to the garden and bury the polluted cutlery – with little labels recording the date of their guilt – up to the neck in the ground. At the kitchen door, however, she cheerfully abdicated, knowing nothing and so regarding herself as innocent of the degree to which Moses was being scorned in the beyond.

The rest of the family – in varying degrees of coherence – proclaimed themselves as progressives, and Leah herself had sold copies of the Communist Party weekly for pocket-money and solidarity at the age of six. Her allegiance, however, had never been any more official than that; she grew up in a period of disenchantment with the party, when a number of its oldest supporters sickened and forsook it over the German–Russian pact.

The South African Communist Party, like its counterparts in the rest of the world, has made costly mistakes; its singularity has consisted not in their bizarreness – though some, like the 'black republic' policy, have been singularly bizarre – but in the speed and thoroughness with which it has managed to recover from them. The 'black republic' policy itself, which was forced upon the party on one of the few occasions when the Comintern even noticed its existence, required the establishment of a black South Africa and led inevitably to the expulsion or resignation of those cantankerous white members who saw in this a racialism in reverse. Hardly had the party recovered by the late 'thirties, when the German–Russian pact sent it reeling again: many of its Jewish members found it rather too difficult to hold down the new propaganda on the 'imperialist war' together with what they had already digested about Hitler and the Gestapo, and threw up their membership. The halcyon days of the Second Front, however, nursed the party back to a state of health that it has never ceased to regard without wry wonder. Prominent white industrialists festooned the platforms at Medical Aid for Russia meetings, while their wives busily helped in organizing film previews. Then, with the end of the war, the 1946 gold-miners' strike and the abortive Sedition Trial of prominent communists that followed, the timid and the prudent fled from even the most pallid association with it, and the party weekly, *The Guardian*, which had watched its readership rocket to over 50,000 during the early 'forties and its advertising revenue swell to the luxury of a reserve fund,

now watched both decline just as rapidly. In 1948 the Nationalists took power, and only the hard core remained for the banning of the party and *The Guardian* in 1950.

Officially, the Communist Party ceased to exist with the
Suppression of Communism Act, though communists continued, of course, their political struggle, bearing their ultimate principles into battle with them like a badge on their
khaki, as volunteers in one or other battalion of the Congress
Alliance. It needed the 1960 State of Emergency and the banning of the non-white political movements, the gauntlet of
terror thrown down with a thud, to make revolution a reality
and re-establish the organization underground. It is a becoming commentary on the muscle-bound anti-communism of the
Nationalists that they should have succeeded in compelling the
Communist Party to the one course of action likely to spread its
influence and prestige furthest among the non-white masses –
the recognition in practice at last of its active revolutionary role.

There is nothing mysterious about the energetic recovery
that the Communist Party has always made from the calamity
of its own mistakes. Until 1953, when the South African
Liberal Party was founded, it was the only political organization in the country that possessed a substantial white membership and yet neither preached a colour bar somewhere in
its objectives nor practised one in its activities. Aspiring
Africans and Indians, rising trade unionists, the intellectuals of
the swelling urban slums, the few university students groping
for a composed ideal of change, found in the party not only a
purpose without compromise, but – to many, far more important – an intellectual friendship across the colour line, without all those prickling discomforts that mark the politics of
patronage. In the homes of white communists, African members of the party, stray sympathizers, or those being groomed
for possible apprenticeship could sip their brandy behind the
curtains, hidden from the liquor laws and periodic township
raids for a while, to enjoy an evanescent escape from squalor and
violence into argument, the climb up the clean rock-faces of the
mind. There, too, behind the curtains, was a live sophistication,

an acquaintance with the music and the painting and the literature of Europe that rustled like dead leaves in the African schools and withered as it sprouted almost in the choked paths of the townships.

Leah introduced me to the twilight territory of the disgruntled white left, that disembodied discontent, unprepossessingly sad, neither accepting the privileges of colour nor working for their elimination, but waiting for some sudden resolution that would automatically resolve its own dilemma as well. The main function of a Jewish mother in South Africa is to marry off her daughter well or, at all events, safely, and Leah's mother regarded my combination of wealth, parentage, and careful dissent – to her daughter's rising irritation – with encouragement. But Leah and I were never in love, just confusingly fond of each other, and though her parents at last acclimatized themselves to this, they continued to show me a constant kindness, which was partly their own easy warmth, and partly, I liked to believe, a fondness for me. I spent much of my time in their Woodstock home and was almost as miserable as Leah when they moved to Sea Point. I had grown so fond of their house, with its large effervescent Coloured family next door, and the whole area with its racial shadings and the rich ragged gaiety of its streets.

Leah was the first real friend I ever had, and our relationship prised open my emotions to the world outside the close security of my home. With her friends, who soon became mine, we went sunbathing to distant beaches, heckled at political meetings, gossiped endlessly about each other's ambitions and restraints in joint exasperation and discovery. I had emerged from school a sort of bolted house, with all the windows shuttered as though to advertise the absence of the occupant. In the astonished pleasure of my friendship, I began one by one to take the shutters down.

Peter, of the strenuous forefinger and the green eyes, came from the thin ranks of the Coloured petty bourgeoisie, which for the most part aped the genteel virtues of the English lower middle class, with a colour rather than a class snobbery, but which also provided almost all the recruits to rebellion. Until the late 'fifties, the Coloured working class lay in a political stupor, soothed by its wage superiority to Africans, its exemption from the pass laws, and its adult male suffrage on the common roll, into stolid acquiescence. Only the Coloured teachers, a few lawyers and doctors, clergymen and small traders, stirred in protest at the numberless discriminations which they were condemned by their race to endure.

In 1943 the Smuts government announced its intention to establish a special Department of Coloured Affairs, and the disaffected Coloured intellectuals, seeing the projected Department as the embodiment of their racial subservience and, worse, an attempt to administer this subservience more efficiently, stirred with sudden revolt. The Coloured had largely escaped the close-cropped subjection of the African. In the Western Cape, where so many of them lived, they might travel on the same buses and trains, sit on the same seats, stroll through the same parks and rest on the same benches, as whites. Unlike the Africans, in areas of Cape Town like Leah's Woodstock, they shared the same street and sometimes the same house with whites. Unlike Africans, they were not forced to carry passes always on their person and deliver them to official scrutiny on demand or face criminal prosecution. Unlike both the Africans and the Indians, they were freely acknowledged as citizens – however inferior – of white South Africa, with the right, virtually uncircumscribed by statute, to live and work and travel where they chose. They did not swim with whites, or drink morning tea with them in town, visit the same cinemas or attend the same well-equipped schools, but this was a rigid social statute, not a legislative one. Their salaries were not nearly as high as those paid to whites, but they were higher than any paid to Africans or Indians doing similar work. Theirs was a dominated and depressed community, rather than a subjugated one. Now the Department of Coloured Affairs threatened all the minute administrative interventions of what had already become, in the Department of Native Affairs, the government of a separate regimented racial colony.

The Coloured community split between those who were prepared to collaborate with the proposed Coloured Affairs Department and those who believed that all its activities should
be shunned. In the same year, the Anti-C.A.D. was established
as a federation of Coloured organizations – tennis clubs, rate-
payers' associations, discussion groups and church committees
– to co-ordinate the boycott and convince the Coloured community at last that its future was inextricably bound up with the
Africans and Indians in one common struggle against white
supremacy. The initiative and control of the movement lay
largely in the hands of Trotskyist intellectuals, most of them
teachers organized into the affiliated Teachers' League of
South Africa, and the boycott campaign led to a fever of political activity among the Coloured people, especially in the Cape,
never seen before. So successful was the boycott itself that the
plans to establish a Coloured Affairs Department were shelved,
and only dusted off and displayed fifteen years later by the
government of Dr Verwoerd.

On the 17th December 1943 the Non-European Unity Movement was formed at a conference in Bloemfontein by the Anti-
C.A.D., the All African Convention and other associated
organizations, to form a united front against white domination
on a 'ten-point programme' of basic democratic demands.

1. The franchise, that is the right of every man and
   woman over the age of twenty-one to elect and be
   elected to Parliament, the provincial councils and all
   other divisional and municipal councils:
2. Compulsory, free, and uniform education for all children up to the age of sixteen, with free meals, free books
   and school equipment for the needy:
3. Inviolability of persons, of one's house, and privacy:
4. Freedom of speech, the press, meetings, and association:
5. Freedom of movement and occupation:
6. Full equality of rights for all citizens without distinction of race, colour or sex:

7. Revision of the land question in accordance with the above:

8. Revision of the civil and criminal code in accordance with the above:

9. Revision of the system of taxation in accordance with the above:

10. Revision of labour legislation and its application to the mines and agriculture.

The supporters of this programme, the Coloured intelligentsia and those Africans – mainly teachers – outside the 31 years old African National Congress, saw in it an assault upon the whole policy of white trusteeship and the first clear assertion of full racial equality. On the principle that white supremacy survived only because the non-whites participated in their own oppression, they decided on a policy of non-collaboration, with the boycott of all 'dummy institutions'.

Peter's father, a clergyman of some personal following and reputation as an orator, was in the Unity Movement, and Peter himself was a vigorous exponent when I met him. He was the first revolutionary non-white in my experience, and I was immediately drawn to the logic of his resistance. I went with him to meetings of the New Era Fellowship, the capital of theoretical dispute in the movement, and tried to keep afloat through the rapids of discussion and frequently rancorous debate. My socialism was passionate but inchoate, and I began to read voraciously in order to give it shape. The Communist Party repelled me by its ritualistic reverence for the Soviet Union, and my distaste was confirmed by the assaults on Stalinism to which I listened in this Trotskyist concourse. On the other hand, the disciples of the Fourth International in the Unity Movement seemed to be devoting their energies to endless bickering among themselves. The personal abuse with which they pursued their fluctuating rivalries appeared to me a substitute for any real political organization, and though I was intellectually attracted to the doctrine of non-collaboration, my emotions were increasingly inflamed by a desire for action. In the end,

I wandered away from the Unity Movement, an unconverted visitor with the textbooks of Marx under my arm. It seemed to me that socialism provided the only answer to the vast political and economic problems of Africa, but that Africa itself had inevitably to develop a new form, shaped by the character of its peoples, instead of borrowing, like the designs for so many tourist souvenirs, the distant European products.

Peter may not have converted me, but the effects of his friendship with me were profound. Gradually I wiped my mind clear of all the make-up without which South African liberalism feels it improper to appear. Gradually I began to feel less the benevolence of my association with him, which characteristically inhibited my criticism of his opinions, and more the pleasure of a mutual, sometimes impatient regard. The first time that I felt completely unconscious of his colour was when, one morning over tea in the university canteen, he lumped all whites psychologically together as creatures of privilege, and I told him that he was talking nonsense. He looked at me and smiled.

Embodying the spirit of traditional liberalism, the University of Cape Town practised academic integration and a strict if irregular social colour bar. Non-white students sat with white ones in the lecture rooms, ambled up and down the campus with them, and – much to the horror of students at the segregated Afrikaans universities – shared the same canteen and even the same lavatories. No non-white student, however, was admitted to the university halls of residence, official dances or sport amenities. It seemed as ludicrously illogical to me as to the most rigorous of racialists that Coloured, Indian and African students should be permitted to use the same lavatories as whites but not the same swimming pool, share the same tables in the university canteen and the same seats at meetings, but not the same dance floor.

The student body itself comprised three clear-cut sections – the Nationalists, who opposed the whole principle of academic integration and agitated for the expulsion of the non-white students; the United Party majority, with a liberal list, which supported the system as it was, academic integration and the traditional social colour bar; and the radicals, organized for the most part into the Students' Socialist Party, who demanded an end to all social discrimination. It was these three groups which jostled for control of the Students' Representative Council, at annual elections in which the poll seldom fell below half of the 4,000 strong student body. Because the preoccupations of the S.R.C. were increasingly racial, the Council's changing composition and resolutions were widely reported in the daily press and absorbed the attention of the university authorities.

The Nationalist government was committed – by the innumerable pledges it had made during its period of opposition and the threats that had accompanied its acquisition of power – to ensure academic segregation throughout the country. Of the nine teaching universities and university colleges, the four Afrikaans language ones – Stellenbosch, Pretoria, Potchefstroom and the Orange Free State – were uncompromisingly white. Rhodes University, at Grahamstown in the Eastern Cape, was white as well, but maintained a supervisory association with the non-white, overwhelmingly African, University College of Fort Hare, at Alice near by. The University of Natal enjoyed segregated white and non-white sections, arranging identical lectures for separate classes, though conferring – let it be confessed – the same degrees. Only the University of the Witwatersrand, in Johannesburg, and the University of Cape Town were 'mixed', although the non-white proportion of either seldom exceeded ten per cent. It was at these two subversive influences that the Nationalists consistently directed their attacks. True, the social colour bar prevented the most blatant breaches of racial purity. But who was to say into what secret passages the contact of study and canteen might not lead white and non-white together?

I entered the university, therefore, when it was in a state of siege, though a siege officially genteel, like an ageing spinster barricading her person against the assaults of vice. The university authorities were fearful of speeding government action by

too forceful an opposition, as though the two mixed universities might somehow be overlooked if only they kept quiet
enough. Increasingly they played down the virtues of racial
integration and concentrated instead upon academic freedom,
their right to admit whom they pleased and teach what they
pleased while receiving ever greater state assistance for both.
They found the socialist students embarrassing, and I was to
have more than one interview with the principal over our
irresponsible provocations.

We ourselves believed that the government would soon
expel the non-white students, and the prudence of the university authorities promised only the most polite opposition.
Above all, a university which permitted integration in the class
rooms and outlawed it from the campus dance or swimming
pool seemed to us a pious fraud which it would be a degradation to defend. In any event, no university could be isolated
from the society of which it was an integral part, and the plea
of academic freedom seemed to us fundamentally a demand for
social irresponsibility. I believed then, as I believe still, that no
educational institute has the right to receive public assistance
for sectarian purposes. No government should prohibit the
existence of a school or university restricted by religion or race,
but no government should be expected to tax the wealth of the
whole community in order to pay for such restrictions. The
struggle against university apartheid seemed unreal to us for as
long as it was not part of the whole political engagement to
reshape South Africa.

I was still in my first year at university when Peter stood for
election to the Students' Representative Council. The counting
took place at Smuts Hall, the large men's residence on the
campus, and I drove Leah and Peter there on election night to
hear the results. But when we entered the front door of the
residence, one of the executive members of the outgoing
S.R.C., a rampaging Nationalist, suddenly barred our way. As
a candidate for election, Peter had unrestricted access to the
room where the votes were being counted. As a Coloured, he
was, by convention, prohibited from entering the residence. I

wanted to argue the point, but Peter strangely cut me short and turned away. As we drove to his home he was silent. But if his mind was anything like mine, it was burnt raw with fury and shame. The following morning we learnt that Peter, with one other radical, had been elected to the Council of fifteen members.

The university was still a dusk in the night around. From the canteen where we would sit arguing for hours over cups of tea, or after a meeting organized by one of the cultural or political societies, Peter and I would drive into town, in the opulent American car that my father had given me, to spend the rest of the afternoon together. The only cafés where we could go were in the squalid Coloured quarter, the only cinemas Coloured ones which offered an unvarying menu of cowboy films. And if we decided simply to walk through the streets together, we would feel creeping over us, like cold shadows, the startled glances of the passers-by. No effort of the will could long fend off a feeling of constraint, of making a public gesture, and our easy conversation would stumble into silence. Once I took Peter home when my parents were away in Europe, but the servants stared at us in bewilderment, and neither of us could escape the sensation of being on show. By unspoken agreement we never tried the experiment again. Instead, one afternoon after the other, we would sit drinking tea in some Coloured café, or watch the tedious fluctuations of a cowboy film.

There were in the city a few night-schools for non-white adults, mainly African labourers and servants, which were run by a voluntary association and staffed by students. From the proceeds of one street collection a year and periodic appeals to sympathizers, the association met the rent of premises and the cost of basic stationery. The schools themselves were makeshift, sometimes no more than one blackboard and a few crowded benches in the corner of a hired hall. Peter regarded them with a mild impatience. One cut a cancer out, one didn't treat it with plasters. We were arguing more bitterly now, as I moved away from the futile infighting of the Unity Movement.

No revolution could be made by waiting for it. While one organized, one had to put one's hand to what one could. Should one want the hospitals closed because the sick would swell the rebellious? I was sentimental, he said, it was a point of priority.

Hiring a small church hall in Tramway Road, the Sea Point school held classes twice a week, for some two hundred students. I helped to teach illiterates there in my first year at university, and then took over the supervision of the school, together with the teaching of the few senior students, for the next ten months. It ripped at the nerves, that hot crammed hall with the shrill competing voices, till sometimes I wanted nothing so much as to fling down the chalk and rush once and for all into the lonely air outside. But there was excitement as well, and a sudden feeling of conquest, as a student picked up a newspaper and wide-eyed read a sentence there, understanding the words at last. The hotel waiters and dock-workers and cooks had a hunger for knowledge that made my own, so easily and carelessly acquired, seem to me a kind of confidence trick. Tired from eight, ten, twelve hours on the ships or in the kitchens, they somehow summoned enough will not only to attend their classes twice a week, but also, in between, to fill pages of their exercise books with undemanded homework.

The beginners were noisy with discovering. It was the senior students who were earnest. For what? That was what Lily asked me, the forty-year-old cook in Standard Six, who wrote about her kitchen table so that you felt the grain of the wood and smelt its sour scrubbed surface. I asked her to stay one night after class. If she passed Standard Six, did she want to study further? She stared at me and then quickly looked down at her shoes. Perhaps, she said. She wasn't sure. One day she might matriculate, I suggested. She said nothing. Well? I asked. And then? she said, looking up at me. I was taken aback. I had not prepared myself for such probing. I didn't know, I answered. Perhaps she could become a teacher. She smiled, and looked down again at her shoes. I snatched up my books, and smiled thinly back at her. For the next three classes she came, and then she didn't any more. One of the men in her class had sometimes arrived at the school together with her, and I asked him where she was. She was sick, he said. And then I forgot her. A few months afterwards I stopped teaching. My second year examinations were close, and campus politics took up most of my time. I lost touch with the school. And then one day the man who knew Lily came to see me in search of a job. I asked him about her. She was dead, he said. Dead? I asked. She had had a cough, he said, dismissing her.

One night, in the middle of 1950, I went to have dinner at the House of Assembly with a Labour M.P. Parliament was debating the Suppression of Communism Bill, which would empower the Minister of Justice to define and punish communist activities with such licence that no one was theoretically safe but the Minister himself from long prison sentences or the milder penalties of confinement to one magisterial district and a ban on attendance at all gatherings for up to five years. Since one of the statutory definitions of communism was the incitement of hostility between different racial groups in the country, the government itself seemed composed of recalcitrant Reds. It was too much to hope, however, that the Minister alone of all his colleagues would submit himself to logic.

A protest meeting had been held that night in the city, but the organizers were fearful of a clash with the police if the proposed demonstration outside parliament took place, and that had been cancelled. After dinner, I listened for an hour to the sterile debate in the House, and then decided to go home. I stopped short at the gated entrance. Coming up Parliament Street was a ragged procession, overwhelmingly Coloured, perhaps two hundred strong, with children bounding at the edges and a few scrawled posters of protest at the Bill bobbing over their heads. Clearly, a small section of the meeting in the city had decided to conduct an unofficial demonstration when the official one had been cancelled. It was pitiable, and I remember wondering to myself how any society could slip into tyranny with just two hundred adults and a few children to demonstrate their protest. Suddenly I heard what seemed like the stutter of a machine gun from the other end of the street.

Police were marching in a tight black square down the street, their boots sounding on it like bullets. They halted before the gates of parliament, no more than two yards from where I was standing, and the commanding officer shouted at the procession:

'We give you five minutes to disperse.'

He hardly waited five seconds. In a kind of cold frenzy, the police rushed at the demonstrators with their batons. And the street was all at once a tumult of screams and bodies. The demonstrators fled, but were seized, beaten and kicked to the ground. In front of me one policeman grabbed a Coloured man by the collar of his jacket and swung his baton, again and again, taunting all the time:

'Loop, jong, loop!' (Run, youngster, run!)

At the bottom of the street, well-dressed whites were spilling out of the Hofmeyr Theatre. The police fell upon those who came within their reach. One man was suddenly jerked off his feet by a policeman and hurled through the plate-glass window of a shop. He was white, and subsequently received substantial damages from the Minister of Justice.

An old Coloured man lay in the gutter at my feet, his head streaming blood. I was rigid with horror. Then suddenly, I found myself next to the commanding officer. I shouted that the old man needed help, an ambulance. The officer looked at me with narrowing eyes.

'If you aren't out of here by the time I count five,' he said softly, 'you will be where he is.' I suppose I should have stood there, staring at him, waiting for him to hit me. For one blind moment I thought of hitting him first, low in the stomach. Then, swept by a feeling of helplessness, I turned and took the few steps back to the pavement. Meanwhile, the old man had staggered to his feet and was stumbling, with an arm flung round the shoulders of a young Coloured, down the street. I caught sight of Amy, a white girl I knew, who was later to join the Congress Movement and spend several months in prison during the 1960 State of Emergency. She was standing on the opposite pavement, looking at the now quiet bodies in the street, and the tears were running down her cheeks. Suddenly she saw me, and we stared at each other in dumb desolation.

I cannot remember how I got to my car and drove home. I remember only pacing the floor at Leah's home, describing what had happened and waiting all the while just to vomit up what I had seen. That night I formed a hatred of police that has never left me, a rising of rage at the sight of the gun and the baton. I felt at last that I knew what Germany had been like in the 'thirties. Phrases that had been no more than the material of persuasion became pictures in my mind, blood streaming from the head of an old man, a policeman swinging a jubilant baton, the machine-gun stutter of police marching down the street. Of all my experiences in South Africa, the scene outside parliament that night bit its way deepest. Before I had talked and thought of revolution. That night I decided that I would give myself, muscle and mind, to making the sort of South Africa in which no such savagery as I had seen would ever again be possible.

Before the Suppression of Communism Bill became law, the University of Cape Town Students' Socialist Party – though the communists in it hardly composed a third of the total – disbanded and advised its members to burn their cards. From then onwards, the radical students concentrated their attention on the Modern World Society, a cultural group which organized lectures on economic and political problems, or devoted themselves to movements outside the university. The struggle against the social colour bar on the campus was pursued by a formless association of individual radicals, grouped by their attachment to particular national movements or their support of a leading figure in campus politics. The preoccupation of the university authorities and most of the students with academic freedom, the island of the campus, seemed increasingly unreal. With the Suppression of Communism Act, the searchlights were trained on us all and the barbed wire stretched everywhere around. We were in one vast concentration camp, and there was no escape until the prisoners could change places with the guards. More and more we demanded that the university should join in the national engagement. More and more we were told in reply that our only safety lay in a careful isolation.

My own campus career began midway in my first year, with my Chairmanship of the Literary Society and, soon afterwards, my Presidency of the Council of University Societies, which I helped to found as a co-ordinating authority for the organization of a student Arts Festival.

Meanwhile, the government was planning a very different sort of festival, to reach its climax on the 6th of April 1962, the tercentenary of Jan van Riebeeck's arrival at the Cape. From the initial publicity it became quickly clear that the government was using the celebration of the first white settlement of South Africa to organize an ecstasy of racial ritual before its own image of Afrikanerdom. The floats proposed for the historical parade to climax the celebrations would have been merely ridiculous had the sponsors wielded any less political power. As it was, the display of barbarism planned for the black participants, with the pattern of civilization and piety planned for the white ones, provided only the most sinister commentary on the government's intentions. The festival was, of course, to be strictly segregated. The blacks would accompany on foot and in picturesque undress the floats on which the Voortrekkers would ride in decorous array. Not that the government altogether ignored the feelings of the non-whites. Segregated seating was provided for those of them who wished to view the spectacle of their ancestors in abject defeat.

The Van Riebeeck Festival Committee invited the participation of the university, and the non-white students, with the white radicals in support, demanded an official boycott in reply. The S.R.C. was required by petition to convene a special mass meeting on the issue, and over one thousand students crowded into Jameson Hall for the debate. The meeting promised from the first to be tumultuous. The Nationalist students, as always, had arrived early and crowded the bays, from which they were able, through the acoustic idiosyncrasies of the hall, to dominate the noise. I had already earned a reputation among them as one of the more dangerous subversives at the university, and when I approached the microphone to speak in favour of boycott, they produced, howling and singing, a sustained uproar. The President of the S.R.C. made a fruitless appeal for silence. I leaned against the table behind the microphone, folded my arms and waited, trembling. It was school all over again, I thought, the bullies were baying. The whole audience seemed to blur in front of me, and when the tumult paused as though for breath, I reached for the microphone and suddenly heard myself shouting. I shouted at the government, with its imperial delusions, and at a university so craven that it would dress itself in chains for the triumphal procession. I denied the legal right of the student body to participate in any segregated function at all. Nowhere in the charter of the university was any student stripped of his right, in consequence of his colour, to participate in every function of the university. That a social colour bar could exist on the campus was due more to the indulgence of the non-white students than to the primitive prejudices of the white ones. But this indulgence was expendable, and I hoped myself that it would never survive the insult of university participation in the racial orgasm of the festival. We were not asking the student body to refuse the invitation, we were demanding it. We would not allow the university so to degrade itself as to bow its head in renunciation of its non-white students and walk under the arch of white supremacy. A feeling of what I can only describe as exaltation filled me as I spoke – I was hitting back at the police, their batons still swinging at the sprawled bodies in Parliament Street, at the Nationalist student barring Peter's way to the bleached sanctity of Smuts Hall, at the small cluster of taunting boys in a corner of the school courtyard. I don't suppose I shall ever speak like that again, in a surge that left me drained and desolate afterwards. It must have been, it seems to me now, a sort of seizure, a convulsion of will to batter that wild blind jeering into silence. As I leaped off the platform and walked shaking to my seat, the whole student body – including the Nationalists in the bays – burst into long applause. The experience of that day

left an indelible imprint on my mind. Ever since, I have
trusted finally to my emotions. I discovered in public speaking
a release from all the distant hurts and submissions. I gained
and have retained a belief in the sheer force of speech, in the
power of the will to overcome.

We won the vote, but the debate dragged on too long to retain the necessary quorum. In the end, the student body did
not participate in the festival, though individual students, of
course, excitedly did.

In my third year, I stood for election to the Students' Representative Council – with two others, on a mandate to eradicate all social segregation at the university. It was a fiercely
fought contest, with a more than usually high poll, and we
missed the co-ordinating force of a Students' Socialist Party
behind us. Traditionally the radicals could count on winning
two of the fifteen seats, and as the election approached, a
rancorous rivalry developed among those supporting our
programme. One of the other two, though not himself a
communist, was considered more congenial to the communists
at the university than I, and I began to receive reports of a
past that I never remember having experienced. One of the
more vociferous of my new antagonists, with an inventiveness
that did greater credit to his energy than to his common
sense, cornered Leah in the canteen and told her that I had tried
to join the Communist Party several times but had been
rejected as politically flirtatious. Leah told me, of course, and I
sought out her informant.

'Merely out of interest,' I said, 'why did you tell what you
must surely have known was a lie?'

He looked at me without the slightest embarrassment.

'We must get Benny on,' he replied.

'I see,' I said, 'and you think that you will get him on like
this?'

He did not answer, but smiled as though we were sharing a
secret.

I stared at him. 'I suggest, in that case, that you have enough
sense at least to feed your stories next time to those who are

likely to swallow them. Cornering my best friend shows a care-
lessness that your colleagues may not appreciate.'

I was not so much disgusted as amazed. The sheer impudence
of his admission disarmed me. The incident was trivial enough,
but I never forgot it. I suddenly felt how corrupt and mean
political competition could be, even within the intransigently
moral left. I myself emerged from that small student election
with few illusions still intact. Ironically, Benny won a seat on
my own excess votes, under the transferable system introduced
a few years before.

The results were an unexpected triumph – all three who stood
against the social colour bar were successful. We could claim a
significant, if not yet major, radical swing of the student body.
The Nationalists won three seats, and the remaining nine were
held by four liberals and five independents of fluctuating United
Party allegiance. At the first meeting of the S.R.C., one
Nationalist, two independents, one Liberal and I were elected
to the Executive, and soon afterwards I managed to get
through the Council a combined liberal-radical motion con-
demning the government for having banned the communist-
sympathizing *Guardian*. In proposing it, I had insisted that the
precise politics of *The Guardian* were irrelevant. A government
that was empowered to ban newspapers for being communist
would soon enough ban them for being radical, and then for
being liberal, and then for being critical at all. The Nationalist
members jeered at my alarmism. The independents protested at
such meddling in national matters; *The Guardian* did not concern the university. But one of the independents was unhappy
with this contention, and after an adjournment during which I
encouraged his conscience, he finally deserted his colleagues.
The vote of the Council was widely reported in the press; the
United Party students were embarrassed, and the Nationalists
furious.

A few weeks later, at the annual conference of the National
Union of South African Students (N.U.S.A.S.), I was elected
National Director of Faculty and Cultural Studies. For the rest
of the year my curricular work persistently dwindled. Many

S.R.C. meetings would exhaust the whole night, and I would totter to my eight o'clock in the morning Latin classes more than three-quarters asleep. I do not suppose that Tacitus has ever been translated with such rapt inaccuracy as he was during the hangovers of my all-night political binges. But I consoled myself with the knowledge that I had already been accepted by Trinity College, Cambridge, to which I had shifted my application from Balliol, after my encounter with *Scrutiny*. Dr Leavis and the Cambridge-centred school of criticism contrasted so sharply with the flatulent reverence of the colonial lecture-room. When I left for England, I would leave my political determinations behind me. I would concentrate on disciplining my mind to what I hoped would one day become creative criticism. But meanwhile, for as long as I remained in South Africa, I felt that I lived, to the rim of my experience, in the struggle – however clumsy or ineffectual – against the government.

At the end of 1951, I took my degree – with majors in English, Latin and Ethics – and decided to spend the next six months, until the 1952 annual conference of N.U.S.A.S. and my departure for England, in studying for a Master's Degree in Latin. As the months passed, the departure itself appeared to me less and less real. I had invested my emotions so deeply in politics that I found it increasingly difficult, when I allowed myself to think of it at all, to visualize my life in an academic context. But the decision to leave appeared irreversible. What would I do if I stayed? I could not take up subversion, as a sort of alternative profession. And perhaps Cambridge would make literary criticism seem exciting to me again. Perhaps I would discover how to write there. At all events, further study would provide me with a dignified excuse for postponing any final commitment of my career.

My last few weeks in South Africa were an orgy of political involvement. Carefully I prepared my address to the Conference of Faculty and Cultural Studies at the annual meeting of N.U.S.A.S. in Pietermaritzburg that July. It was absurd, I claimed, for university students to organize cultural activities or examine their curricula in blind indifference to the society of which they were inextricably a part. The university was the teachers who taught in it, the subjects and the students they taught. A government that wished to turn the schools and universities of the country into concentration camps of the mind was the inevitable and passionate concern of any student who believed in free inquiry. Faculty and cultural studies involved an analysis not only of what students wanted from their universities, but also of the degree to which the government would help or hinder them in their search. If they found that the government was pursuing a policy which could only end in their own intellectual enslavement, then they could not escape the duty of doing all they could to change its character.

In the Student Assembly of N.U.S.A.S., to which I was a delegate from the University of Cape Town S.R.C., I moved that the whole organization should adopt as a basic objective, the political, economic and social equality of all peoples in South Africa. The debate that followed was among the most turbulent and bitter in the organization's history. We were accused, with justice, of attempting to reshape N.U.S.A.S. into a political movement, when it was a union specifically of students and should remain so. I maintained that the distinction between students and ordinary citizens in any society was fatuous and false. The very composition of the universities in South Africa reflected closely the arrangement of the society to which they belonged. That there were hardly three hundred non-white students out of a total of four thousand at the University of Cape Town was not due to the effects of pigment on the brain. It was due to the racial character of the government, which pursued the intellectual depression of the non-white peoples as a matter of policy. A National Union of Students that concerned itself exclusively with the affairs of its affiliated universities and never with the political, economic and social structure which made these universities what they were, was pursuing the hollow consolations of the schizoid. It would be rejected both by the government, for whose policy it showed an inadequate enthusiasm, and by the popular

D

movement directed at changing the whole character of the society.

In the event, we lost the vote by a narrow margin – 19 to 23, or thereabout. The organization was forced, during the years that followed, to take an increasingly active part in the political struggle. For the universities, passionately as they wanted to be left alone, lay provokingly in the government's path. Inevitably they were flattened by the passage of Christian National Education. Under the ludicrously named Extension of University Education Act, passed in 1959, non-white students were forbidden entry to the mixed universities; separate Coloured and Indian educational systems were established, and Africans were herded into special tribal colleges, where courses in Xhosa Architecture and Zulu Physics might be pursued in secure isolation.

I went straight from the conference to Johannesburg, where my father met me with a bundle of newspapers under his arm. Without comment he pointed to the headlines – STUDENT LEADER ATTACKS GOVERNMENT – and the full reports of my speech to the Faculty and Cultural Conference. I knew he was glad that I was going. I asked myself whether I was glad as well. But I found that I felt nothing at all. As I gathered my hand luggage and walked to the plane for London, I felt as one does between sleeping and waking, in a dusk of experience.

During the Spring of 1962 I visited Cambridge on some business. My train had arrived an hour before my appointment, and I ambled for a while through the colleges and streets. I might never have studied there, for all I remembered of the place. The two years I had spent there seemed to have passed without leaving a single mark on my emotions. When I walked through Trinity College I felt a flicker of recognition, but it was a kind of *déjà vu*, and I found myself thinking repeatedly, of course I was there, I used to cross that court in the dusk, with the chimes of St John's, and eat in that hall, under that portrait, with the clatter of cutlery around.

It was not that I was happy or unhappy at Cambridge. It seems to me now that I never really cared enough to be either.

My two years there were a sort of emotional sequestration. I was going to be an academic, and I resolved to prepare myself properly. I read voraciously, often for sixteen hours a day – Jacobean plays and Victorian novels and eighteenth-century moralists, the poems and pamphlets of Milton, my special study, the literature of Medieval Latin, my selected language. My memory is of people, not of experiences, or consequently of the places which experience might have invested with some emotion. From the lectures of Dr Leavis, which I attended assiduously, I learnt at last to reassess the clichés of English criticism, to reject intimidation by authority or repute. Whether or not his particular revaluations of the revered in English literature, like Milton, were wholly or even partly justified, he taught his students to think by denying their second-hand assumptions. Above all, he taught us how to read, not lazily glancing past, but picking a way, with precise foot-holds, through the text. It was not always easy, but it was honest. One night I took my own poems, from their security in a book on old English silver, read them carefully and tore them up.

Of all those I met at Cambridge, however, the one whom I remember most sharply was Enid Welsford, my tutor in the English moralists. She was a tiny woman, with a lined round face under straight grey hair and a formidable flow of energy. I had read her book on the history of *The Fool* in my second year at the University of Cape Town, and been stirred by her study of *King Lear* into weeks of immersion in Shakespeare. It had been the only emotional detour I had taken from my pre-occupation with politics. From her work I expected her to be a practising Christian, but never one so tender and intense, with so passionate a gentleness. She must have understood sin – she knew her way through Jacobean drama better than anyone I've ever met – but only as an argument, not as a temptation. I was astounded at her innocence. And I loved it. We discussed Machiavelli and the Cambridge Platonists and God for hours on end over glasses of her sherry, and I felt for the first time in my life a serious tug to theism. For a few weeks I even carried on a short intellectual flirtation with Christianity. But my scepticism was insuperable. I remember her face when I told her that if ever I believed in God, it would be because I believed in the existence of hell. She stared at me in disbelief, and then pain. It made a difference, I explained, that I should have grown up during the rampage of Nazism and then been swept by the frenzy of South African politics. She was even kinder to me after that than she had been before. I think she regarded me, ever afterwards, as morally crippled.

In April 1954 I sat for my Honours in English and passed in the first division of the second class – a just return for having identified, with such supreme assurance and abundance of argument, a poem in Victorian hexameters by Arthur Clough as typical first world war free verse. I had hoped, of course, to get a first, acquire a fellowship at Cambridge and postpone any further decision on my future career. Instead, I now took a flat in Hampstead and wrote a dissertation on *Paradise Lost*, which I dispatched to several universities in the United States with inquiries into the fellowships they offered for doctorate study. I then started writing a play on the Immorality Act, the 1949 measure which makes physical relations between white and non-white in South Africa a crime. Reading it now is a protracted embarrassment; the whole vibrates on a constant high note of political hysteria. At the time, of course, I thought it was marvellous, and spent hours in imagining the varied successes of its production.

In August my father died, soon after my return to London from a holiday in Morocco, and I flew to South Africa. We had never been close – he had been bewildered by my inexhaustible capacity for diverging from the norm, and I had never made any effort myself to appreciate what he measured as important. I had, however, grown increasingly aware of his massive, helpless generosity, and his death ripped the packaging of his presence, and so numberless silent restraints, suddenly from my life. My share in his estate, and the trust which he had established for his children many years before, promised me an annual income of at least one thousand pounds for life. I returned to London, and left almost immediately for Rome.

Around the six months that I spent in Italy there hovers in my memory still a constant glow. It was a life of clear jubilant irresponsibility. I would spend day after day lying in the sun on one of the Tiber boats, with a lunch of pasta and red Chianti as the only interruption. At night I would go with my friends for a walk up the Via Veneto to sneer at the tourists, or sit over interminable coffees, watching the pavement traffic, or search out a film hilariously dubbed, and then play poker till the morning. I had arrived without knowing anyone but a young man, of the impoverished and minor Roman aristocracy, who had shared for several months with me the same girl-friend. He had appeared in London to pursue his sudden suspicions, and we had genially decided that the object of our attention was not worth the rivalry. Accordingly, to the young girl's discomfort, we had become fast friends and dismissed her from serious consideration together. It was he who found a room for me with a lower middle-class family in the Via Andrea Doria – they sold furniture on hire purchase and were constantly changing the tables and cupboards in my room – and introduced me to his own circle of friends in Rome.

Our poker sessions, fast with the five low cards removed, often went on till eight o'clock in the morning, while on one occasion four of us sat down at ten o'clock on Thursday evening and only broke off for breakfast on Saturday morning. In between, the game fluctuated, as the exhausted gave place to new arrivals, or the young wife of the friend in whose flat we were playing forced a way for food through the cards. The end was unfortunate only for me.

I lost eighty thousand lire – about fifty pounds – but I could afford comfortably to pay it, since I had just received a large draft from home, and considered my loss a small enough return for the experience. My friends supposed that I had limitless resources – I was a foreigner, after all – and fought off my efforts to pay them for no more than one dignified day.

I fell helplessly in love with Rome, with the streets, and the battle to stay alive in the buses, the sunburnt stone by the river, and the quick pleasure of the Romans themselves in their city.

I found myself thinking less and less about South Africa, and feeling less and less committed to my success. On the crowded train to the beach at Ostia, lying on the grass at dusk in the Borghese Gardens, or – in a brief break from Rome – careering on a motor bike around the Dolomites, I no longer cared how the races in South Africa resolved their disputes, or whether I ever wrote more than a few dutiful letters home. A friend, who had shared my flat in Hampstead and assumed possession of it when I left for Rome, wrote to tell me that my dissertation on Milton had won a scholarship to the University of Chicago and a fellowship at the University of Virginia. The news startled me; I had forgotten about the dissertation altogether. That night I went with three of my friends to the Terme di Caracalla, to watch – the singing was manifestly subordinate – a production of *Aïda*. We sat in the third row from the back, among tumultuous appreciation of the events on the stage so far below, and sung with excitement when an elephant and two moth-eaten camels appeared in the triumphal procession. Suddenly – during the impatient muttering that accompanied the inadequacies of the death duet – I thought to myself, do I want to go to America at all? And I realized that, more than anything else, I wanted to go on doing what I was doing, in a long luxuriant stretch of the senses. For the rest of the week I did everything with a desperate intensity, as though I would never enjoy the chance to lie soaking up the sun on the Tiber, or amble along the Via Andrea Doria at night, in quite the same way again. On the Sunday afternoon, I was sitting at a pavement café with two of my friends. We were not talking, just staring at the passers-by and smiling in silent satisfaction at each other. And there flashed through my mind a vision of myself and my friends in ten years and twenty years from then, sitting at the same table and smiling, wryly at each other and at ourselves. I was twenty-three years old. And a little fear stirred the short hair at the back of my neck. I got up from the table.

'I am going,' I said.

'Where?' asked the first of my Roman friends lazily.

'Back to London.'

He sat upright.

'Why?' he asked, astounded.

I searched for an answer.

'I don't know,' I said, shrugging my shoulders. 'It's just that if I don't go now, I shall stay here for ever, and I'm not sure that I want to.'

In hysterics of movement we rushed to my room, packed my bags – my two friends all the while passionately protesting – and fled to the station. Within two hours I was on the train for the South of France and London.

I did not hesitate between Chicago and Virginia, though the University of Chicago had much the shriller reputation as a centre of creative study. I accepted the fellowship in Virginia, fundamentally, I suppose, because I wanted to live in a traditionally Southern state, with its tensions so similar to those in South Africa. I wanted already to go home. But, of course, I had planted my persuasion in altogether different ground. I had decided to do my doctorate on the American novel, and the South had produced – or significantly influenced – many of those authors whom I particularly wished to study. I spent a few fevered days in London preparing for what I believed would be a stay of several years in the United States, and went by ship to New York. There I stayed for two months before proceeding to Charlottesville.

My grandfather had been the only one of several brothers to leave Lithuania at the end of the last century for Southern Africa. The rest of his family had followed the well-beaten path to America, though they had found there little of the swift prosperity which report had promised them. One of them had married a Catholic – his son became a priest – and was dropped from the family recollections. The oldest, an orthodox Jew, had registered an early success with a soda water factory, but had resolutely refused to deliver his products on the Sabbath and had soon succumbed to his more worldly competitors. Another brother, who developed a strong socialist streak, had worked, from the moment of his arrival throughout the years of depression, at a multiplicity of different jobs, all equally ill-paid. Yet he had managed to steer his son and two daughters through school, and in varying ways they had inherited his resilience and stubborn dissent. The elder of the two daughters had set herself up as an interior decorator and had acquired for herself a loyal and profitable following. I grew to like her and her husband, the manager of a Wall Street brokerage firm, enormously, and she was to help some months later in launching *Africa South* to the American public. They both had that tireless push, the demanding trust in themselves, which seemed to mark the first generation immigrant community and fade in its children.

Moving from New York to Charlottesville was like leaving a crowded street for a small and silent cul-de-sac. Virginia itself was not the Deep South, I discovered to my dismay, but merely its shallows. And Charlottesville was a constant back-tracking on itself. The Deep South had produced a culture, heavy and stagnant perhaps, like an overblown magnolia, but all its own. Charlottesville seemed to me a pallid exercise in the derivative. The windows of the smarter shops were filled with English tweeds, and it was fashionable to get drunk on Scotch whisky. The racial patterns of the South were reproduced in the segregated university and schools, but with an effete traditionalism, unfortified by any apparent passion. The university itself had been the creation of Jefferson. But the creator might as well have been Bonny Prince Charlie, for all the legacy that survived.

Accommodated in the graduate school, I found a flat congeniality in the students around me. They were welcoming and warm, and I found their spontaneous ease, their readiness to show themselves without embarrassment, a delight after the constriction I had experienced at Cambridge. The students at Charlottesville and at Cape Town seemed much more like each other in their emotional generosity than either were like the students at Cambridge whom I had met. But in intellectual initiative, Virginian students belonged to a museum world, in which the basic American assumptions were on display behind locked glass, to be seen and even – with permission – photographed, but never handled. My room-mate, a Virginian who carefully covered his face every night with a green, peppermint cream to suck dry his complexion, while otherwise preserving a firm image of the football star, rigorously refused to be drawn into any dispute over the cult of American free enterprise. With astonishment he would listen to my indictments and then shrug his shoulders and ask me questions about Europe. He planned one day to visit Germany and Switzerland; he had heard that they were both neat and sanitary countries. One night I at last succeeded in involving five of my neighbours in a discussion on politics. When one of them condemned all socialism out of hand, I argued that the United States itself was far more socialist than its citizens apparently believed. Graduated income tax, high death duties, and the federal manipulation of the economy, condemned as Bolshevik hardly thirty years before, were now the foundations of American enterprise. They looked incredulous and then bewildered. Suddenly one of them plunged. 'Well, if it is socialist, I don't like it.'

With my classes themselves I was bored almost to violence. I had arrived in Charlottesville contemptuous of literary criticism by biography. I did not care to discover why Hawthorne had started work as a surveyor in the custom house at Boston, or when Melville had first gone to sea. I wanted to discuss the texts, to dispute interpretations, not tabulate anecdotes or dates. Even my thesis on the American novel, which had so stirred my interest to begin with, palled under the tedium of excavating biographical irrelevancies. In retrospect, I suppose that my irritation had less to do with the type or quality of teaching than with my own emotional discrepancies. I was emerging from the hiatus of Cambridge and Italy, and my commitment to South Africa was all the stronger for being rediscovered. The news that reached me from home overwhelmed me.

By the South Africa Act, through which the Union of South Africa had taken shape in 1910, the vote of the Cape Province's African and Coloured males on the common roll had been entrenched in the constitution. Indeed, there is little doubt that a union of Natal and the Cape with the Afrikaner dominated Transvaal and Orange Free State would never have been constituted, had the Cape's demands to secure its non-white franchise not been met. Only a two-thirds majority of the Assembly and Senate sitting together could remove any of the rights entrenched in the South Africa Act. And only once had this been achieved, when in 1936 the United Party – formed by a fusion, two years before, of the Nationalist and South African Parties – had passed by a two-thirds majority of both Houses the Native Representation Act, to remove African male voters in the Cape from the common roll and provide them instead with white representatives elected on a separate franchise.

The rump of the Nationalist Party, which had refused to enter the 1934 coalition, had propagated instead an opposition policy of still more sweeping white domination. And it was this rump which had swollen in popular support, achieved the undisputed leadership of Afrikanerdom, and won – with its soon absorbed ally, the Afrikaner Party — a close victory at the general election of 1948. Dr Malan, the new Prime Minister, had immediately set himself to remove the forty thousand-odd Coloured male voters in the Cape from the common roll. But he controlled only 79 seats of the 153 in the House of Assembly and had no hope of mustering the two-thirds majority required for the amendment of an entrenched constitutional right. He introduced a Bill in 1951 to remove Coloured voters none the less. It was passed by a simple majority of the Assembly and – after intricate argument on the supremacy of parliament over the constitution – ruled invalid in 1952 by the Appeal Court. A torrent of bitter criticism by government spokesmen swept the judges. Paul Sauer, one Cabinet Minister, sneered at 'the five old men of Bloemfontein'. Eric Louw, another, proclaimed that parliament 'cannot be subjected to the whims of the courts'. Dr Dönges, a third, said: 'The people must now decide whether to trust a Bench appointed and paid by a government but which is not responsible to anyone, or the parliament elected by the people which has to get a mandate from the people at least every five years.' J. G. Strijdom, soon to become Prime Minister himself, cried that it was 'a terrible mistake ... to take the view that because a man is a judge he is, therefore, like a being from heaven who only sees matters in an unprejudiced light. The judges are ordinary people. . . . It is very clear, according to reports which appeared in the newspapers and from the remarks of the judges, that from the beginning they had already made a study of the case and it was already decided what their judgment would be.'

The government accordingly introduced the grotesque High Court of Parliament Bill, to constitute parliament as a court of appeal superior to the Appeal Court on matters affecting the constitution. A few months later the Appeal Court held the measure to be 'invalid, null and void, and of no legal effect'. The 1953 general election increased the government majority substantially, but still left it short of a two-thirds majority in the Assembly or Senate. Dr Malan then introduced the South Africa Act Amendment Bill, to repeal the entrenchment clause affecting voting rights in the South Africa Act itself, but despite his strenuous appeals to the opposition for support in resolving the constitutional crisis, the two-thirds majority remained as elusive as ever. In 1954, he made his last attempt, with the help of the Conservative Party, a group of break-away United Party M.P.s, but his Separate Representation of Voters Act Validation and Amendment Bill failed to achieve a two-thirds majority at a joint sitting of the Assembly and Senate. He retired from the premiership.

His successor, J. G. Strijdom, abandoned argument for the axe, and reshaped parliament itself. The Senate consisted of 48 members – 8 elected by each of the four provinces, 8 nominated by the government, 4 elected by Africans, and 2 elected and 2 nominated to represent South West Africa. The election of the 32 senators to represent the provinces had, ever since the establishment of the Senate by the Act of Union, been on a basis of proportional representation. The Senate Act of 1955 almost doubled the membership of the Senate, from 48 to 90, loosened the qualifications for admission, adjusted the representation of each province to the size of its white population, and introduced the system of 'winner takes all', by which the majority party in any one province took all its Senate seats. In consequence, the Nationalist Party, with its slender majorities in the Cape and the Transvaal added to its domination of the Orange Free State, emerged with 57 of the 65 seats allocated to the provinces and, with the government nominees, possessed in the new Senate a total of 78 seats, to 8 for the United Party and 4 African representatives. A joint sitting of Assembly and Senate would now provide a secure two-thirds majority for any legislative measure required by the government.

Strijdom, however, had not forgotten the courts. He appointed additional Judges of Appeal, almost doubling the toal, and pushed through parliament the Appellate Division Quorum Act, which provided that appeals challenging the validity of any Act of Parliament should be heard by the new full bench of eleven judges. The Hon. Percy Hugh Fischer, former Judge-President of the Orange Free State Supreme Court and son of Abraham Fischer, one-time President of the Orange Free State Republic, commented: 'The public has been faced with the appointment of five additional judges to an existing court of six. . . . With regard to constitutional matters, the public is of course aware that the present government, through some of their members, have repeatedly expressed their disapproval of recent decisions of the Appeal Court. The public is also aware that the present government, through these Ministers, have threatened to take steps to prevent a repetition of such decisions. . . . Essential to the due administration of justice is the reliance of the public on the integrity of the bench. To raise a doubt as to such integrity, even if it be in respect of one class of case, will in all probability raise doubts as to cases in general. It would seem that a greater injustice could not be done to the bench of the Appellate Division than the manner of appointment adopted by the government in enlarging the bench and altering the quorum.'

Even some of those in South Africa who believed in the need for permanent white rule reeled from the implications of the government's new measures. Political struggle within the white community had, till then, followed constitutional forms. Now the government had decided to eradicate democratic processes from white South Africa, as white South Africa had itself eradicated them among the blacks. We were, inevitably, emerging from an era of racial rule into one of fierce authoritarianism. Even to South Africa's non-whites, already experiencing the anguish of white supremacy, the abandonment of constitutional rule would make a difference. The manipulation of the courts, of parliament itself, promised a swift slide into terror. It was the logic of domination.

A group of white women, indistinctly liberal in character, formed the Black Sash to defend the constitution. Its members bore silent witness to the government's assaults by wearing black sashes and standing with bowed heads in public places, or wherever possible along the routes that individual Ministers travelled. I learnt from home that my sister, quiet and withdrawn, almost bashful as she was, had joined the movement. I knew suddenly that I had to return, not because I felt that I could accomplish anything significant against the government, or even because I felt it an unavoidable gesture to all I valued most, but because I passionately wanted to go home, to be part again of the struggle against violence and cruelty.

I delayed for three weeks while I considered what part I might profitably play in opposition. I had had, during my visits to New York, various discussions with leaders of the National Association for the Advancement of Coloured People, together with other individuals and organizations interested in Africa. Everywhere I had encountered a strong wish for an international magazine that would study developments in Africa and relate them to the world beyond. And I myself had long thought necessary a periodical which would assemble the different militant groups of opposition to the government in South Africa into a kind of intellectual united front. All at once, it seemed to me that this second objective would be more feasible – politically and commercially – if it were allied to the first. I knew at last what I would do on my return. Still I hesitated. My family would vigorously oppose my engagement in opposition politics, and I did not fool myself that I could act without endangering those about me. One night I lay awake, arguing myself into a decision. But I knew all the time how I would decide. To remain any longer outside the struggle in South Africa was an agony and a humiliation.

I went to see the head of the English department, and found him sympathetic. I resigned my fellowship and sent a cable to my family that I was coming home. I had been in Charlottesville hardly six months. And, except for the fortnight's visit after my father's death, I had been away from South Africa for nearly four years. As I packed my suitcases I found myself throbbing with excitement. I had always been short on the love I had given to people and to places. Suddenly it seemed to me that I loved South Africa with the whole surrender of myself. I took the train to New York, and some ten days later, in February 1956, the plane to Cape Town.

CHAPTER FOUR

PUBLISHING

I ARRIVED home to the bewildered reproaches of my family. They displayed a strenuous distrust of publishing, suspicious of its capacity to consume large sums of money without apparent returns, and fearful of the consequences that my proposed collision with the government would carry. I had discarded an academic career of adequate if not exceptional success for what promised to be alike an economic and political embarrassment. With disconcerting justice, they reminded me that cases of unsold magazines were gathering damp in the cellar from my last expedition into print.

Musa had been an effort of my first year at the University of Cape Town, a national cultural quarterly which had creaked through a single issue. A young girl from Johannesburg, who taught with me at the Sea Point night-school, and was later to marry my cousin, had joined me in constructing it as a vehicle for our careers; but as neither of us had possessed any idea of where we wished to go, we had soon tired of the trip and abandoned it altogether. Within a lurid maroon and silver cover, we had earnestly published articles by various authorities on theatre and painting, poetry and music in South Africa. But our diligence had faltered at reading proofs, and the result had staggered the most sympathetic understanding. Our own editorial had invoked the muses with elegant rapture, and my own contribution had consisted of a short satire on the prose poems of Lord Dunsany, so delicate that no one had any idea of what it was about, let alone at whom it had been directed. In the event, we had published 1,500 copies and sold 6, though a lavish distribution to newspapers, relatives and friends had brought the total disposed of to a slightly less ludicrous figure.

All the same, some 1,200 copies had remained, and my father
had helped to meet the printing bill with an unspoken astonishment at the waste. It was useless to explain to the members
of my family that I had returned from America for a very
different venture.

I had no clear idea myself of how to set about establishing
the magazine that I wanted. I had been away from South Africa
so long, and my view of it had gradually blurred in the mean-
time. Surely the centre of Cape Town had never been so
cramped, with the bottom of the principal street in clear sight
of the top. There was a small town closeness about it, a slow
gossiping on pavements in the inert heat that muffled the
clashes of colour in the country beyond. The beaches seemed
the same, with their week-day circles of young women in languid
conversation on the sand while their children paddled among
the rocks, and an occasional black maid, in uniformed green,
stared sideways at the sea. On the week-ends, the same crowds
spurted on to the beaches, to lie in separate small puddles and
absorb the sun. Only the suburbs seemed to have changed,
swelling in their course along the coast to well beyond Camps
Bay, across the peninsula to Muizenberg and Simonstown,
northwards to the Afrikaans-speaking encampment of Bellville. And, with the suburbs, the slums, too, seemed to have
spread – a vast acne at Windermere in the shadow of the
mountain, and at Nyanga, the new African township and
squatter camp, hidden by the bush from the wide road to the
airport. The whites seemed as breezily arrogant as ever, the
Coloured as placid. Only the Africans, rather more of them in
the streets than I remembered, glanced sometimes their fierce
rejection.

On the Reef, or in Durban and Port Elizabeth, the atmosphere was taut. But in Cape Town the complacency seemed to
have survived unchanged, and parliament then in session, in
the gardens at the top of Adderley Street, might as well have
been mutilating the statute book of some distant state, with
which the city maintained close but circumscribed relations. In
the urgency of Johannesburg I might have felt it necessary to

launch the magazine at once, hoping that it would remain afloat while I gave it direction and shape. In Cape Town there seemed time enough to consider the design and canvass an influential participation.

I carefully calculated my chances of success. My father had settled 10,000 5% preference shares in Greatermans on each of his four children, and my own holding – in the politically depressed market – had a value of some £6,250. The capital of the family trust could not be touched, but provided each of us with £500 a year. The Estate could only be distributed in 1964, and meanwhile had to meet considerable death duties. It would, however, pay a further £500 a year to each of us. I could accordingly count on an annual income of £1,000, and the full £6,250 realized by the sale of the preference shares as backing for the magazine. Stories subsequently circulated of the vast fortune at my disposal. Dead South Africans are always richer than live ones, and my father was widely believed to have left his children several hundred thousand pounds each. But the truth was much less accommodating, and I knew from the outset what a struggle publishing would entail.

The high infant mortality rate in progressive publications – the few who survived invariably succumbed before adolescence – made the capital seem intimidatingly inadequate. True, the magazine would be aimed at an international readership, and I could hope for a larger circulation than the 2,000 to 3,000 readers which domestic precedent promised. But I doubted if I would find advertising abroad, and I early assumed that I would get none in South Africa. I had no illusions about the readiness with which the business community would support radical criticism of the government and the racial structure which supported it. I suspected then what my experience later consistently confirmed, that money in South Africa had become the hostage of power, not – as formerly – power the hostage of money.

Most Marxists I have met outside, and many inside the country, seem disconcerted by the divorce between money and power in South Africa. They assume that in a highly industrialized state, with clearly defined classes, law is the instrument of capital and power the pursuit of profit. This had been generally true up to the fall of Smuts in 1948, though the structure of white supremacy, promoted at the polls, had demanded and obtained sacrifices in industrial efficiency by tying work, as well as wages, to colour. With the mass circulation papers as their mouthpiece, mining and manufacturing had moulded the economic policy that parliament cast. It had been possible for *Trek*, a short-lived free-lance radical magazine, devastatingly to satirize John Martin, the Chairman of the Chamber of Mines, as the real Prime Minister of South Africa, the power behind the ornamental façade of Smuts.

With the victory of Afrikaner nationalism in 1948, however, successful for the first time without the constraint of any English-speaking alliance, a gulf developed between political power and wealth. Mining had always been the preserve of British capital, and the fast growing distributive and manufacturing network of South Africa's war-time and post-war industrial revolution was overwhelmingly dominated by the English-speaking whites of the cities. Only agriculture, of shrinking significance to the economy, remained largely an Afrikaner possession. Yet the government elected under the leadership of Dr Malan contained no English-speaking representatives at all and enjoyed a record of rigorous hostility to the control of wealth by foreign capital and the English-speaking community.

South Africa began more and more to assume a fascist rather than a capitalist shape. It became a state governed by, and for, a huge racial oligarchy of white farmers and industrial workers, prepared to collide with capital in the promotion of its power. Capital itself felt menaced on two sides – by the aggression of Afrikaner rule from above and by developing non-white discontent from below. Of the two, it consistently preferred the first, showing itself ever ready to retreat before the force of Afrikaner nationalism rather than risk its survival in a revolution of colour. It ceaselessly complained, often threatened, and sometimes for a moment uneasily stirred, but it never rebelled.

It let the government make the kills, and satisfied itself with a share of the carcass. In defeat it revealed itself as greedy and craven, sullen without courage, cruel without strength. It had once been the lion in South Africa's racial jungle. It was now the hyena.

A magazine of opposition to the government could either prosper on the support of the business community, by attacking non-white resistance movements while carping at the extremities of Afrikaner rule, or suffer the boycott of the business community by encouraging non-white resistance to the ravages of Afrikaner rule and English-speaking exploitation alike. I saw no reasonable choice. To attack white supremacy without attacking at the same time its economic prop seemed to me absurd. Race rule in South Africa rested not on the coercion of government alone, with its police and its army, but on the collaboration of commerce and industry. It was possible to break the power of Afrikaner nationalism by substituting for it the government of capital. But this would merely change for a new evil, an old one. The two fought together against the disciples of a non-racial democracy, and the disciples of a non-racial democracy would have to fight against the two together, in turn.

It was not, after all, the 'Slegs vir Blankes' (Whites Only) prohibition painted on the park benches, the police silencing a protest with their batons and their guns, even the starched white parliament, by which the oppression of black South Africa could best be measured. It was the bleak interminable poverty, from the first cry to the last dry cough, the tiny arid patches of land in the Reserves, suffocated by the few weak roots that they supported, the huge mining compounds and the lonely rural slums, the corrugated iron and box-wood shanties of the festering townships. White supremacy was the one black in four who died in infancy, the one in two who died before the end of childhood; it was the seven out of every ten Africans who lived in the richest part of the country, the industrial Witwatersrand, and yet could never climb above the breadline; it was, most of all perhaps, the pass laws, the silent severing of husband from wife, of father from children, in order to provide white South Africa with an unencumbered cheap migratory labour force. I was a socialist, and I could no more blind myself to the economic shape of apartheid, than to the colour of the clothing it wore.

Beyond the sterility of the official parliamentary opposition lay movements of varying militancy and strength. Outside of the Communist Party, which unappealingly reflected the fluctuations in Soviet policy, only the South African Labour Party pretended to a programme of economic radicalism across the colour line, though even then it muted its objectives so as not to jar too violently the sensibilities of its few remaining white supporters. While it had been a stridently white labour party, mouthing the prejudices of its electorate, it had been able to participate in the parleys of power; in fact, it had reached its zenith in the coalition with the Nationalists under Hertzog during the 'twenties, when it had assisted in placing on the statute book the pattern for industrial apartheid. With the United Party as the mouthpiece of commerce, manufacturing and the mines, the Labour Party had faced its real challenge for worker support from the Nationalists; and it had failed, not only because the Nationalists had been able to conscript the emotional battalions of Afrikanerdom, but because it had itself been consistently outbid in anti-colour fervour.

Its failure had been inevitable, for the peculiar appeal of a labour party must be to labour, and the real labour force of the country had increasingly become non-white. By the end of the second world war, the 'civilized labour policy', which the Labour Party itself had played so prominent a part in evolving, had combined with rapid industrialization to give the white working class a supervisory complexion and an aristocratic mentality. The aim of the Nationalist Party, to 'keep the Kaffir in his place', had been less political and social – though both these drums had been loudly beaten too – than they had been economic; the Nationalists had pledged themselves to ensure that the status of the white worker was raised, while that of the black was militantly maintained if not degraded still further.

The only survival possible to the Labour Party, therefore, lay in cutting its umbilical cord with the white electorate, accepting the loss of its thin parliamentary representation, and striving to become a party of the real working class, the non-white proletariat, so providing the inevitable revolution with a socialist leadership and objective. That it should have chosen not to do so, was not its own agony alone, but the agony of a whole country rushing headlong to revolution without a single cohesive socialist force to guide its subsequent direction.

At the time of my return to South Africa at the beginning of 1956, the Labour Party was already living a posthumous existence. Returned with six members to parliament in 1953, on an electoral pact with the United Party, it had helplessly watched its support in the country die, and its appearance of political animation depended upon its three main spokesmen in parliament – Alex Hepple, the leader, Hymie Davidoff, and Leo Lovell – who sustained, with the African Representatives, the only real parliamentary opposition to the government. Hymie Davidoff and Leo Lovell were family friends through their association with the Jewish Board of Deputies and the South African Zionist Federation, while for Alex Hepple I was to discover a growing affection, gratitude and admiration. All three, from my first application to them, were to help in launching *Africa South*, and Alex Hepple particularly was to assist its progress by his advice and the articles which he always agreed so readily to write. For the 1958 general election the United Party repudiated its electoral pact, and the Labour Party lost all its seats in the three-cornered contests that it was accordingly forced to fight. With its disappearance from parliament its public image disintegrated altogether, leaving behind nothing but a remembrance of its courageous last days and a lesson in the retribution of political schizophrenia.

The failure of the Liberal Party, founded in 1953, was congenital, springing from the personality of the traditional movement that had produced it. Liberalism in South Africa had never come to terms with its circumstances – it had taught where it should have learned, petitioned where it should have campaigned, protested where instead it should have resisted. It had clung to the crumbling ledge of evolution long after it had become obvious that the only escape from the rocks below lay in the risk of climbing. And this failure of political recognition had merely mirrored the lack of any economic one. Largely middle class in outlook, South Africa's leading liberals had been unable – or unwilling – to see the struggle against white supremacy as a struggle against economic domination, with colour merely painting the distinction between driver and driven. They read Exodus as though Pharaoh's heart had softened at the eloquence of Moses, as though the Jews had gone out of Egypt only to worship their god freely in their own way, not also in order to escape the brick-fields and the whips of Pharaoh's task-masters. In its preoccupation with individual freedom, liberalism assiduously dodged the implications of communal servitude – as though an African could be free on 3s. a day in the gold mines, whether or not he might gain the right to sit together with whites in the same bus and even in the same parliament. The Labour Party had failed to produce a popular movement of political power because its economic vision had been restricted to a shrinking white working class. The Liberal Party failed at the outset because it possessed no economic vision at all.

At the beginning of 1956, it was dancing a dizzy polka before the qualified franchise, while its leadership displayed a mystic elusiveness over the methods by which this constitutional compromise was to be accomplished. The whole movement appeared as a salon culture, to which sofas were more the instruments of change than barricades. Yet, under the guidance of Alan Paton, it contained some of the most incisive minds in the whole commitment against white supremacy, propagandists whose value to any intellectual campaign against apartheid was unassailable. And already its younger members, with the encouragement of Paton himself, were reaching for a new and vital policy. They would grow in numbers and influence, as white supremacy struck out ever more savagely at all those who opposed it, and at last they would transform the programme of the party to an acknowledgment of economic realities. They would adopt universal adult suffrage as an immediate objective, and participate in campaigns of unconstitutional resistance, and in the 1960 State of Emergency some of them would be imprisoned for months without charge or trial.

When I set out to establish *Africa South*, I rejected the then dominant Liberal outlook, as I rejected the official policy of the Labour Party. Yet both groups denounced the whole doctrine of permanent race rule promoted by the government and its official opposition. It seemed to me possible for the magazine to provide a platform on which spokesmen of the Liberal and Labour Parties might sit with those of the non-white political movements and free-lance rebels like myself. I approached prominent Liberals, like Alan Paton and Margaret Ballinger, to associate themselves with it as sponsors and contributors. Their agreement, together with that of the Labour leaders and prominent independents, like Dr Ellen Hellmann, former President of the South African Institute of Race Relations, and, above all, Ambrose Reeves, Bishop of Johannesburg, was to assist in giving the magazine from its inaugural number a broadly humanist complexion, identifiable not with any party, but only with a general democratic dedication.

The Non-European Unity Movement, to which I had been so attracted during my first few months at the University of Cape Town, appeared to have degenerated altogether into sterile bickering. Its policy of non-collaboration increasingly provided an excuse for mere inaction, and its principal organ of opinion, *Torch*, reverberated with abuse of all those against whom its Trotskyist Coloured leadership bore any grudge. Only in the Transkei, where its African constituent, the All African Convention, enjoyed some influence, especially among the teachers, had the movement displayed any willingness to come to grips with the government, and against the proponents of this sudden militancy the pages of *Torch* carried paragraphs of snide invective. The interminable discussions on revolutionary methods and objective, which had dazzled me briefly seven years before, now seemed more than ever a mere glitter of sound. With the leadership of the A.A.C. and especially with Dr A. C. Jordan, Lecturer in Bantu Languages at the University of Cape Town, and his wife Phyllis, both of whom were to contribute regularly to *Africa South*, I discovered once more a rewarding friendship. But the Trotskyist disputants filled me with a tedious distaste, and I made little effort to draw them into the magazine. It is doubtful, anyway, if effort would have accomplished anything. The first issue of *Africa South* was greeted with a fury of derision by *Torch*, which castigated it as a liberal–colonialist conspiracy.

It was to the African National Congress that I felt most closely drawn. It was a mass movement, revolutionary in objective and employing unconstitutional – though still non-violent – techniques of struggle. It seemed to me the one proper instrument of change in South Africa, since only mass action appeared capable of toppling white rule, while the younger socialist leaders of the movement recognized the need for an economic revolution if change was to have any real and lasting popular meaning. It was these Africans, together with the Coloured, Indians and whites who thought as they did but who could not similarly channel the course of revolution, who would fulfil individually the group function of a Socialist Party. Certainly, if they failed, the Communist Party would take squatter's possession of the vacant lot, and there construct its first African edifice of power out of the desires and despairs of an awakened proletariat.

The African National Congress was no new organization. In 1882 a Native Education Association had been formed in the Cape, and two years later had issued the first organized African protest against the pass laws. In 1884 a Native Electoral Association had been founded at King William's Town in the Eastern Cape, in order to organize the African vote for the Cape general election of that year, and in 1887 a conference there had selected a delegation to protest at the raising of the franchise qualifications. By 1904 the Natal Native Congress had been formed, and, by 1907, a similar organization in the Transvaal.

In 1909 a National Native Convention had met to discuss the implications of South African union and had decided to send a delegation to Britain in protest at the colour bar in the proposed constitution. A qualified African male franchise in the Cape had been secured, but no vote of any kind for election to parliament had been granted to Africans in the other three provinces. All protests had, of course, been ignored by the British government – the Africans possessed no resources for political blackmail – and union of the four provinces had followed on the 31st of May 1910. On the 8th of January 1912, the South African Native National Congress, later to change its name to the African National Congress, had been formed at a conference in Bloemfontein, to agitate for political reform.

With the passing in 1913 of the Land Act, which deprived Africans of all land rights outside the Reserves, the new Congress had launched its first major campaign, organizing protest meetings in many parts of the country, and sending a further futile deputation to Britain. In 1914 it had even supported the war effort, in the hope that its gesture would be rewarded with concessions when victory came; but this hope had proved hollow, and Congress had dispatched still another deputation to Europe in 1919, to put African grievances before the British government and the League of Nations. Meanwhile, slowly, reluctantly, it had started on the road to revolution. In 1918 it had threatened a general strike, in support of an African demand for a wage rise of 1s. a day and in protest at the heavy sentences passed on striking municipal sanitary workers in Johannesburg. Soldiers had marched on Johannesburg, and eight Congress leaders had been arrested.

Such was to be the pattern of the years to come. In 1934, the bulk of the Nationalist Party under General Hertzog and the South African Party under General Smuts had fused to form the United Party, with Hertzog as Prime Minister and Smuts as his Deputy. Enjoying a massive majority in parliament, the new administration had decided to settle 'the Native problem' once and for all. By the 1936 Native Trust and Land Act, parliament had sanctioned the purchase of seven million morgen as a final settlement of African demands for more land, so providing for a maximum African ownership of 13% of the country's total area. At the same time, the 1936 Native Representation Act had amended the constitution to remove African male voters in the Cape from the common roll, providing instead three seats in the House of Assembly and four in the Senate for Europeans to represent African interests, and establishing a Native Representative Council as a sounding-board for African complaints. The African National Congress, while protesting passionately at this new assault on African rights, had permitted its members to serve on the Native Representative Council, and a dissident group within the movement, formed in 1943 as the African National Congress Youth League, had arisen to demand a boycott of the Council and a programme of greater political militancy. By 1946 Congress itself had decided to boycott the Native Representative Council in protest at its political impotence, and three years later had adopted the Youth League's Programme of Action.

In 1946 the Presidents of the African National Congress, the Transvaal Indian Congress and the Natal Indian Congress had signed the Xuma–Dadoo–Naicker Pact of co-operation in the common struggle against white supremacy, and this alliance had been fortified by the Nationalist victory in 1948 and the 1950 Suppression of Communism Act, with its assault on all organized non-white opposition to the government. In 1952, the Joint Planning Council of the African National Congress and the South African Indian Congress had launched a defiance campaign against the race laws, and all democrats irrespective of colour had been invited to join. During the next eight months, over 8,000 men and women of all races had gone to jail for civil disobedience, and the campaign had at last been shattered only by the Criminal Laws Amendment Act of 1953, which prescribed severe penalties – including whipping and up to three years' imprisonment – for breaking any law by way of protest.

In 1953, the South African Coloured People's Organization (S.A.C.P.O.) and the white Congress of Democrats (C.O.D.)

had been formed, and these had at once associated themselves with the African and Indian Congresses in resistance to white domination. On the 26th of June 1955, at Kliptown in the Transvaal, delegates of the four organizations, with wide representation from the African and Indian urban masses, had formed the Congress Alliance, with a Freedom Charter of aspirations and demands. This Charter, mildly socialist in character, had become the faith of a new inter-racial mass revolutionary movement.

It seemed to me unthinkable that I should publish any magazine without the support – or, at worst, the connivance – of the Congress Movement. Were the A.N.C. leadership alone in any degree hostile, the whole gesture of an intellectual front against apartheid would be ultimately theatrical, isolated from the mass which could give it significant force. For a time I even considered placing my resources and services at the disposal of the A.N.C., on the sole condition that they were both employed in publishing a magazine. Yet it seemed to me that a propaganda association of different political groupings against white rule, if only an alliance of print, would serve the interests of Congress better than any organizational mouthpiece. And I was, as well, not sure that I could fit my strident individuality into the frame of any one political movement. Whatever allegiance I felt to the common programme of the Congresses, I wanted to remain finally free to criticize any decision of the leadership that I believed to be wrong. It was an arrogant reservation, but one which my whole experience and personality had shaped. I had been impetuous in my very resolution to return. I wanted to retain my right to be impetuous again, if I ever felt it necessary. Looking back now at my short career in South African politics, I am glad, above all else, that I doggedly preserved my independence of judgment and action. The part I played might well have been more valuable to the cause I wished to advance, had it been controlled by membership of a political movement. And it may have been more considerable. I never had a chance to lead, because I never showed a readiness to serve. Yet, in return, I never made a mistake for which I could blame

anybody but myself. What I said or did carried the whole of me
behind it, my own doubts and my own determinations. And
though, in consequence, I was often sorry, I was never
ashamed. *Africa South* was a mirror of idiosyncrasy. That was
its weakness and also, I like to think, its strength.

I approached Chief A. J. Lutuli, President-General of the
African National Congress, Dr G. M. Naicker, President of the
Natal Indian Congress, and Len Lee-Warden, African Representative in the House of Assembly and President of the Congress of Democrats, to sponsor the magazine. Mr Lee-Warden
agreed at once, but both Chief Lutuli and Dr Naicker pardon-
ably preferred to wait for the evidence of the magazine itself.
Their agreement, soon after they had received copies of the
first issue, constituted for me the first accomplishment of the
magazine, and one which assured political significance to its
production. My gratitude to those who agreed to sponsor from
the outset is boundless; they took me on trust, for I had done
nothing upon which they could have formed a reasonable
judgment of my intentions and integrity. As he would be so
often in the future, the Bishop of Johannesburg was an invaluable reassurance to me and to others. His immediate support for the whole concept of the magazine helped to make its
materialization possible. But without the association, once the
magazine had appeared, of the President-General of the
African National Congress, *Africa South* would have remained
for me a fundamental failure, a flourish at the mere edges of
the crowd.

From the beginning I had planned the magazine as an international effort. The creation of a united front against apartheid
in South Africa was to be complemented by an influential
democratic association outside. My own ideas of international
pressure were still nebulous, but I recognized how formidable
were the forces at the government's disposal and believed that
rebellion could succeed only with intervention of some sort
from abroad. Since direct foreign investment in South Africa
topped one thousand five hundred million pounds, of which
over nine hundred million pounds were British and nearly

three hundred million pounds American, I did not suppose that the West would welcome a revolution which, in dismantling white rule, might tamper with the structure of capitalism. All I could hope to do with the magazine was to help create a climate of opinion in the West which would make any intervention in support of white supremacy improbable. In the prevailing weather of 1956, it seemed reasonable to expect no more than mere connivance at change in South Africa. Any assistance would have to come from independent Africa, slowly spreading southwards down the map.

I applied myself to finding influential figures in Britain and the United States prepared to associate themselves with the magazine. In Britain, Joyce Cary, the novelist, the Rt Hon. Arthur Creech-Jones, M.P., former Labour Secretary of State for the Colonies, Kingsley Martin, Editor of the *New Statesman and Nation*, and Rev. Donald Soper, the Methodist leader, were among those who responded, while in the United States, with the assistance of the National Association for the Advancement of Coloured People, I acquired thirteen sponsors, including Louis Fisher, the author, Thurgood Marshall, Special Counsel to the N.A.A.C.P., Dr Reinhold Niebuhr, the theologian, Victor G. Reuther, of the United Automobile Workers, and Willard Townsend, Vice-President of the A.F.L.–C.I.O. trade union federation.

There was to be an ironic prelude to publication. While I was assembling quotations from printers, I heard that a number of liberal professors and lecturers at the University of Cape Town were contemplating a magazine of their own. We held three meetings to discuss a joint project, but failed to agree. I was clearly more radical in approach than the academics and, since I would be providing the capital, I demanded the final say in shaping the policy of the magazine. The academics claimed to be providing the reputations, without which the capital would be useless, and proposed a divided control. We parted on the worst of terms, with two magazines projected. In the end, theirs never appeared, and I was angrily to encounter several offers, during the years that followed, of sufficient capital to promote the magazine as I wished, together with demands for a say in shaping its policy.

For five pounds a month and a five shilling charge for electricity, I took a small office – some 6 feet by 12 feet – up two flights of stairs on the top floor of an old office block in Church Square. From the window I could look down on the Houses of Parliament opposite – a defect discounted in the rent – and after inserting a large director's desk that I had bought for seven pounds at a sale, had just enough width for a chair and six inches of play. From a firm of prosperous lawyers I filched a young girl recently arrived from England to be my secretary at £40 a month – she was persuaded by my idealism to a cut of £10 from her previous salary – and surrendered the chair to her. I sat on a small stool reserved for visitors or, when there was a visitor to occupy it, perched on the desk.

I eventually settled on the Cape Times [1] as my printer, and prepared the promotion brochure. After several depressing attempts at acquiring an appropriate cover design from commercial artists, I approached the country's most distinguished sculptor, Lippy Lipshitz, with foreboding. He cheerfully agreed to try, and emerged two days later with a design of sophisticated simplicity, a sculptured African profile, which I immediately bought and which was to become the emblem of *Africa South*.

I do not remember having considered any other name for the magazine, though doubtless I did. I wanted to emphasize, concisely and unemotively, that the scope would cover all of black Africa. I assumed that *Africa South* would be taken to mean Africa south of the Sahara. I was wrong. Most people whom I carefully questioned seemed to think that I had inverted South Africa for some arch political reason. And from the moment of the magazine's appearance, a number of my friends started calling me Segal Ronald.

The brochure was a small stapled eight-page booklet with

[1] The company, one of the largest in South Africa, printed *Hansard* as well as the *Cape Times*, Cape Town's English-language morning newspaper, which it owned.

the Lippy design on the cover, a short statement of objectives – that the magazine would analyse developments in Africa and support the struggle against race rule wherever it was waged – a list of sponsors, and a subscription form. In a convulsion of optimism I ordered 100,000 copies, and then visited an agency that dealt in postal circularization. Not surprisingly, the agency was unable to provide me with a list of liberal South Africans. It had, however, divided the South African whites with whom it exclusively dealt into English and Afrikaans speaking, upper, upper-middle, lower-middle and working classes. How it managed all this from a scrutiny of the names I was never able to discover, but my trust was complete. On the assumption that we might sell 5,000 copies of a magazine containing 128 pages, $8\frac{1}{2}'' \times 5\frac{1}{2}''$ in size, at a retail price of 3s. 9d. each, I calculated that I would lose £2,000 a year. To drop the price would increase the loss alarmingly. To raise it would reduce the proposed circulation, I suspected, before my own opinions had had a proper chance to do so. The less I spent on promotion, the more I would have for the magazine itself. I accordingly settled on a circularization of 40,000 brochures, to encompass the English-speaking upper and upper-middle classes, with the Afrikaans speaking professional class – the agency promised a special effort at identification – in the Union and Southern Rhodesia. It seemed a beginning.

Some three hundred responded with subscriptions, and three dozen with letters of abuse or threats. To a representative in Britain and a public relations firm in the United States, I shipped the remainder of the brochures, and received in return a further three hundred subscriptions. At least the magazine would be read by more than the six who had bought *Musa* seven years before.

Enjoying a virtual monopoly over the distribution of magazines and newspapers in South Africa and the Rhodesias, the Central News Agency had never conducted itself kindly towards publishers of small periodicals and radical opinions. I approached the company's Cape head with a scepticism only less massive than that with which he received me. I heard his excuses – I was to hear them often enough afterwards from similar organizations in other countries – with argumentative respect. The company could not afford to gamble on any new venture. I suggested that it take copies on sale or return. The company could not afford to risk huge freight charges for magazines that could not be sold. I promised to meet the cost of railage myself if the receipts from sales did not cover it. The company was wary of political magazines, which showed a distressing propensity for involvement in libel. I offered to meet myself any damages for libel that the company might suffer. The gentleman raised his eyebrows in search of collateral. I mentioned in passing that my father had been Managing Director of Ackermans and Vice-Chairman of Greatermans Stores. The gentleman stirred with interest. Clearly the magazine I projected was unlikely to be too radical. Besides, as he was kind enough to observe, one of the company's busiest branches was located in the Cape Town head office of Ackermans. I saw no reason to remark that his attitude to *Africa South* was unlikely to have any bearing on the lease of his branch. We chatted amiably about the government over cups of tea. When I got up to go, he assured me that the company would handle the magazine on terms which we might settle in subsequent conversations and correspondence. I went back to the office and treated my secretary to a milk shake.

To a letter of sustained panic, my cousin Sylvia, who had survived my visit to America without undue bitterness, replied by agreeing to supplement herself the costly labours of the public relations firm I had employed for the magazine. In the event, this entailed the keeping of complicated accounts and innumerable melancholy approaches to bookshops and distributing agencies. At last we found a news agency which agreed to take the magazine, on sale or return, at half the American selling price of seventy-five cents a copy. All my own efforts, with those of such friends as I could conscript in London, failed to acquire the co-operation of any distributing network there. Such a market for the magazine as I could

reasonably hope for in Britain, I would have to make with the
help of small bookshops up and down the country.

I wondered then, as I wonder now, how far the free publication of opinion exists in the West. The monopoly of newspapers, magazines and books held by the state, directly in
communist countries or indirectly through the operation of
censorship in societies of the totalitarian right, soon enough
induces an intellectual paralysis. Yet only sanctimonious propaganda, it seems to me, can justly claim much more for the
fastnesses of democracy. It is true that communist newspapers
and magazines are published in several states of the anti-
communist West, while no anti-communist literature circulates
legally in communist states. Here, certainly, exists a fundamental difference between the two kinds of society. But publication under capitalism is an industry like the manufacturing
of cosmetics or dehydrated soups, subject to the same pressures
for profit and with the same genesis of ever greater combines in
the search to diminish costs and competition. When it is remembered that four men control almost the entire newspaper
industry of Britain, and that two concerns dominate the distribution of periodicals, the right to the publication of opinions
seems a dangerously conditional one.

For the first issue of *Africa South* I sought a representative
apologia for apartheid, and a series of replies by authorities in
specific fields. For the defence, I found an enthusiastic advocate
in Japie Basson, the young Nationalist Member of Parliament
for Namib in South West Africa, who was reputed to be the
most radical and imaginative of the younger apostles. He was
the only Nationalist I was ever to entice into the pages of
Africa South; others, whom I subsequently approached, considered the magazine too repugnant even as a channel for
proselytizing the enemy. In 1959 Basson himself would be
expelled from the Nationalist Party for publicly criticizing
Verwoerd's expulsion of the African representatives from
parliament, and would then establish an ineffectual National
Union in electoral alliance with the United Party.

In his article for the magazine, he was passionate if elusive.

E

The white South African nation did not wantonly wish to dominate the Bantu. It wished only to preserve its own character among the numerically stronger and culturally different Bantu nations, in a homeland that it had so laboriously led to peace and prosperity. It recognized that its present policy of paternalism towards the Bantu could not endure; that the boy became a man; and that the Bantu nations, too, had legitimate national aspirations, with a right to the highest possible development of their talents. Naturally it welcomed the valuable assistance of the Bantu in the economic development of its own living space. And in return it was more than willing to help the Bantu to a higher cultural level and standard of living. But it believed that where two nations, each with its own aims and desires, had to live and develop under the same political ceiling, a brute struggle for supremacy, with all its attendant pain and injury, was bound to ensue.

The only dynamic solution which had so far offered itself to white South Africa, and which had proved successful on the Indian as well as the African, sub-continent, was that of apartheid, of 'Separate Development or National Separateness'. It aimed at the establishment of one or more permanent national homes, with eventual home rule, for the Bantu, alongside a permanent national home for the (white) South African nation. As the Prime Minister and leader of the Nationalist Party, Mr Strijdom, had so clearly expressed it in his first Christmas message to the Bantu in 1954: 'The government will, as in the past, continue to lead you along the path of self-development to maturity ... to self-reliance and independence.' There was nothing necessarily repressive in the principle of apartheid. Intrinsically it was a policy of equal opportunities and equal privileges, in distinct and independent spheres of activity.

Against this argument I assembled several articles, each of which concentrated upon a specific corrosion of apartheid and contributed to the overall indictment. The Vicky cartoon which I solicited provided a matchless illustration – it depicted a plump white figure in a squalid slum, wagging one figure at a ragged black child, with the words: 'Don't you

understand? We're doing this for your own good!' I presented
the original to the Bishop of Johannesburg, who hung it de-
lightedly on a wall in his study. Further articles analysed the
white opposition in South Africa, African political movements,
the doctrine of passive resistance, United States policy in
Africa, Britain's colonial record, and the current political tensions in Nigeria and the Gold Coast. The issue concluded with
a short story by Harry Bloom and a poem by Professor Guy
Butler of Rhodes University.

My own editorial, 'In Sight of the End', reflected the reasons
for which the magazine had been founded with an urgency and
alarm that seemed to many histrionic at the time, but which turned
out even less lugubrious than the future might reasonably have
excused. I predicted that the African representatives would soon
be shuffled out of the parliamentary pack, while the Labour Party
would lose its place in the 1958 elections. The United Party
would be the only opposition left, till the government lost
patience with its dummy and dealt it out of the pack as well.

'If Liberty is indivisible, Tyranny is indivisible also. Neither
can have any regard for the Colour Bar. And so every Parliamentary Session is inundated with Bills conferring extraordinary powers on individual Ministers, every Session dis-
bands with a Cabinet momentarily dazed by the authority it
has voted to itself. But the next Session is a return only to
fiercer demands more fiercely demanded. The more power the
Government seizes, the more it reaches for, till no more will be
asked because there will be nothing left to give.

'We are being driven along towards the disaster of a total
Police State, and while most White South Africans do not even
notice it because the whips are as yet being used upon other
people's backs, the rest are too afraid of the whips to say anything in protest. It is not easy to cry out your horror aloud when
you may lose what you consider the right, and what the Government prefers to call the privilege, of a passport, not easy when
you may have your house searched in the middle of the night
for evidence of "treason", your movements limited to a
particular district by Government order, your associations

restricted to only those gatherings the Government permits you
to attend.... It is not easy to run the risk of five years in jail for
propagating what the Government ludicrously calls Communism, to lose your job, your property and your liberty because
you believe in and practise your right to political opposition.

'All this is not easy. But it represents a risk we must all find
the courage to take. For sooner or later the risk will be forced
upon us. And it is better, surely, that we should take it now,
among the last hesitations of the twilight, than later, in the
dumb lonely agonies of the dark. Above all, we must realize
that we cannot fight tyranny in fragments. The dissipation of
our resistance to it through civil wars over trivial differences of
approach can only lead to the collapse of all resistance in South
Africa before the undivided, indivisible onslaught. If it is
treason in South Africa for White democratic opinion to ally
itself with Black, it is a judgment we must necessarily suffer
and be proud to call down upon ourselves.'

The first issue was published at the beginning of October
1956. The *Cape Argus*, Cape Town's evening newspaper, remarked on the indiscriminate capitals with which the editorial
was peppered and complained that so much was the wrong
way round – the design on the cover in white with the colour
used as background, and the name of South Africa reversed.
It admitted the standing of contributors like the Bishop of
Johannesburg, but disputed the value of confirmed colonial
critics like Fenner Brockway. The *Cape Times* was more in-
dulgent and gave the magazine a measured welcome in a
special editorial. We had printed 15,000 copies; we distributed
several thousand abroad as inducements, and sold just over
7,000. The Central News Agency, to its frank astonishment,
sold almost 2,000 copies alone. It was a far from spectacular
success. But in comparison with past progressive publications
of a similar kind in South Africa, it was a triumph, if a rather
expensive one. The issue had cost some £1,200 to print, while
shipping and railage costs, office expenses and contributors'
fees, all but swallowed the receipts. I had resolved to pay £7
a thousand words for contributions, in the belief that magazines

which depended on voluntary articles inevitably found themselves short of worthwhile material and forced to publish makeshifts instead. It was a resolution which I never regretted, though it cost more than £1,000 a year to maintain. I found that even the most politically committed of my contributors were prompter in delivering their material because they knew that they would receive a cheque in reply, while I myself found it less embarrassing to solicit articles. A cursory examination of outgoings and receipts was accordingly dismal. At the current rate of expenditure, the magazine seemed likely to dissipate its capital within two years.

Soon after the first appearance of the magazine, I received a telephone call from Professor Nicolaas Olivier of the Bantu Studies Department at the University of Stellenbosch and the South African Bureau of Racial Affairs (S.A.B.R.A.), an organization of Afrikaner intellectuals – mainly academics and clergymen, but with a scattering of politicians like Japie Basson – who propagated a policy of real racial separation. These were the confident carriers of Afrikanerdom's conscience, the apostles of sacrifice in the cause of racial peace. If ever the Nationalist Party were to retreat from its policy of ruthless white domination, and promote a programme of territorial partition instead, they would be the accessories before the fact.

Professor Olivier expressed his interest in the career of *Africa South* and invited me to dinner with his associates in S.A.B.R.A. at Stellenbosch. If I wished, he added uncertainly, I might bring with me a few of my friends who were interested in discussing S.A.B.R.A.'s policy. Did the invitation cover Africans? I asked. There was a pause. He had no objections at all himself, he explained, but his colleagues might not feel easy. It was to be a social evening, after all. I thanked him and said I would come.

I collected two journalists of liberal cast and set out with them for Stellenbosch a few days later. We met our hosts at a hotel in the centre of the town, had two rounds of preparatory drinks, and then filed into the dining-room, where I was seated at table between Olivier himself and Professor J. L. Sadie, another member of S.A.B.R.A., who enjoyed some repute as an economist of influence with the government. The conversation took an unhappy turn from the start. Over the soup – recalling the published impressions of a recent visitor to South Africa, who considered the Africans happy because they smiled and sang – I discoursed breezily upon the deceptiveness of appearance, how miserable a street crowd in London generally looked, and how jubilant the passers-by in Barcelona. Yet it was absurd to assume from this that the English were discontented with their government, and the Spanish contented with theirs. 'But the Spanish *are* happy with things as they are,' Professor Sadie observed. 'I know.' The rest of the meal passed in fitful silence.

When we had withdrawn for coffee in the lounge, we began discussing government policy with some earnestness. Of course, my hosts declared, there were aspects of Nationalist policy that disturbed them, but with the substance of it they agreed. Only the establishment of separate Bantu homelands could provide both black and white in South Africa with justice and security. I pressed them for details. How would the country be carved? Who, for instance, would receive the gold mines? The gold mines had been developed by white capital and skills, I was told. Not by black labour? I asked. And who might expect to keep the cities? They were also white creations, one of my hosts replied. But, of course, they would have to sacrifice much of their black labour force. Not all? I interrupted. The convivial polish on the discussion was visibly fading. An elderly academic explained that black labourers were likely to work in white South Africa for many years to come, and would probably always represent some portion – though a minor one – of the total working force. 'And if the blacks reject partition altogether?' one of my journalist companions asked with impatience. 'Because they believe the whole country to be as much theirs as yours?' It was an inflammatory question. 'Let us be realistic,' one of the younger S.A.B.R.A. intellectuals barked back. 'Partition is not the

same as unconditional surrender. We are not without resources.' The party disintegrated with polite allusions to the
possibility of further discussions. Professor Olivier looked distressed. His evening had not gone as he had planned it. I was
not surprised.

The second issue, published at the beginning of January
1957, had collected the sponsorship of Chief Lutuli and Dr
G. M. Naicker, and contained contributions from Walter
Sisulu, banned Secretary-General of the African National Congress, Ezekiel Mphahlele, soon to leave for Nigeria and enjoy
a success with his autobiography, *Down Second Avenue*, and
Tom Mboya, General Secretary of the Kenya Federation of
Labour but not yet a member of the territory's Legislative
Council. We printed 8,000 copies and sold some 4,500. I was
not depressed. I had expected the drop. I only wondered with
what fury hundreds of curious but politically conventional
South African whites must have abused their initial extravagance. And I was encouraged by the direction which the
magazine seemed to be taking. The first issue had been earnest
but dull, with most of its contributors representative of
intellectual liberalism. The second issue was brittle but
provocative, with flares of feeling that gave excitement and
immediacy to the criticism. There were background studies,
but reports on current developments as well, like Mphahlele's
article on the Evaton riots in the Transvaal, and an analysis by
Professor Hobart Houghton from Rhodes University of the
Tomlinson Report on the feasibility of territorial segregation.
The blend of academic analysis with passionate comment, of
incident with trend, set the pattern for all the issues to follow.
Die Transvaler, the Johannesburg Afrikaans-language daily
which Dr Verwoerd had edited from 1937 to 1948 and which
remained his mouthpiece, reviewed the second number of the
magazine in a special editorial, entitled 'Die Dood in die Pot'
(Death in the Pot), a rather strained metaphorical description of
the function that the newspaper considered *Africa South* to be
performing. We were stirring up death in the pot for South
Africa and, with the rest of the English-language press, could

not expect the government for ever to ignore our irresponsible slanders and provocations.

At the beginning of November 1956, Russian tanks crushed a rebellion of the Hungarian people, and white South Africa exploded into demonstrations of protest. Afrikaner university students paraded frenziedly in Pretoria and Stellenbosch, while men and women from the plushest English-speaking suburbs rushed into the centre of the cities to collect and give money for relief. I was astounded. The Russian intervention seemed unpardonable to me, and I engaged in bitter dispute with my communist friends over it. Their excuse that the Soviet Union had acted in protection of its own security seemed cynical beyond my most lurid expectations. If the Soviet Union was justified in suppressing all revolt in order to surround its borders with a slavish conformity, the United States and Britain might be forgiven for identical conduct in areas like Latin America, South-East Asia, and Africa that they regarded as their own strategic spheres of influence.

All this, however, did not make the genuinely passionate reaction of white South Africa any less extraordinary. Was it rational that those who had subjugated so many themselves could denounce with manifest sincerity the subjugation of Hungarians by Russians? For the third issue of the magazine, I prepared an editorial on 'Hungary and South Africa'. The truth, it seemed, was that the normal white South African did not think in terms of freedom at all when he thought in terms of Africans or Indians or Coloured. Hungary and South Africa presented totally different issues to his mind, because Hungarians were white, and white men were born to certain inalienable rights. If non-whites were white, they would be human as well, with title to personal freedom and security.

'The South African government, without seeing anything bizarre in its gesture, grants a token £25,000 for the relief of Hungarian refugees. The impudent hypocrisy of one tyranny's assisting, in the name of freedom, the victims of another, makes one wonder at the extent to which even the South African government is capable of moral effrontery. It cannot be believed that the Minister of Justice, by whose edicts so many men have been prohibited from expressing their political convictions, can remain chastely unaware of the work of his department. Yet in his New Year message to the country, he declared that we should all thank God that South Africans were living in a free country and should consider ourselves lucky and be grateful that we lived in such a South Africa. The picture of nine million Africans sinking on to their knees in thunderous gratitude for the liberties they enjoy in South Africa is a profoundly improbable one. And the kindest thing one can say about its author is that he is living in a moral dream-world of his own.

'And so white South Africa deceives itself perpetually, deceiving itself nowhere so completely as in its faith that the non-whites too are taken in by the moral fraud. The whites may not think of the Africans and Indians and Coloured people in terms of rights and freedom at all. But the non-whites do. They know that they are oppressed and they know to what rights as men they are naturally entitled. If the government does not see reason in time and continues to reply to their cries for liberty with batons and Sten guns, bannings and prison sentences, if its only reaction to the suffering of the non-white peoples is to increase it, one day sooner or later what has happened in Hungary may happen in South Africa too. And the men and women of South Africa who have never known what it is to order their lives in freedom, may take for themselves what they have so brutally for so long been denied. And when that happens, not the least tragic aspect of it all will be the utter moral astonishment of most of the white population. Not even in the final disaster that they are so scrupulously preparing for themselves, will they understand.'

In a sudden gesture of reverence for the basic aspirations of men to liberty, the South African government, in the early morning of the 5th of December, arrested 156 leaders of the Congress Movement on a charge of high treason, alleging that they had conspired to overthrow the government by force. I was stunned as I read the names of those who would now be standing trial for their lives. Three of them were sponsors of the magazine, Len Lee-Warden, M.P., Chief A. J. Lutuli and Dr G. M. Naicker. Many, like Sonia Bunting and Ruth First, had become close personal friends. It was an assault upon the whole movement for non-racial democracy in South Africa, and one which, if successful, would reduce all legal opposition to the arid bickerings of the United Party. If *Africa South* was to have any meaning at all, I felt, it would have to make clear its hostility far beyond the safe equivocations of the daily press. The hinge of the trial was to be the Freedom Charter. I decided to republish the text in full. Advocate V. C. Berrangé had delivered, in his opening address for the defence, a scathing attack on the indictment. I decided to republish his speech, despite the contention of my lawyer that a quarterly did not enjoy the same privilege as a daily newspaper, and that my failure to balance the address by the defence with the address by the public prosecutor, to which it was a reply, might be held as contempt of court.

Yet all this seemed to me an inadequate gesture. I planned to dedicate the third issue of the magazine 'TO THE 156'. My lawyer, himself a progressive of long-tried courage, whose wife was subsequently to be arrested in 1960 under the State of Emergency, heard me with horror. He agreed that a gesture was essential, but he asked me to consider whether I could not make one, equally pointed, that would not so needlessly provoke the magazine's prosecution for incitement or contempt. A magazine committed to the policies of those on trial would be more than ever necessary now. We argued for hours, and in the end resolved upon a slight amendment. In the centre of the first page of the third issue, published at the beginning of April 1957, was printed, in bold capitals –

TO
MR. L. LEE-WARDEN, M.P.
CHIEF A. J. LUTULI
AND
DR G. M. NAICKER
THIS ISSUE IS
DEDICATED

Within a few days of the arrests, a group of prominent liberals, under the leadership of the Bishop of Johannesburg and with the full backing of the Congress Alliance, launched the Treason Trial Defence Fund to raise the vast sum of money that would be required for an adequate defence. I agreed to become Organizing Treasurer for the Western Cape and set about energetically raising funds. I loathed the work, and only the fury I felt at the arrests and the course of the trial enabled me to continue with it for the two and a half years till my banning under the Suppression of Communism Act. Some of my family's friends refused to contribute, and I never visited their homes again, or agreed to be present when they visited my mother's or sister's. Anyone, I felt, who refused to help at least in paying for the defence of the accused and so upholding their right to trial, associated themselves with the government's persecution. In the event, I was astonished at the response I encountered from those I approached. Despite their horror of political involvement, their exaggerated fears of sudden retribution, many of the city's most respectable businessmen slipped envelopes of old dirty pound notes into my pockets, with passionate appeals that I should not list their names or send them receipts. My committee was to raise in the next three years some £13,000, part of it from two auctions in Cape Town for which painters and writers all over the world sent contributions.

The Executive Committee of the Fund in the Western Cape was largely a list of influential names, headed by the Archbishop of Cape Town as President. The fund-raising itself was done by a Treasurer's Committee, which consisted, in the main, of Congress members, with spasmodic recruits from the respectable beyond. The wives or husbands of the accused themselves joined cheerfully in the least pleasant of the Committee's activities, the collection and selling of cakes, vegetables and jumble, the dreary tramp through office blocks in the city, where they often received more threats and abuse than money. I acquired a deep respect, almost awe, for the dogged gaiety which they always displayed. It was difficult sometimes to believe, at meetings of the Committee, that the husbands or wives of those in the room with me were on trial for their lives.

The Africans on the Committee would organize concerts, jumble sales, and prayer meetings, bringing to me the trivial amounts which had been wrung in pennies and small silver, at so great an outlay of effort and sacrifice, from African labourers and their families. I never felt sentimental about non-white resistance in South Africa, but I never receipted the trickle of money from African areas without a small heave of the heart.

One night at a meeting of the Executive Committee, I clashed with the Archbishop of Cape Town, then Dr Geoffrey Clayton. We were discussing my fund-raising programme. I reported that one prayer meeting at the African township of Langa had raised over £30, and I proposed that we should further encourage such functions. The Archbishop turned purple. Prayer meetings, he said, were for prayer, not for the raising of money, however admirable the cause that might benefit. I controlled my own temper, quickly rearing at what I felt to be a cruel misunderstanding of the motives behind these meetings. For many Africans devout in their Christianity, prayer was a political petition, and the coins they gave to defend their leaders on trial were each an act of charity. I said that it would be wrong to dictate to the Africans how they should give their money. In deference to the Archbishop's views, I would not myself propose prayer meetings to them, but I was not prepared on any account to dissuade them. Happily, at this point tea arrived, and we did not return to the subject afterwards.

It was often with barely concealed irritation that I swerved my attention from *Africa South* to the work of the Fund. Yet now, in retrospect, that work seems to have given me as deep a satisfaction as the magazine itself. *Africa South* was my own effort, and at times I felt its isolation cold. It was on the Treasurer's Committee that I experienced again, as in my years at the University of Cape Town, the excitement of a shared political effort, the open joy of shared accomplishment.

In the end, it was not the dedication of the third issue, or the republication of the address by the defence, that produced any obvious public effect. While I had been gathering material for the second issue, Guy Butler, Professor of English at Rhodes University and Editor of the bilingual literary magazine *Standpunte*, had brought me the typescript of a long satirical poem, written by Anthony Delius, a journalist on the *Cape Times*, who was then travelling in the United States. It had been submitted to *Standpunte* for publication, but Butler had reluctantly recognized that it was far too provocative for his Afrikaner associates on the editorial board. I had eagerly agreed to consider it for publication in *Africa South*.

It had taken me two days to make up my mind. The poem was in three sections, each several hundred lines in length – the first a discursive introduction, the second a portrait of the South African parliament, and the third a fantasy of parliament's sudden appearance and stubborn survival in hell. I had decided to publish the second and third parts in successive issues. And so, in the third number of the magazine, there had appeared Delius's satire of parliament, with its savage assaults on individual members and party programmes.

He had drawn especially sharp portraits of Strijdom's two principal assistants – Charles 'Blackie' Swart, then Minister of Justice and now President of the Republic, and Eric Louw, then as now Minister of External Affairs.

> The closest friends of this upright sectarian,
> Are Mutt and Jeff of this odd ruling set-up,
> A long neurotic and a short vulgarian,
> And each a master of the comic get-up;
> Bills which opponents hold in gravest doubt
> Are those which these two laugh the most about.
> One looks an ageing elongated fairy,
> Or, possibly, a sort of bleached giraffe,
> This minute agitated, the next airy,

A tape-worm's pallor and a horn-bill's laugh ...
The Minister of Order he, who foils
Plots mostly laid in his imagination
And with a weird and spastic ardour toils
With agitation against agitation.
For the new order he has changed the law,
Replaced it with his own judicial system,
Police are practically his private corps,
And 'communists' are those who most resist him.
Yet he can joke, and no one can be cheerier
Increasing floggings, Sten-guns and hysteria.

And there sits Tommy Vlenter, least a novice,
A sallow tokolos, but worldly wise,
With great dexterity and knack of office,
As head of Defamation, nails the lies.
He can be poisonous but never pompous,
His dignity escapes him like an elf,
He scoops the gutter first in every rumpus,
If praise is slow to come, he'll praise himself.
He has a human weakness for the press
And reads his speeches there with shining eyes.
Those praising him he quotes to great excess,
The rest – distortions, calumny and lies!

Delius had not restricted himself to the government.

Across the way the weary Opposition
Nods forty heads above one nice reflection
– A dream as well – to find a proposition
That's vague enough to win the next election;
And round this high abstraction, brisk
Old goats of happy expectation skip –
The Government across the way will risk
Too much, and crash from a stupendous slip.
Triumph (some say) is won with greater ease,
However many hearts and years it breaks,

If faith's not pinned to forthright policies
But hope is fixed on Government mistakes ...
Besides, God knows what quarrels, splits, divisions
Might come among them if they took decisions.

And he had composed a lament for the busily distracted
liberals in the United Party.

Ten little liberals waiting to resign,
One went and did so, and then there were nine.

Nine little liberals entered a debate,
But one spoke his heart out, and then there were eight.

Eight little liberals saw the road to heaven,
One even followed it, and then there were seven.

Seven little liberals caught in a fix,
One stayed liberal, and then there were six.

Six little liberals glad to be alive,
One turned a somersault, and then there were five.

Five little liberals found they had the floor,
One spoke for all of them, and then there were four.

Four little liberals sitting down to tea,
One choked on a principle, and then there were three.

Three little liberals looking at the view,
One saw a policy, and then there were two.

Two little liberals lying in the sun,
One turned dark brown, and then there was one.

One little liberal found nothing could be done,
So he took the boat for England, and then there were none.

The third issue of *Africa South*, produced at the beginning of April 1957, was a publisher's daydream. Newspapers, even the government-supporting ones, seized on the satire in momentary relief from the monotonous tension of South African race politics, and almost drove the public into the bookshops. Stocks were exhausted within hours of appearing in the shops, and I was flooded with re-orders. The excitement quickly ebbed, of course, but left behind it many new readers of the magazine. The circulation jumped to over 7,000.

I had dinner with Hymie Davidoff at the House of Assembly and suggested that he attempt to quote sections of the satire during a debate. He roared with laughter at the probable consequences and agreed to search out an appropriate occasion.

In South Africa, railway station and airport bookstalls are operated and controlled directly by the Department of Transport, which none the less, at least at that time, permitted the sale of anti-government literature. To my application, however, that *Africa South* should be sold at railway stations and airports, the Department had replied with an unelaborated no. I told Hymie Davidoff, and he agreed to bring the matter up in the House during the debate on the railway estimates. It was a hilarious occasion. He rose, on behalf of the Labour Party, to demand an explanation for the refusal by the Department to allow the sale of *Africa South*. The Minister of Transport replied that the magazine had a bad smell. Several government back-benchers shouted that it was 'communistic'. Davidoff seized his chance. He read out the list of sponsors as evidence of the magazine's respectability. He himself had found nothing bad-smelling or communistic in *Africa South*. No one, for example, could call the poem which he was about to read a communistic poem. The House was entitled to judge for itself. And he proceeded to quote those passages in the poem which attacked individual Ministers. After a few minutes, the Speaker called him to order, but he protested that his point would soon become clear and he was permitted to continue. Soon the Nationalist benches were in uproar, with one member yelping over and over again, 'This is getting into *Hansard*!' At last, some ten minutes after he had begun, Davidoff was ordered to resume his seat, but with his purpose effected. The daily press snatched with glee at the occasion and reported it in lavish detail, while *Hansard* duly appeared with chunks of the poem. Leslie Rubin, African Representative, also quoted from the poem in the Senate, where he managed to have rather more recorded in *Hansard* than Davidoff had done, because most of the Senators were, following their usual practice, dozing at the time, and only woke up to what he was saying some time after he had begun.

The combination of the poem with the dedication of the whole issue and the inclusion of the address for the defence in the treason trial, had proved too much for the *Cape Times*. While the third issue was in the process of being printed, I had been summoned to a meeting of the principal directors of the company. They had suspended work on the magazine. Even if they were not sued for libel, they feared possible prosecution for contempt of parliament or court. I had insisted that they proceed with work at once, or face a claim for damages. I had agreed that they enjoyed the right to refuse to print any issue, but only on receipt of copy, not at so advanced a stage in production that I would be forced to postpone publication for more than a month. In the end, we had taken joint legal opinion, and I had accepted a few slight excisions in the poem. The directors had agreed to continue printing, but suggested that I find another company to handle subsequent issues.

Their prudence reverberated through the offices of other printers I then visited. One had a contract for school textbooks from the government, and feared that this would be threatened by the provocations of *Africa South*. Another, with a large plant, half of which was reportedly idle, replied that it had more work already than it was able to handle. Eventually, I took the magazine to the Pioneer Press, a small company which was already printing *New Age*, the Congress-supporting weekly. Len Lee-Warden, M.P., himself facing trial for high treason, and a former German refugee, Adolf Grandé, were the owners. Grandé was not surprised by my encounters with the established printing world. He had seen the same polite disengagement in Hitlerite Germany.

On the 20th of February 1957, Dr Verwoerd introduced the Native Laws Amendment Bill in the Assembly. Clause 29(c) stated that no church, school, hospital, club or place of entertainment, existing since the first day of January 1938, to which an African was admitted, might continue to operate within any urban area, except one restricted to African residents, without the approval of the Minister of Native Affairs. No meeting or gathering might equally admit an African without the approval of the Minister, who was empowered to impose conditions or withhold permission altogether. Archbishop Clayton, the day before his death, addressed a letter to the Prime Minister on behalf of the Anglican Church.

> The Church cannot recognize the right of an official of the secular government to determine whether or where a member of the church of any race (who is not serving a sentence which restricts his freedom of movement) shall discharge his religious duty of participation in public worship, or to give instruction to the minister of any congregation as to whom he shall admit to membership of that congregation.
>
> We recognize the great gravity of disobedience to the law of the land. We believe that obedience to secular authority, even in matters about which we differ in opinion, is a command laid upon us by God. But we are commanded to render to Caesar the things which be Caesar's, and to God the things that are God's. There are, therefore, some matters which are God's and not Caesar's, and we believe that the matters dealt with in Clause 29(c) are among them. It is because we believe this that we feel bound to state that if the Bill were to become law in its present form, we should ourselves be unable to obey it or to counsel our clergy and people to do so.

We therefore appeal to you, Sir, not to put us in a position in which we have to choose between obeying our conscience and obeying the law of the land.

Similar declarations followed from the Roman Catholic, Presbyterian, Baptist and other Churches, while clergymen of the Dutch Reformed Churches made covert representations of their own to the government. On March 21st Dr Verwoerd submitted a redrafted clause to the House of Assembly in a two-hour speech. It dealt with schools, hospitals, clubs, places of entertainment, meetings, social gatherings and, in a special section, with the Churches.

The Minister may by notice in the *Gazette* direct that no Native shall attend any church or other religious service or church function on premises situated within any urban area outside a native residential area, if in his opinion:

(i) the presence of Natives on such premises or in any area traversed by Natives for the purpose of attending at such premises is causing a nuisance to residents in the vicinity of those premises or in such area; or

(ii) it is undesirable, having regard to the locality in which the premises are situated, that Natives should be present on such premises in the number in which they ordinarily attend a service or function conducted thereat, and any Native who in contravention of a direction issued under this paragraph attends any church or other religious service or church function, shall be guilty of an offence and liable to the penalties prescribed by section forty-four:

Provided that no notice shall be issued under this paragraph except with the concurrence of the urban local authority concerned, and that the Minister shall before he issues any such notice, advise the person who conducts the church or other religious service or church function of his intention to issue such notice and allow that person a reasonable time, which shall be stated in that advice, to make representations to him in regard to his proposed action: and provided further that in considering the imposition of a direction against the attendance by Natives at any such service or function, the Minister shall have due regard to the availability or otherwise of facilities for the holding of such service or function within a Native residential area.

The main feature of the change was to remove responsibility for observing the law from the Churches themselves to the Africans. It was a cruel and cowardly gesture. The Christian Council of South Africa strongly protested.[1] And even those whose attitude to organized religion was impatient or indifferent, were no less appalled by the other provisions of the Bill. For these promised to conclude all social and cultural contact between white and black, close down the clubs which fostered such contact, and prohibit even the private party, the conversation over dinner and coffee, behind closed doors. Even worse, perhaps in its long-term effects, the Bill threatened to destroy all political activity that straddled the colour line, to separate opposition into the categories of race.

For the fourth issue of the magazine, I invited Dr R. H. W. Shepherd, President of the Christian Council of South Africa, to analyse the religious implications. He concluded his article with a ringing sentence: 'Beza spoke for the Church of the ages when he said to the King of Navarre: "Sire, it belongs in truth to the Church of God ... to receive blows and not to give them, but may it please you to remember that it is an anvil that has worn out many hammers." '

I asked Alan Paton to examine the political and social implications of the Bill, and he did so eloquently in an article which we entitled 'Association by Permission'.

The many racially oppressive Acts which the government has passed, have revolted, or wounded, or disgusted, or depressed, or angered people like myself, according to the state of our minds and souls. But somehow the Native

[1] 'We shall be forced to disregard the law and to stand wholeheartedly by the members of our Churches who are affected by it.'

Laws Amendment Bill seems the most terrible of all. It is like the closing of the last door, the pulling up of the last bridge into the white fortress, behind whose battlements the white people of South Africa will spend the rest of their historical span; we, the white people of South Africa, are sealing ourselves off from the rest of our continent, and indeed from the rest of the world, leaving open only the sea-lanes to Europe, the continent we have already rejected ...

There can be no doubt that, even with the drastic penalties of the Criminal Laws Amendment Act in mind, the idea of disobedience has been alive in the minds of many opponents of the government. Just as church leaders have openly stated that they cannot accept the exclusion of any person from a church on grounds of race, just so other persons, some churchmen and some not, cannot accept the right of the Minister of Native Affairs to forbid political or social association with Africans. There is no bravado about this, for no one can contemplate lightly the serving of a long prison sentence. One would do it only because it would be the only thing to do.

Of course, the Bill was passed.

Sex has always been the obsession of racially organized societies. In 1927 the Immorality Act had been passed by the South African government to make 'illicit carnal intercourse' between Africans and whites punishable by five years' imprisonment. This, however, had left open the broadest thoroughfare of racial mixing, that between the country's three million whites and the one and a half million Coloured who were themselves in part the consequence of almost 300 years of miscegenation. In 1949, the year after they had seized power, the Nationalists had pushed through parliament the Mixed Marriages Act, which prohibited all marriages between non-whites and whites. The Churches had noisily protested that marriage was a sacrament, beyond the racial mutilations of the state, and all critics had remarked that a Coloured and white could legally engage in sexual relations outside of marriage, while marriage itself had become a crime. For once criticism produced some effect. In 1950 the South African government had amended the Immorality Act to make its provisions apply to sexual relations between any non-white and a white.

The result of the various sex laws might have been anticipated by their framers had rather less passion and more thought gone into their consideration. There was a persistent increase in prosecutions for statutory sex offences, while the publicity given to the cases in parliament and the press served merely, it seemed, to stimulate further contraventions. Every year the number of whites imprisoned for breaking the Immorality Act bounded upwards, while the proportion of the offenders who were policemen suggested that the guardians of the law in South Africa were no more sensitive to the ideological importance of its provisions than those whose sensitivities they were employed to enforce.

The government had only one reply to the mounting statistics – an increase in the maximum penalty for statutory sex offences. Once more, in 1957, it amended the Immorality Act, this time providing for prison sentences of up to seven years. It was to be doubted, of course, that anyone willing to risk going to jail for five years would be deterred by the possibility of having to go for seven. But how else was respect for such laws to be inspired? There were growing demands from the government back-benches in parliament that the press be prohibited from reporting Immorality Act prosecutions. It was bad enough that so many whites should care so little for the protection of racial purity. It was much worse that everyone should know it.

Meanwhile the erosion had spread across the frontier, and in May 1957 the Southern Rhodesian Legislative Assembly debated racial mixing under its own jurisdiction. The Immorality and Indecency Suppression Act, passed in the muscle-bound colonial days of 1903, had prohibited illicit sexual intercourse between African males and European females. A Mr

Buchan moved an amendment to extend the provisions of the law so as 'to prohibit illicit sexual intercourse between a European male and an African female'. He made his own attitude significantly clear:

> One has only to look back to Roman times, as recently as that, to appreciate the consequences of the inherent dangers of the introduction of new blood strains of slaves from the conquered territory. There is not one single thing of which I am aware that can condone in any shape or form the evils of miscegenation, and while strong, lusty and victorious men are not likely to be subject to what one might term biological inhibitions, it remains to those who follow on to endeavour to stabilize the position as soon as possible.

A number of members, led by the Prime Minister himself, the Rt Hon. Garfield Todd, begged the Assembly not to follow the dangerous precedent of South Africa. Mr Todd himself called the Bill 'frankly a racial measure and not a measure which is concerned with morality'. The Assembly, however, rejected his arguments and, by sixteen votes to eight, set itself to follow in hot pursuit the example of its neighbour. Todd's own opposition was to be politically expensive. It contributed significantly to his rejection as leader by the ruling United Rhodesia Party, and so as Prime Minister, in 1958.

I was horrified by this spead of racial lunacy, and in my editorial for the fifth issue of *Africa South*, 'Sex and Sedition', I expressed my horror with a force that made the magazine as suspect in Salisbury and Bulawayo as it had already become in Cape Town and Pretoria.

'There is nothing more certain in Africa today than that Southern Rhodesia will find it increasingly difficult to work its new law and increasingly necessary to make it work. Like South Africa, it is committed to the success of its sex legislation, for the legislation must succeed if the state in its present form is to survive. In a society dominated by a racial minority, any racial mixing presents the ultimate sedition. And the state must arm itself against it as against a moral fifth column threatening its whole nature. Yet sex legislation of a completely racial kind can never succeed. And its failure corrupts from within the very structure of the state that it exists to protect. In its career the whole hopeless, helpless insanity of white domination is symbolized, the self-accelerating speed of its decline, the inevitability of its essential collapse.'

In Southern Africa itself, and abroad, *Africa South* was acquiring an influence and a following. In the fifth issue I was able to announce that Victor Gollancz, the publisher, Jo Grimond, M.P., leader of the British Liberal Party, John Gunther, the author, the Rev. Martin Luther King, Jr, leader of the Negro struggle for civil rights in the American South, Mrs Eleanor Roosevelt and the Rt Rev. John Leonard Wilson, Bishop of Birmingham, had joined the sponsorship committee of the magazine. The circulation had reached 7,500, but with advertising revenue no more than a trickle, and most of the sales still conducted at sacrificial cost through the news agencies, the closure of the magazine loomed in sight. I dismissed my secretary, who migrated to Johannesburg and married. From then onwards I handled the magazine alone, from the typing of letters to the parcelling of subscription copies, with which I staggered to the general post office every three months. I approached the Bishop of Johannesburg, to whom I had grown increasingly close in our shared work for the Treason Trial Defence Fund. He immediately agreed to do what he could and approached Canon Collins of Christian Action in London. In the years to come, Christian Action was to send several thousand pounds to keep the magazine alive. From issue to issue, I did not know how much I would get or whether, at the last moment, I would find myself without money at all. But the money always came, and it was always the Bishop of Johannesburg who encouraged me during my periodic bursts of despair. I have never ceased to regard whatever achievement *Africa South* may have been, as partly his.

On the 26th of June 1957, the second anniversary of the

Congress of the People at Kliptown, and the fifth anniversary
of the day on which the 1952 defiance campaign had been
launched, the African National Congress and its allies organized
a series of demonstrations against government policy. Each
area was left free to decide its own form of protest, and
throughout the Witwatersrand, the industrial core of the
country, the Africans stayed away from work, despite the
massing of police and the threats of dismissal by employers.
The stay-at-home there was described by police chiefs as a
'wash-out, only 50% successful'. The newspapers, however,
which had predicted a fiasco, were soon revising their columns
to explain away the 80% response.

Christopher Gell, who edited *Africa X-Ray Report* and
received a stream of visitors, seeking his advice and judgment,
from the iron lung – or, for brief periods, the bed – to which
polio had confined him, wrote for the fifth issue his report of
'A Day to Remember'. He did not exaggerate the African
reaction in areas like Cape Town and Durban, or mistake the
overwhelming success of the Witwatersrand protest – as did
some Congress leaders – for the outbreak of revolution. And
he described in moving detail the response of Port Elizabeth,
where Africans boycotted the buses, stopped work early, and –
'As daylight ebbed and the street lights of the white city began
to sparkle below them, "European" housewives in the fashionable suburbs on the northern slopes of Port Elizabeth's hill
were astonished to see the glow of bonfires illuminating
the flat, black anonymous space which accommodates 60–
70,000 Africans in their segregated dormitory suburb for the
night.'

Gell, who was to die soon afterwards, recognized the difficulties of resistance in South Africa, but passionately believed
in the possibilities of its success.

'The Nationalist Party will continue to control parliament,
the police, the armed forces. The outward show of "white
domination" will remain quite a while as living people calculate these things, though not very long as history reckons.
There will be still greater oppression, suffering, deprivation of

personal liberties (white as well as non-white), before we reach the lowest point in our appointed course. The façade will not crack just yet.

'But the non-white majority now *knows* it is only a façade. Deep in their hearts the non-whites, and particularly the Africans, treasure the certainty, proved by the evidence of their own eyes these last six decisive months, that working-class solidarity based on the indispensability of labour to an industrial economy is a liberatory weapon against which there can be no lasting defence.'

The fifth issue also initiated a series of articles on the treason trial, which were to follow the turns and twists of the Crown case, through evidence forged by the police and sudden changes in the terms of the indictment, till the trial finally came to its end with acquittals in March 1961. Principal witness for the prosecution was Andrew Murray, Professor of Philosophy at the University of Cape Town, who had lectured to me during the second part of my course in Ethics there. It was his evidence that provided the whole crazy paving of the Crown case – that the accused, in their capacity as leaders of the Congress Movement, had conspired to overthrow the government by force and put in its place a communist dictatorship of the proletariat. Professor Murray waded through the thousands of documents seized in police raids over a period of years, including hundreds of routine organizational circulars, private letters, publications freely sold on the bookstalls, and such oddments as a Russian recipe book and two notices – found at an all-day conference where lunch was being served to delegates – one of which read *Soup With Meat* and the other, *Soup Without Meat*. Tony O'Dowd, himself a barrister employed by the defence team, concluded his introductory article by quoting a list of propositions which Professor Murray had identified as communist.

> That the property-owning class, referred to as the bourgeois or capitalist class, must be destroyed.
> That the South African state has reached the stage

wherein capitalist imperialism has developed or is developing into fascism.

That the South African state is a colonial state wherein the liberatory movement must be promoted.

That ownership of property means control of political power.

That banks shall be transferred to the people.

That Russia must be defended at all times and remains the homeland of the revolution.

That action should be militant.

That contact must be made with youth associations and women's associations.

On the 17th of November 1954 the government had appointed a Commission of Enquiry into Undesirable Literature, and at the end of September 1957 this Commission at last issued its report. Government spokesmen had for years been threatening to deal with the press, overwhelmingly English-language in circulation and correspondingly critical of Nationalist policy. The combined circulation of the government-supporting Afrikaans newspapers was 350,000, while that of the English ones was 1,450,000, or over four times as great. Since the non-white readership was far too small significantly to affect the ratio, and Afrikaners constituted over 60% of the total white population, many Afrikaners were clearly reading newspapers in a subversive language. It was unthinkable that they did so because such newspapers were better. Either they were seduced by the crime and sex reporting in some sections of the English press, or by the lively and critical treatment of politics in others. Whatever the cause, the government had no intention of permitting such seduction to persist.

The Commission drew attention in terrified italics not only to the existence of subversive writings, but to the flourishing market in pornographic literature. 'As the torch-bearer in the vanguard of Western civilization in South Africa, the European *must be* and *remain* the leader, the guiding light, in the spiritual and cultural field, otherwise he will inevitably *go* under. The undesirable book can and must be drastically combated because it is obviously a spiritual poison.'

The report itself recommended the establishment of a special Publications Board to exercise control over the production, purchase and distribution of all books, magazines and news-papers. No periodical might be published, no publisher pro-duce, and no distributor sell books or periodicals unless registered by the Board. And the Board itself, sustained by severe prison penalties for the publication of undesirable literature, was to be guided by a set of bizarre definitions:

In particular, printed matter or other objects, or any part thereof, shall be undesirable if they:
(b) are subversive of or endanger, or tend to be subversive of or to endanger, the morals or moral conceptions cherished and respected by the ordinary, civilized, decent, reasonable and responsible inhabitants of the Union; or
(e) eulogistically depict, represent, describe or portray, or tend to eulogize, miscegenation, sexual relations, intermarriage, or other intimate social intercourse between Europeans and non-Europeans; or
(f) tend to engender or have the effect of engendering friction or feelings of hostility between the European and non-European population groups of the Union or between its various non-European racial groups; or
(g) propagate or tend to propagate the principles of com-munism, or promote or tend to promote the spread of communism, or propagate or further or tend to propa-gate or further the achievement of any of the aims of communism.

I devoted the editorial in the sixth issue of the magazine, January–March 1958, to the Commission's report, pointing out that the market for pornography and cheap crime books among the whites was not a cause, but just another symptom of the general decay. For the white South African, however carefully he insulated himself, there was no real escape from the colour problem. He woke up with it to the sounds of a servant in his kitchen, and went to bed with it when he latched the door at night. Assiduously it followed and caught him up. Some refuge, however temporary, was vital, a little while to fill his eyes and ears with something else. Yet the Commission expected him to display moral judgment in his choice of escape. How could he? When the whole condition of white South Africa was dictated by its capacity to do without a moral sense altogether? The real printing presses of the crime and pornography paper-backs were the government benches of the South African parliament. The crime wave swelled up from the statute book.

The ultimate objective of the Commission's report I emphasized, however, was political control. Were its recommendations accepted, and the special Publications Board established, the organs of political dissent would be bled to death in South Africa, under the pretence of treating pornography and subversion.

In the event, protests from *Die Burger* and other Nationalist newspapers which feared the effects of a rigid censorship on themselves prevented the immediate assassination of the English-language press. Instead, the government shrewdly bided its time, till the newspapers, already cowering, at last agreed to commit suicide. On the 13th of March 1962 the Newspaper Press Union, an association of proprietors, announced in Johannesburg that it had adopted a code of conduct and a voluntary Board of Reference for newspapers and periodicals. The code itself pledged 'no wilful departure from facts either through distortion, significant omission or summarization'.

News reports should be free from colouring, slanting or emphasis. Excess in reporting and presentation of sexual matter should be avoided.

Comment should be free from malice and not actuated by dishonest motive. While the press retains its traditional right of criticism, comment should take cognizance of the complex racial problems of South Africa, the general good, and the safety of the country and its peoples.

Then, at the end of April 1962, the government introduced the Publications and Entertainments Bill, establishing a Publications Control Board 'to examine any publication or object and to state whether that publication or object is in the opinion of the Board undesirable or not'. The Bill empowered the Board to prohibit the publication or exhibition of any object, and prescribed severe fines and terms of imprisonment for illegal circulation or exhibition. The definitions of 'undesirable' were even more bizarre than those proposed by the Commission of Enquiry into Undesirable Literature four and a half years before.

> The publication or object shall be deemed undesirable, if it or any part of it
>
> (*a*) is indecent or obscene or is offensive or harmful to public morals:
> (*b*) is blasphemous or is offensive to the religious convictions or feelings of any section of the inhabitants of the Republic:
> (*c*) brings any section of the inhabitants of the Republic into ridicule or contempt:
> (*d*) is harmful to the relations between any sections of the inhabitants of the Republic:
> (*e*) is prejudicial to the safety of the State, the general welfare or the peace and good order:
> (*f*) discloses indecent or obscene matter in relation to any judicial proceedings.

Publications of the Newspaper Press Union, however, were exempted from the terms of the Bill. For them, submission had already made the Bill superfluous.

The editorial in the sixth issue of *Africa South* ended with a profession of faith. What I believed then I believe as passionately now:

'In South Africa today, those in power remain in power only through the ruthless exercise of force against an increasingly hostile population, and they hear in any criticism made or reported by the press the voice of that population raised in inflexible protest against them and what they are doing. They would silence that voice, because they are stupid men and they believe that if they can kill the voice of the opposition, they can kill as well its will to overcome them. That is not so. And how can it ever be so? As long as there are men and women alive in South Africa to whom the right to live lives free of fear and violence, the right to possess and to enjoy, the right to preach and to pray are rights without which life is void of value, so long will a free press survive in the hearts and minds of South Africans, however deep its public grave is dug.'

I considered it a vital function of the magazine to popularize the recent discoveries of research into African history. The slave-traders of the eighteenth century had excused their raids on Africans by denying them an equal humanity. Africans transmitted stories from one generation to another without writing them down. Their dress and languages were undeniably different. They had not invented the gun or massed fleets with which to convert and plunder Europe. And two centuries later, in the parliaments of Cape Town and Salisbury, the guardians of white supremacy, from similar premises of superiority, were denying Africans equality in the control of the state. Even those who felt that such conduct was uncharitable were disconcerted by African inadequacies. Why, after all, had Africans never exploited the natural resources of their continent? Where had been their cities and courts, their universities and exchequers? Was it not possible that their historical backwardness mirrored some inherent inferiority? The Egyptians, of course, had left monuments to their pride towering behind them. But then, were they a black people, after all? The Zimbabwe ruins had long presented something of a puzzle. But they were probably the foot-prints of King Solomon's vanished colonizers.

I did not suppose that the intransigents of Afrikanerdom

would be converted by the consequences of any research. They would not be persuaded of African equality even if, in their vociferous Christianity, they were shown incontrovertible evidence that Christ had been black. The Dutch Reformed Churches would merely reform themselves again to acquire a less embarrassing political testament. But I believed that there were many whites, of both language groups, whose growing discomfort with crude racial repression might be fortified by an accurate assessment of African history. Before they could emotionally concede the inherent equality of black and white, they needed to clear their minds of the accumulated junk which their schools and politicians had deposited there. It would matter to them that the eleventh-century empire of Ghana and the fourteenth-century empire of Mali should have controlled considerable armies, maintained law and order over vast distances, and constructed complex cities. It would matter that Zimbabwe should have been built not by King Solomon or the ubiquitous Phoenicians but, from the eleventh to the sixteenth centuries, by the forefathers of those very Africans who now worked in the kitchens and factories and mines of South and Central Africa. Belgian excavators had even discovered that Africans, not physically unlike the contemporary Luba population of the area, had mined and forged copper in Katanga at least one thousand years before Union Minière.

For the sixth issue of *Africa South*, I accordingly invited three renowned researchers into African history to contribute articles. Roger Summers, Keeper of Antiquities for the National Museums of Southern Rhodesia, wrote on Zimbabwe; Gervase Mathew, the archaeologist, described the opulence of the East Coast trading culture; and Dr Saburi Biobaku, Director of the Yoruba Research Scheme in Nigeria, dealt with the political and artistic achievements of Yoruba society. Basil Davidson, who had done so much himself to publicize the results of new research into African history, wrote a special introduction in which he pointed some of the implications. At the start of the sixteenth century, there had been little difference between the cultural level of Lisbon or London and that reached by several

African societies. Yet three and a half centuries later, in the hey-day of Victorian rediscovery, the gap had become enormous. Was not part of the reason that Europe, plunging into industrialization and trade, had emerged with technological supremacy and fallen upon Africa as a defenceless source of slaves? Was it not conceivable that the hand of the European had guided 'not away from chaos, but towards it'?

Careless for once of the extra production costs, I increased the size of the magazine by a four-page art paper insert, with Benin and Ife bronze heads reproduced in black and dull gold. It made an eloquent witness. Numbers of readers wrote to applaud the articles, and some confessed to their glad retreat from traditional preconceptions. I continued the series in subsequent issues, publishing studies of various African art forms and political arrangements. It remains for me one of the real accomplishments of the magazine that it should have provided many whites in Southern Africa with a glimpse of African history to which their eyes had for so long been closed.

The success of the poem by Delius in the third and fourth issues of the magazine had encouraged me to search for further satire. If one could only get white South Africa to laugh a little at its rulers, it might begin to find its own obsessions absurd. One day there arrived by post at my office a number of short prose satires, entitled 'Grim Fairy Tales', by a Johannesburg school-master. I published them jubilantly in the sixth issue and, when they arrived in response to my pestering, further tales in subsequent numbers. E. V. Stone satirized Dr Verwoerd's mystic apologia for the repressions of apartheid with deftness.

'Once upon a time, long, long ago, there lived in Egypt a Pharaoh who had a Bright Idea. He would sit looking out of his palace of a morning and see the long lines of toiling slaves, all busy making bricks without straw, and it distressed him greatly to see how they were discomforted by the flies. Accordingly, being a very benevolent despot and having the welfare of his slaves at heart, he gave orders that henceforward all taskmasters were to carry whips.

F

'The slaves seemed a trifle anxious about this and sent a deputation to Pharaoh to point out that it would be cruel to whip them to work. Pharaoh was very indignant and very upset that the slaves should ever have thought that such was his intention. "Why," he said, "you poor ungrateful wretches, the whips won't be used to whip you. They are for swatting the flies as they land on your backs." '

In May 1957 Joost de Blank, Suffragan Bishop of Stepney, was elected Archbishop of Cape Town by the clergy and laity of the Western Cape with the assent of all the Bishops in the Church of the Province. On the 23rd of June he arrived in Cape Town, but soon left on a round-the-world trip and only returned in October to assume his official duties. I met him soon afterwards, when he agreed to become Honorary President of the Treason Trial Defence Fund in succession to the former Archbishop, and it was to him that I went when, early in 1958, I was approached for help by a group of Africans from Windermere.

The Transvaal Local Government (Stallard) Commission of 1921 had defined the conditions for the residence of Africans in the urban areas of white South Africa.

'The Native should only be allowed to enter urban areas, which are essentially the white man's creation, when he is willing to enter and minister to the needs of the white man, and should depart therefrom when he ceases so to minister.'

It was this attitude that had qualified before, and was to qualify since, the legal migration of Africans to the rich industrial regions of the country. White South Africa wanted cheap black labourers, but not the settled communities, the families, which would overwhelm, in their inevitable surge, the beach-heads of white domination. Successive South African governments passed laws and promoted a sprawling administration to ensure that only able-bodied African males would be received in the cities, while the old, the sick, the women and the children were left behind in the Reserves to scratch survival from the overburdened earth. Yet, despite all their efforts, the black areas of the towns and cities swelled with an illegal flow

from the Reserves – wives and children who somehow eluded
police vigilance to skulk in the shanties which their husbands
and fathers had built. Periodically, the Department of Native
Affairs would initiate a sweep of the African areas, beating the
shanties for documents, sending back to the Reserves the
illegal immigrants they found and levelling the shanties themselves. For the men, after all, there was ready accommodation
in the sterile 'bachelor' quarters of the locations.

After 1949, when Dr Werner Eiselen became Secretary of
Native Affairs, this policy was pursued with particular ruthlessness in the Western Cape, which the government suddenly
proclaimed, in a programme of ethnic adjustment called the
Eiselen Scheme, as a preserve of Coloured labour. On the
ragged fringe of Cape Town, in the shadow of the mountain,
spread Windermere, an eczema of shacks made from rusted
tins, boxes and newspaper, without lights or drainage, where
15,000 men, women and children clung frantically together.
And now Windermere was being subjected to one of those
periodic sweeps, and African women and children found there
without proper documents were being put on trains for the
Reserves. The husbands and the fathers would return from
work at dusk to find their shacks levelled and their families
gone.

I appealed to the Archbishop, and he protested to the Cape
Town City Council, whose servants were undertaking the destruction of the shacks on orders from the Department of
Native Affairs. The City Council resolved to investigate, and
arranged a meeting of its own representatives and officials
from the Department of Native Affairs with the Archbishop
and other prominent clergymen. I attended the meeting at the
Archbishop's invitation. There is no record of what was said
there, and my memory may have misplaced a word or jumbled
a phrase, but the gist of the conversation between a spokesman
for the Department of Native Affairs and the Archbishop himself I will never forget.

The Archbishop began by remarking that he had come,
without prejudice, to discover the motives for the assault on

Windermere. He could not claim to know the country, he had but recently arrived. Yet what he had seen of events in Windermere – he had visited the area himself – deeply distressed him. The government spokesman explained. 'These people,' he said, 'are in the area without permission. Permits are granted for residence in Cape Town only to those Africans for whom jobs are available. The government has clearly and repeatedly proclaimed that those without opportunities for employment, the women and children, should stay in the Reserves or leave only when they have official permission to do so.' The Archbishop nodded his head. 'I see,' he said. 'And what of the men? Is it a condition of their employment that they should be separated from their wives and their children?' 'There is no reason,' replied the official, 'why the men should come here. There is an abundant labour supply in the area. If they do not wish to be separated from their families, they should remain in the Reserves.' 'You will forgive my ignorance,' said the Archbishop quietly, 'for I must repeat that I have not been long in this country, but can you tell me what opportunities exist for employment in the Reserves?' The official hesitated. Pressed for a reply, he at last confessed that the Reserves could not support their present population, and that adult males were forced to leave in order to support their families. The Archbishop stared at him. 'Am I to understand,' he asked, 'that the only choice before the African is one between starvation and the break-up of his family?' The official stared at us all. 'I am a civil servant,' he said. 'I am not responsible for government policy. I carry out my orders, as any loyal civil servant would do.' The meeting drew quickly to a close.

I decided to concentrate in the seventh issue of the magazine on the cruelties of government labour policy. Phyllis Ntantala, the wife of Dr Jordan, wrote an account of the women abandoned by their husbands for work in the cities. Entitled 'The Widows of the Reserves', it was a passionate testament to the desolation of migrant labour, and was subsequently reprinted and quoted in numerous articles and anthologies of African writing abroad. Ruth First, in an article illustrated by the

British artist Paul Hogarth, dealt with the conditions of African farm labour in the Bethal area, and Christopher Gell added an Eastern Cape postscript. James Fairbairn, the South African correspondent of the *New Statesman*, described African resistance to government policy in the Transvaal tribal area of Zeerust, with the indiscriminate violence of its repression. And in an article, entitled 'The Fight is On', the Archbishop publicly proclaimed his disgust with government policy and his determination to oppose it.

'The whole system of migratory labour has corrupted the Union and should be rooted out. It has degraded the African, but not nearly so much as it has degraded the European who condones and encourages it.

'I am prepared to believe that there is a good deal to be said for a just and equitable distribution of land between the races on a basis of common discussion and mutual agreement. Apartheid on such terms may even be justifiable and sound. I am not so wedded to a materialistic Western civilization as to believe that it is the saving Messiah for all men everywhere. Many may one day thank God that they were never contaminated by it.

'But an equitable division of territory has nothing in common with a devilish policy that breaks up homes, that refuses to recognize the family as a unit, and that works to create a cheap migratory labour force with no rights of its own.

'Such a policy is damnable. Christians must resist it by reason of their Christian faith.'

The article received wide publicity in the daily press, while the Nationalist newspapers furiously denounced the Archbishop's intervention, and in particular his description of government policy as 'devilish'.

I had visited Windermere and seen the level places where homes had recently stood. And I had been appalled, not so much by the policy of the government itself, which I had seen in as corrosive a manifestation before, as by the readiness of the City Councillors, some in apathy, most in fear, to yield their services to government command. One afternoon, lying on the lawn outside my sister's house, I wrote my editorial for the seventh issue of the magazine. In the clarity of the late summer light, the Windermere demolitions seemed to loom before my eyes, and I felt an ache of guilt at my own submission.

I remembered that visit I had paid, some four years before, while hitch-hiking across France during a Cambridge vacation, to the ruins of Oradour-sur-Glane. Once it had been a community of 650 people, a village like all the other villages of France, with a few shops, a café where the men could sit through the long evenings around a bottle of wine, and a church built high to stand guard over the squat, sturdy houses. Then war had been declared, and the Nazis had fallen upon France. On a hot summer afternoon – Saturday, the 10th of June 1944 – the German S.S. Division 'Das Reich' had entered Oradour in a column, gathered the villagers into the church, and then shot them, men, women and children. Having done at last with the people, the soldiers had marched back through the streets, blowing up the houses and shops, one after the other, till only the church remained standing with its dead inside.

At the beginning of 1953, in the city of Bordeaux, the French government prosecuted twenty-one surviving members of the German S.S. Division 'Das Reich' for the murder of Oradour. The defence held that Hitler himself had been the real culprit. Some of the accused were Alsatians who had been forcibly enlisted in the German army. Had they deserted, they would have invited instant reprisals upon their families. And the German accused had been young men, obeying the orders of their military superiors. 'If Hitler disposed of their bodies,' the prosecution replied, 'did he dispose of their will?'

Writing my editorial, I asked myself whether the countenanced killing of Windermere, by the submissive civil servants and city council, was any different from the killing of Oradour. And if it was not, then it seemed to me that all of us who watched it, without rising up to stop it, were guilty.

'There are many ways of killing a man. Shooting him is just quicker and cleaner than most others. He can be starved to death, slowly, so that the dying is hidden away in the years. Or he can be held fast in the sort of life that rots his body and his heart together, till even his capacity for wanting is worn away, and he fumbles his own way to the grave. No one has killed him with a twitch of a trigger, no one but those dying about him has seen him die. And no one feels any guilt, for so many are guilty, and guilt sufficiently shared lies as lightly as innocence. Yet he has been killed for all that, and his murder demands an accounting.

'The killings of Windermere will be neither so quick nor so clean as were those of Oradour. And many more will die, men, women and children, than died on that hot summer afternoon in the village church. Nor will the bodies ever be counted so that a man may say, "Here died so many men, women and children, on such a day." For who can tell the number of the women sent back to the Reserves who will shrivel up inside with the sterile land, the children who will scratch in the dust outside the hut in the morning and lie there in the dust with the flies under the same sun, the men who would have been men in the thrust of their time and who will grow instead an ageless old, imprisoned children, in the bleak labour barracks of the 'bachelor' camps.

'If there is any meaning at all in being a man, then are we guilty, all of us, of the massacre of Windermere, since we will watch it happen and, watching it happen, will do nothing to stop it. We have not ordered the murders, nor, once they have been ordered, have we busied ourselves strenuously to obey. Yet we, even we, who say to each other, it is a cruelty and an ugliness beyond sanity, it is not men that do these things, and we would not do it or help in the doing of it, even we are guilty also.

'Like the German who watched from his window the Jew being beaten up in the street beneath him and cried in his heart, it is wrong and I would not have it so, but if I run downstairs and throw myself between, surely I will be taken to one of their camps or be killed here below, in the street, with the Jew – as the German at the window was guilty, of the death of the

Jew and all the deaths that followed, of Belsen and Oradour-sur-Glane, so are we guilty also. For what is done is done because we let it be done. Surely, it is we, even we, who by our silence and our quiet bodies are destroying the shacks of Windermere and the living and the not yet living that they guard.'

CHAPTER FIVE

REQUIESCAT

On the 16th of April 1958 white South Africa, disembarrassed for the first time of its small Coloured contingent, massed at the polls to give the Nationalists an increased parliamentary majority. The United Party gained seats only from Labour, the representatives of which were eliminated from parliament altogether. The election seemed to mark a last rupture with the possibilities of constitutional change. The results were unambiguous. The electorate believed in white supremacy and meant to maintain it whole at any cost. In the eighth issue of the magazine, for July–September 1958, I published a cartoon which pictured the Cabinet as pushing the coffin of democracy into its grave. My editorial, entitled 'Requiescat', was the dirge.

'Mr Ben Schoeman, the Nationalist Minister of Transport, proclaimed at an election meeting in Bellville on March 24, 1958, "Supremacy means that you have the political power in your hands and that you can be overthrown only by a revolution." More arrogantly than anyone else has Mr Schoeman portrayed the rigidity of the parliamentary pattern. The white electorate did more in the general election than vote for apartheid. It voted, ultimately, for revolution ...

'Can the non-whites be expected to endure such oppression for ever? For as long as they believe in the possibility of relief through the law, so long will they canvass their case by plea and by protest. But their trust is expendable. And when they no longer believe they will ever achieve their rights through the peaceful procedure of government, will they not rise up, in the courage of their despair, against the authors of their agony? The whites, indeed, are allowing them no other choice.'

My lawyer and I spent two hours in argument over the wording. He insisted that the paragraph on non-white rebellion was open incitement, and that I was risking several years in jail as a result. In the end, we compromised by changing the order of the words and adding question marks to the end of two sentences. I was learning to find my furtive way through the dark corridors of South African law. If I wrote, 'the non-whites cannot be expected to endure such oppression for ever', I was inciting them to rebellion. 'Can the non-whites be expected to endure such oppression for ever?' left the possibilities open. Increasingly, these legal quibbles depressed me. Each amendment of my text seemed to me a surrender, and each time I agreed to one, as a concession to common sense, I felt ashamed. I believed now that revolution was inevitable. More and more I felt that *Africa South* was not playing its proper part in assembling the instruments of change. The magazine, it seemed to me, could serve a significant purpose only if it entered, despite the legal traps strewn everywhere around, the territory of incitement.

The weeks following the general election were filled with a sense of dank futility, like a constant grey drizzle. The three-day stay-at-home, called by a special National Workers' Conference, with the backing of the Congress Movement, to coincide with the general election, had failed dismally. The government, with diligent assistance from the employers and the press, had conducted a campaign of intimidation against which the organization of the stay-at-home had clearly not succeeded in making the African masses proof. My allegiance to Congress made me anxious to discover and publish excuses rather than criticize. But, while recognizing the dangers of recrimination, I felt that apology was no substitute for success. More than ever it seemed to me necessary that the leadership of Congress should engage itself in a clear examination of the forces it faced, and consider, at whatever cost to traditional designs, the whole strategy of change.

It was in this mood that I received one day an article from Julius Lewin, Senior Lecturer in African Administration at the

University of the Witwatersrand and a prominent liberal. Entitled 'No Revolution Round the Corner', he subjected white
rule in South Africa to a scrutiny unblurred by wishful thinking. It was a devastating analysis. In 1957 Professor Crane
Brinton, the Harvard historian, had published *The Anatomy of
Revolution*. Studying the English revolution of the seventeenth
century, the American and French of the eighteenth, and the
Russian of the twentieth, he had established four factors as
common to them all. First, the revolutionary movements had
originated in the disaffection of relatively prosperous people,
who had suffered frustration rather than a crushing oppression.
Secondly, in all four societies, during the years before revolution, there had existed bitter class antagonisms of a complex
kind. Men and women, above the level of the degraded poor,
had regarded with rancour and revolt the exclusive ranks of a
socially privileged class. Thirdly, the machinery of government in all four countries had been inefficient, partly through
neglect, partly through a failure to change old and exhausted
institutions. Economic expansion and the development of new
moneyed classes, new methods of transport and commerce, had
laid an intolerable strain on administrative machinery adapted
to more primitive conditions. Finally, the armed forces themselves had been widely disaffected. And Professor Brinton had
concluded: 'No government has ever fallen before revolution-
ists until it has lost control over its armed forces or lost the
ability to use them effectively; and, conversely, no revolution-
ists have ever succeeded until they have got a predominance of
effective armed force on their side. This holds true from spears
and arrows to machine guns and gas.'

Lewin took the four factors isolated by Brinton, and
measured South Africa against them. He found the first two
applicable to Africans in the Union. They were relatively prosperous, and indeed the loudest discontent came not from farm
labourers, or peasants in the Reserves, but from the African
middle class – such as it was – and the urban working class.
The machinery of government in South Africa was not, however, on the whole, inefficient. Indeed, since it was manned

almost exclusively by Afrikaners in sympathy with the government and its policies, it was much more reliable than it would be in the hands of a different set of civil servants, whose greater technical efficiency might be offset by their political neutrality or opposition.

Non-whites had no access to modern weapons and no training in their use, and the loyalty of the men who did handle such weapons was of a different quality from that found outside Africa. The attitude of soldiers and policemen towards non-whites was notorious. No realist could believe that the loyalty of the armed forces in South Africa was open to subversion, above all in a real racial crisis. The race riots that did take place periodically were localized and therefore subdued without much difficulty. Least of all in so large a country with such poor communications as South Africa could rioting spread into revolution.

To the apostles of passive resistance, Lewin provided small comfort. He dealt bluntly with the defiance campaign of 1952–3.

'At no time did the campaign shake – though it did anger – the government; nor does anyone who was wide awake in that period honestly think that it ever looked like producing anything remotely resembling a truly revolutionary situation. Since that time the severe new laws, passed as a direct result of the campaign, have sufficed to suppress any inclination to organize another campaign on similar lines. It is one thing to go to prison for two weeks and another to go for two years and to be flogged into the bargain.'

Finally, he discussed the possibilities of mass industrial action.

'If and when urban Africans did strike in large numbers, their place would be taken and their work carried on somehow by white workers or by other Africans brought, if necessary, from neighbouring territories where Africans are more backward and much less politically conscious than they are in the Union. Add to this the fact that African workers predominate in hardly any service or industry where stoppage or slowing down would at once create a national crisis impossible to resolve. The gold mining industry is not such an industry. Even if it were, the experience of August 1946 showed how a strike could be dealt with and terminated within a week or two.'

I hesitated for more than a week before deciding to publish the article. Clearly, a significant function of revolutionary propaganda was to sap confidence, both inside the country and beyond, in the ability of the government to retain control. An article like Julius Lewin's served, on the contrary, to fortify such confidence. Yet, clearly too, a revolutionary leadership that fed off its own propaganda would soon enough fall into a stupor of self-satisfaction. It seemed to me more urgent, in the weeks of depression following the failure of the stay-at-home, to prod resistance thinking into a scrutiny of its problems than to propagate a distrust in the security of racial rule.

My decision was shamelessly a political one. I have never believed that the function of a newspaper or magazine is to publish the facts, regardless of the consequences. No editor, for example, would be justified during a war in publishing information of value to the enemy. And this was not denied by a press as jealous of its freedom as the British when Britain itself was at war. We in South Africa were already in a state of un-declared civil war, and I should not have had the slightest compunction in returning Lewin's article – despite its un-deniable quality – had I felt its publication to be on balance detrimental to the movement of non-white emancipation. I recognized, of course, that the principle I followed could not be denied other editors, who suppressed facts and information in the furtherance of racial suppression. I never condemned them for flouting some absolute standard of journalism. I be-lieved then – and I have not changed my view – that it is sheer cant to talk of an absolute standard of journalism, as though the press operated in a sort of social vacuum. Those who sup-pressed analysis or news of value to the non-white resistance movement were guilty not of the suppression, but of the policy

which inspired it and of the harm done to the resistance
movement as a result.

I invited Dr H. J. Simons, then Senior Lecturer in Native
Law and Administration at the University of Cape Town, and
a trenchant theorist of the left – he was detained for months
without charge or trial during the 1960 State of Emergency –
to write 'An Addendum' to the article. He began by applauding
Lewin's 'Freudian device of bringing submerged ideas to the
surface'. But, despite the limits placed by the Suppression of
Communism Act on the free discussion of revolution, he
considered it necessary to provide three further observations.
Despotic governments flourished most in stagnant societies.
In South Africa, on the contrary, there was a feverish movement of men and capital. The urban population had increased
between 1900 and 1958 from 23% to 44%, so that five and a
half million people now lived in towns which had contained a
bare one and a quarter million at the turn of the century. In
addition, this flow was directed in the main towards the large
industrial centres. Over three million people, or 60% of the
total urban population, were now concentrated in the four
biggest metropolitan regions, which together produced nearly
80% of the gross value of manufactured goods. And social
relations, too, were changing rapidly. Only two-fifths of the
white urban population were manual wage-earners, and of
these 82% were skilled, 15% semi-skilled and 3% unskilled.
Inevitably, as a result, Coloured, Indians and Africans were
increasingly moving into the professional, administrative,
commercial and technical occupations which had once been
considered a white prerogative. Already they formed 17% of
all skilled workers in industry, and 66% of the semi-skilled.
This change in the industrial sector was mirrored in the political one, where the 'most formidable of all political combina-
tions', the alliance between workers and intellectuals, was
assuming the initiative.

Finally, Dr Simons put the South African struggle into its
world context. The government had earned the unenviable distinction of making the most enemies in the shortest time. By

repudiating both liberal capitalism and socialist equality, it had incurred the enmity of both camps, while – in its insistence upon white supremacy – it had become the symbol of racialism and the main target of the anti-colonial front. Yet it was unlikely that other countries would apply trade boycotts or other sanctions to restrain South African vices. The country was 'safe' for trade and investment, and could be depended upon to pay its debts. Capitalists preferred a strong authoritarian government that was on their side in the Cold War to a liberal, progressive but neutral or hostile government.

'The climate of world opinion is, none the less, having a great and visible effect on opinion at home. Our white population, which plumes itself on belonging to the Western Christian Capitalist way of life, and to which Africa is as much a "dark continent" as it is to Europe, is feeling isolated, humiliated and afraid, in spite of its defiant protests. The collapse of colonialism and the racial myth has stripped it of its ideological pretensions ... The moral basis of the system has collapsed, and no society can survive if those who control it lose faith in their claims to dominate.

'More important is the effect on the subject peoples. They have seen the tide of colonial liberation spread through Asia into Africa; they feel that it is eroding the foundations of white autocracy in all territories. They may not get much in the form of material aid from abroad, but they know, and the knowledge will percolate through the masses, that the rest of the world is on their side.'

Dr Simons could not have been called extravagantly hopeful over international intervention to topple white supremacy, and in this he was largely joined by the Congress leadership. I considered such intervention – economic or military – against South Africa in the first place, equally improbable, but I more and more cherished the possibility of international action over South West Africa which would inevitably spread to the Union as well.

In the European scramble for Africa during the late nineteenth century, Germany had seized the south-west corner, and in the wars of rebellion and repression that had followed, established its authority there with vigour. The Hereros alone had been reduced from over 80,000 to 15,000 within the span of one generation. Then, with the defeat of Germany in the first world war, the Principal Allied and Associated Powers had assigned the territory to His Britannic Majesty, to be administered on his behalf by the government of South Africa as a Class C Mandate, or an integral portion of its territory, 'subject to the principle that the well-being and development of the indigenous peoples form a sacred trust of civilization'. This act had been approved on the 17th of December 1920 by the Council of the League of Nations, with the provision that, as other powers administering Class C Mandates, South Africa should submit reports to the Permanent Mandates Commission of the League, and subject itself to the Commission's supervision.

The pattern of race relations in South Africa was soon enough reflected in its administration of the mandate. Under the constitution granted in 1925, the white inhabitants of the territory received the right to elect members to a Legislative Assembly, while one member of the Advisory Council was to be chosen on the grounds of his 'thorough acquaintance with the reasonable wants and wishes of the non-European races in the territory'. The international conscience, sufficiently belaboured by events in Abyssinia and Spain, had no time for developments in South West Africa during the 'thirties. With the end of the second world war, however, and the stirring of nationalism throughout the non-white world, South West at last became an issue. In 1946 Field-Marshal Smuts raised at the United Nations the wish of his government to integrate South West as a fifth province of South Africa. But the U.N. required evidence of the benefits that the South African government had conferred on the indigenous peoples of the territory, and even bent an ear to the petition of Hosea Kutako, Paramount Chief of the Hereros, that South West Africa be removed from South African administration altogether and placed in the hands of the Trusteeship Council.

In 1948 the Nationalists swept into power and resolved upon an inflexible control of South West Africa. In 1949, with the double purpose of swelling its parliamentary majority and giving some constitutional shape to its practical annexation of the territory, the new government – by the South West Africa Affairs Amendment Act – conferred six seats in the House of Assembly and four in the Senate on South West, for occupation by those of European descent. Then, in a letter dated the 11th of July 1949, it advised the United Nations that, in the interests of efficient administration, it would forward no further reports on the territory. On the 28th of November 1953, the United Nations General Assembly established a Committee on South West Africa, to examine information and documents and to receive reports and petitions until such time as agreement could be reached between the U.N. and the South African government.

Despite the judgment of the International Court in July 1950 that South West Africa remained a mandate, subject to the supervision of the United Nations as heir of the League, and that the South African government had an administrative obligation to promote the material and moral well-being of the territory's indigenous inhabitants, the Nationalists challengingly extended the policy of apartheid to South West. In 1954, they even removed the control of these indigenous inhabitants from the general administration of the territory to the protective custody of South Africa's own Minister of Native Affairs.

In an article for the fifth issue of *Africa South*, Jariretundu Kozonguizi, then a student at the University of Cape Town and now a petitioner to the United Nations, had detailed some of the consequences of South African rule. £40,000 were spent each year on hospitals for the white population of 50,000, while only £20,000 were spent annually to maintain the hospitals of some 400,000 non-whites; 22 million hectares of land were occupied by non-whites; and nearly 38 million hectares by the whites. Of the £800,000 spent on education in the 1952–3 financial year, over £650,000 had been spent on white schooling.

Wages for African labourers varied generally outside the small free market of the towns from £2 to a mere 18s. a month. And the whole battery of South African race laws operated in the territory, from the sexual flack of the Immorality Act to the multitudinous arrests of pass administration.

The twelfth session of the U.N. General Assembly appointed a Good Offices Committee, with representatives from the United Kingdom, the United States and Brazil, to discuss with the South African government a satisfactory settlement of the differences between South Africa and the United Nations over the status and administration of South West. In the middle of 1958 Sir Charles Arden-Clarke of the United Kingdom, and Vasco Leitao da Cunha of Brazil, visited Pretoria. Then suddenly, at the end of June, a special South African Air Force plane touched down at Windhoek, the capital of South West Africa, and discharged the two emissaries into waiting cars, which carried them off speedily to a hotel in the city. There, reportedly on South African government instructions, they shut themselves up in their rooms. The following morning they were rumoured to have been released for a short while and taken on a stealthily conducted tour, exhaustive enough to bypass altogether the main African area. The administration then informed the press that they were to visit Gobabis, and they left instead for Kietmanshoop. Later it was announced that they had visited Okaukuejo and Namutoni in the Etosha Game Reserve. They did not meet a single non-white leader in the territory. But then doubtless the Paramount Chief of the Hereros, or any of the other petitioners to the U.N., excited less interest than the indigenous wild life of the territory.

I was, as so many others who had invested so much of their faith in U.N. intervention over South West, furious at this furtive, ignominious trip. I decided to visit the territory myself at once, to check the movements of the U.N. emissaries and, if gossip on their conduct had a basis in fact, publish an attack on the mission in time for the U.N. debate on its report. Rumours were rife of a secret understanding between the South African government and the Good Offices Committee which would save the face of the U.N. while surrendering all international claims over the territory to ultimate South African control. If such an agreement indeed existed, I hoped that I would find evidence of it in South West Africa itself. *Africa South* was already circulating widely among the Afro-Asian delegates to the United Nations. If the Good Offices Committee planned any concessions to the South African government, I intended that the evidence in which they rooted them should be adequately analysed in the magazine.

My trip to the territory had a sentimental resonance. My grandfather had pioneered the Mariental district and was still commonly spoken of as the 'Oubaas' there. The two days that I spent in the small town were like browsing through an old photograph album, in which the figures suddenly stood up from the pages and spoke. Old Afrikaners who had known my grandfather for thirty years and more, and freely acknowledged their gratitude to him—he had carried much of the area on credit during the depression years – would come up to me in the lounge of his hotel or at a counter of his shop, to talk of their recollections. On the hot red dust tracks around the flat low buildings, or on the swimming tarred road before his shop, I slowly acquired a vision of the grandfather my childhood had never encountered, the rough thick-set piercing blue-eyed man, in waistcoat and rolled-up shirt sleeves, hard drinking, gruffly kind, suspicious and soft, tempestuous and maudlin, and strenuously alone. At last I understood why he had left £250 in his will to the Dutch Reformed Church and £250 to the local mission, why the town had gone into mourning when he died, and why the old Jew was a presence still, four years afterwards, to the karakul farmers of the whole district. And I measured the pathos of that decision he had once defiantly made – to plant trees in Mariental for his grandchildren to enjoy.

The white population of the territory, in between anxious discussion of the rains, exuded a quiet satisfaction at the visit of the U.N. emissaries. The gossip seemed solidly based. The trip had displayed all the elements of chase in a paper-back thriller, and those non-whites in the territory who knew of it at all, had discovered it by rumour or reports in the press. After several escapes from the surveillance of the Special Branch, more dutiful in the territory than in South Africa itself, I realized that I had gained all I prudently could and flew back to Cape Town. For the ninth issue of October–December 1958, David Marais, the *Cape Times* cartoonist who did a regular cartoon for *Africa South*, drew the Good Offices Committee as two old men, with blinkers, led on nose-rings and ropes by Eric Louw, South African Minister of External Affairs, through the desert, with only South African policemen for company. From Hosea Kutako, Paramount Chief of the Hereros, I received a protest at the activities of the U.N. mission which I published as 'An Open Letter to the United Nations'. In my own editorial, which I entitled 'The Pattern of Betrayal', I described the mission's visit, quoted Eric Louw's complacent remarks on the 'more reasonable and conciliatory attitude towards South Africa shown by a fairly large number of (U.N.) delegations', and speculated on the possibilities of a secret agreement.

'Doubtless a number of motives conspire to persuade the Committee that the time for concession has arrived. The General Assembly can hardly allow the Union to continue snubbing its decisions on South West. The authority of the United Nations is fragile enough already, without the organization's having to submit to the defiance of its gallery. The administration of South West Africa has become an annual abasement – the General Assembly is unable to persuade South Africa to submit, while the Afro-Asian bloc is unwilling to let it cease trying. Inevitably, the United Nations must either contemplate economic sanctions and, if these do not help, some form of military intervention, or succumb once and for all to South African intransigence.

'A solution must be found but, in finding it, the General Assembly would do well to remind itself of Abyssinia and the last abject days of the League. For surely, if the non-white peoples of the territory are betrayed to their oppression, they alone will not endure the anguish. On the grave of their trust, the United Nations itself will stand the tombstone.'

I was bitterly attacked in the Senate, by Eric Louw and others, for my reference to economic sanctions or some form of military intervention. It was doubtless a possibility which the South African government wished to ban even from mention. And the Minister himself, after quoting extensively from the editorial – without qualifying its complaints against the Good Offices Committee further than to call them insulting – dealt at some length with my family and the source of its wealth in South West Africa. I was not alone in supposing that the unexpected direction of his assault pointed a threat.

I had been anxious for some time to visit the United States again in order to see if the circulation of the magazine there could not be substantially expanded. I now had a further and urgent interest in going. I wanted to discuss international action over South West with Afro-Asian delegates to the United Nations, and those leaders of Congress with whom I consulted agreed that the issue demanded an immediate canvass. The trip, however, seemed forbiddingly expensive, and I was reconciled at last to an indefinite postponement when I heard from the American Committee on Africa that they might be able to organize a lecture tour for me. It would not meet my air fare, but might cover my living costs in the United States and enable me to promote the possibilities of intervention among a much larger section of the American public than the magazine reached. In October I flew by way of Accra and London to New York and arrived in time for the debate in the United Nations Trusteeship Committee on the report of the Good Offices Committee. My suspicions were confirmed. The report which had emerged from the discussions in Pretoria and that singular incursion into South West Africa dealt sympathetically with the South African government's willingness to discuss the partition of the territory. I had several meetings with Afro-Asian members of the Trusteeship Committee, who launched a concerted assault upon the report and in particular upon the form which the visit to South West Africa had taken.

The bulk shipment of the magazine to the United States had arrived, and I arranged that copies should be sent to those delegates who did not normally receive them. It soon became clear that any plan for partition of South West was unacceptable to the vast majority of U.N. delegations, and the report of the Good Offices Committee was speedily shelved.

My few days in New York I spent almost entirely at the United Nations, in urgent discussion with such delegates as I could corner on the possibility of international economic sanctions against South Africa. Among the representatives of the other African states in the General Assembly at the time, I encountered a passionate commitment to action against apartheid. Even those who represented cautious and conservative regimes regarded race rule in South Africa as a personal affront. But I realized that effective action was impossible for several years to come. The African ranks were too thin and required many more recruits before they could move the weight of realism from the international conscience. Most Asian delegates were sympathetic but unpromising. And India, which non-white South Africa regarded then as the only state influential enough to promote an international initiative, was the most disappointing of all. Since soon after the war, it had conducted an official boycott of South African goods which had cost it in cold economics much more than it had gained. In one General Assembly session after the other, it had taken the lead in indicting South Africa for its racial policies. Yet recently, a number of African delegates warned me, there had been a change in the Indian attitude – a change, they remarked in puzzlement, more of mood than of matter.

I was excited at the prospect of meeting Krishna Menon, head of the Indian delegation. Everywhere I had heard criticism of his arrogance and caprice, but most of the criticism had come from those on the right, who expressed their strongest hostility to his neutralism. I myself was ready to revere him for his refusal to put India in pawn to East or West. An African delegate took me up to him in the cocktail lounge and introduced me. Bending over his stick, with a few Indians in defer-

ential attendance upon him, he listened to me. Then, with
thinly disguised impatience and looking periodically at his en-
tourage for approval, he explained to me that the mood of the
U.N. had changed in the years of the Cold War. The moral
fervour of the early days had frozen into cynicism. The best
advice he could give was that we should depend in South
Africa upon our own efforts.

'You have your revolution,' he said, 'and I think I can promise you the warmest welcome here.'

Unreasonably, perhaps, I would have preferred a little encouragement, however hollow, to the cruelty of that exercise in
realism. I tartly suggested that Mr Menon might have been dismayed after one of his speeches in Britain during the 'thirties on
the need for Indian independence, had a member of his audience advised India to depend on its efforts alone and cheered it
meanwhile with the promise of a warm welcome to the international community afterwards. Mr Menon stared at me for a
moment and then said:

'You speak to the Ghanaian delegation. We have taken the
initiative too long in African affairs. Let the African states
demand sanctions, and I think I can promise you at least that
the Indian delegation will abstain.'

Shying from the humiliation of any further discussion, I
muttered that I would carry back the comfort of his advice to
the South African Indian community and withdrew. In retrospect, I suppose that he was probably justified in bringing me
up hard against the realities of international conduct. I learnt
from my short talk with him more of the mood in which decisions at the United Nations were taken than I could ever
have done from days of passionate planning with delegates
from the new African states. He administered to me the same
shock that I had administered to the more complacent Congress
leaders by publishing Julius Lewin's article in *Africa South*.
What I still cannot excuse is that he should himself have displayed the cynicism with which he castigated the United
Nations. I would have been angry but grateful had he merely
stripped me of my illusions in the force of international

morality. That he should have accepted the situation as one which India would not strain itself to change, abandoned non-white South Africa to its agony alone.

The next few weeks I spent in travelling across the United States from New York to San Francisco, lecturing sometimes to three or four different audiences a day. In the main, they were members of foreign policy associations or university student bodies, and I enjoyed abundant opportunities to meet and talk with individual Americans from widely different geographical and economic backgrounds. I was excited by their frank hunger for information, but appalled by their political conformity. Perhaps it was because McCarthyism had not altogether receded and I caught the last rustlings of its presence, but I sensed a real fear of dissent, especially among students, where I had least expected to find it. Increasingly I included an assault on American foreign policy – the coupling of revolution with hostility to America's interests, of economic radicalism with Soviet conspiracy – in my lectures on South Africa. Yet question time remained sacred to careful questionings of fact. There was never any of that fervent discussion with which a political speech to students at the University of Cape Town would have been followed. After one lecture that I had given at the University of Chicago, and a more than usually starched question time, a group of students invited me to a party which they were having that night. I eagerly accepted, and some time between eleven o'clock and midnight I found myself listening over cans of beer to a passionate assault on the idiocies of the Dulles-dominated State Department. The criticism was penetrating and informed, and it was largely socialist in its assumptions. I thought for a moment of asking why I had had to wait for the beer before hearing it. But the very surge of excitement with which the students talked, like some sudden release from solitary confinement, gave me my answer.

What oppressed me was not any antagonism with which my criticism of American policy was occasionally greeted – on the contrary, I enjoyed that, and remember with pleasure a long debate I had with a professor at the University of Colorado –

but the far more frequent, rigidly polite neglect. The audiences would ignore my references to American policy, even my particular attack on the American Embassy in South Africa for its assiduously segregated functions, and pepper me with questions on every part of Africa, the racial and political conflicts in each.

More and more I felt a furtiveness in American conformity, a careful keeping of counsel. I had visions of a vast subterranean river of radical sentiment, swollen by an infinity of lectures and books, which would one day break unexpectedly through the surface and sweep away the accumulated bigotries of years. And this, it seemed to me, was not a disconsolate prospect.

I learnt, too, how absurd were the traditional political compartments into which the various regions of America had been placed. Such articulate radicalism as I found, I met, together with an unrestrictive internationalism, along the North Pacific Coast and in the mid-West. It was the Eastern seaboard, with its European preoccupations and Cold War pathology, that seemed to me to have assumed the contemporary isolationism of the white world. Possibly my experience was exceptional, but I encountered the most passionate interest in the Afro-Asian world at a conference in Manhattan, Kansas, called by the Governor, to which delegates from all parts of the state had come. Nowhere else, outside the beer-drinking catharsis of the Chicago student party, did I discover so profound and open a concern with the short-sightedness of the American administration in its attitude to Afro-Asian affairs.

All the while I enjoyed the tour enormously. I did not know that I was being trailed by grooms of the South African government. I was to discover that several months later, after my passport had been seized, when Eric Louw announced in parliament that the government had reports of my addresses and that I would not be permitted another opportunity to slander my country abroad. Only at the end of the trip, when I was speaking at a college outside San Francisco, did I collide with any defence of white South Africa. At the end of my speech, a man of manifestly uncollegiate dress and years, rose to ask me why, if my analysis of South Africa were correct, international investors continued to risk considerable capital there. He himself was employed by Charles Engelhard, who had recently extended his interests from platinum to gold and been instrumental in forming the American South African Investment Company. I replied that international investors had been stupid before, in China to mention only one example, and I saw no reason to suppose that Mr Engelhard was any more intelligent than they had thought themselves to be. The discussion ended there, but I wondered for some time afterwards whether Mr Engelhard's employees were generally given to attending college lectures.

A few days before my departure for home, I addressed at the Harvard Club, on behalf of the Treason Trial Defence Fund, a group of rich Americans, all of whom had been lured by an invitation from Eleanor Roosevelt, Senator Javits, and a grape-juice multi-millionaire. Mrs Roosevelt herself, whom I had always regarded with awe, filled me now with an admiring affection. I had met her first several weeks before, on the day after her return from a trip to the Soviet Union, and had been dismayed and then delighted to find a frail, large, tired woman, spontaneous and kind and overwhelmingly human. Her eyelids had repeatedly struggled and then closed with exhaustion as we talked, and she would jerk them open with a tender unspoken apology. Though South Africa must have been the most distant of her preoccupations, and her schedule already bursting at the seams, she somehow stuffed a meeting on South Africa into it.

Her speech at the Harvard Club was tremendous in its quiet. She began by admitting how little she knew of South Africa beyond one experience she had had at the United Nations meeting in Paris soon after the end of the war. The South African delegate had announced that his government would never permit the native races to share in the control of the country. She had met him subsequently in the lobby. 'He asked me what I thought of his speech, and I said that I had never heard anything quite so wicked, as to take from a people all hope, all possibility of ever peacefully acquiring some say in the government of their lives.' I was profoundly stirred. The audience, though strenuously deferential, was manifestly less moved. We hardly raised enough to meet the expenses of the function. I suppose that I should not have been disappointed. The Treason Trial Defence Fund did not rank as a charity for tax purposes.

The meeting, however, was not without its success. Before it began, I had held a press conference together with Senator Javits, and when I had complained of the American Embassy's conduct in South Africa, the carefully colourless cocktail parties and the lack of any contact between the ambassador himself and the non-white political leaders, Senator Javits had announced to the assembled journalists that he would make it his business to investigate the matter and demand a change in policy if my account proved to be correct. I cannot, of course, bear witness to the energy of his inquiries. But several months later the American ambassador to South Africa was replaced, and his successor paid several visits to non-white political leaders, including Lutuli, despite criticism in the Nationalist press. Recently, indeed, a few unprovocative non-whites have been present at Embassy parties.

I was in the United States when the tenth issue of the magazine went to press, and it was only through the amenability of two journalist friends, with conscripts from my family, that the issue appeared on time. In the weeks before my departure for the United States, I had solicited and edited the necessary articles. In the end, I had decided not to write an editorial at all, but to publish in its place a biography of Dr Verwoerd – entitled 'A Racialist's Triumph' – which I had commissioned from Stanley Uys, political correspondent of the Johannesburg *Sunday Times*.

On the 24th of August 1958, J. G. Strijdom, Prime Minister of South Africa, called by his followers 'the Lion of the North', had died. When I remembered the many mutilations of his rule, I found the public condolences of English-speaking

South Africa sanctimonious and infuriating. I have never had
patience with the courtesies of death. A criminal does not
erase his crimes by dying. And the crimes of Strijdom were
still alive on the statute book. But I recognized much of the
regret for what it was – a terror of his probable successor.
Again, it seemed, we would have cause in South Africa to say,
he was bad but a worse is to follow him. For over his grave
there now fell the cold shadow of Dr Verwoerd.

Born in September 1901 at Amsterdam, Verwoerd had
emigrated to South Africa as a child and early assimilated the
racial obsessions of Afrikanerdom. Indeed, as though to compensate for not having been born an Afrikaner, he had set out
to become one by the very zeal of his self-adoption. Having
studied at the University of Stellenbosch, he had rejected the
Abe Bailey scholarship to Oxford that his academic record had
earned, in proof of his anti-British resolution, and enrolled instead at the Universities of Hamburg, Leipzig and Berlin.
Returning to become Professor of Applied Psychology at
Stellenbosch (1927–32) and then Professor of Sociology and
Social Work (1933–7), he had increasingly engaged in the
political struggle of the Afrikaners for control of the country.
Sometimes this engagement took a strangely revealing form,
as when, during the 'thirties, he had protested, with five other
University of Stellenbosch professors, at the South African
government's decision to admit a shipload of German Jewish
refugees.

From 1937 to 1948, as Editor of the Johannesburg Afrikaans
daily *Die Transvaler*, he had pursued an unwaveringly anti-
Semitic and anti-British course. Attacked by Johannesburg's
English-language *Star* for his Nazi sympathies, he had sued for
damages in 1943. It was one of his less astute moves. The
Witwatersrand division of the Supreme Court had ruled against
him – because, he was later to claim, the judge was Jewish.
Mr Justice Millin had found that he 'caused to be published a
large body of matter which was on the same general lines as
material coming to the Union in the Afrikaans transmissions
from Zeesen and which was calculated to make the Germans

look upon *Die Transvaler* as a most useful adjunct to this propaganda service ... There have been proved two very grave cases of the publication of false news, in reckless disregard of whether these were true or false; six cases on the whole less serious, but still clear cases of falsification where news originally correctly reported was falsely restated for the purpose of editorial comment; and two cases in which news was falsified by means of misleading headlines ... His legal right to publish what he did is not in question. The question is whether, when he exercises his legal right in the way he does, he is entitled to complain when it is said of him that what he writes supports Nazi propaganda and makes his paper a tool of the Nazis. On the evidence he is not entitled to complain. He did support Nazi propaganda, he did make his paper a tool of the Nazis in South Africa, and he knew it.'

Such a man had dominated the government's colour policy as Minister of Native Affairs since October 1950. What his succession to the premiership would produce, his eight years of ruthless control over the country's Africans promised with terrifying precision. Till the last moment, it seemed reasonable to hope that the Nationalists would reject him as their leader. Charles Robberts Swart, the senior Cabinet Minister and Acting Prime Minister, was, after all, the obvious candidate for succession. Dr Eben Dönges, Minister of the Interior and leader of the Cape Nationalists, might at the last moment rally the scattered ranks of those hostile to the dominance of the Transvaal extremists. The balloting on the 2nd of September was unprecedentedly secret. The windows of the parliamentary caucus room were covered with cardboard, and special ballot papers were issued to avoid any forgeries. At the first ballot, Swart polled 41 votes, Dönges 52, and Verwoerd 80. Swart was eliminated, and at the second ballot, Dönges polled 75 votes to 98 for Verwoerd. We had as our Prime Minister a man who had diligently, ceaselessly assisted the Nazi cause in the second world war.

I had told Stanley Uys that I wanted at last to discard all caution. I would publish whatever he wrote. He produced a cleverly documented portrait, of a ruthless and consistent fanatic. From the opening sentence – 'Like so many racialists, Dr Verwoerd had his early training in anti-Semitism' – he caught the spirit of Verwoerd's accomplishments.

'An aloof, academic man, Dr Verwoerd has compensated for his lack of ability to rouse passions by practising the art of mass psychology. As the fledgling Professor of Applied Psychology at Stellenbosch University, he contributed a paper to the S.A. Journal of Science (1928) on the psychology of newspaper advertisements. He gave, as an example, an advertisement for a stomach medicine. It showed a dog, with a child firmly gripped in its jaws, standing sturdily in the middle of a rushing stream. The caption read "Saved!" By the same technique – the simple association of ideas – Dr Verwoerd has persuaded Afrikanerdom, presumably, that he is its saviour.

'With the crude, but effective, art of the mass propagandist, he has almost succeeded in convincing Afrikaners (and perhaps others, too) that to criticize him is tantamount to heresy. Minutes after the result of the leadership ballot had been announced to the caucus, he was staking his claim to divine rule: "I believe that the will of God was revealed in the ballot." Two days later, in a national broadcast, he repeated: "In accordance with His will, it was determined who should assume the leadership of the government in this new period of the life of the people of South Africa." '

Uys compiled most of his indictment from remarks made by Verwoerd himself.

'Where does one begin with this man who, after becoming Prime Minister, boasted that instead of "mellowing", he would remain a "devil"? His speeches teem with remarks like this one: "It is in no way a pleasant duty to have people, even though they are Natives, imprisoned." He has closed the doors of more schools and opened the doors of more jails than any other South African in history. Once, surprisingly, he bowed to public opinion: he abandoned (temporarily?) a scheme to establish a labour camp (a concentration camp, in fact) for African political offenders. It was the method, not the principle, that worried him: "The policy of the department has always been to scatter rather than to concentrate the deportees." '

Soon after my return from the United States, one of the journalists who had helped to produce the tenth issue was sitting in my office.

'The one thing I regret,' he said, 'is that I was not able to see Verwoerd's face when he read the article.' A wild idea leapt in my mind. I scribbled 'With the Compliments of the Editor' on the back of a copy of the tenth issue, and handed it to him.

'Send it into Verwoerd by messenger,' I said, 'and then run up to the press gallery and watch his face as he gets it.' The journalist looked at me for a moment and then rushed from the office. Half an hour later he was back.

'I got to the press gallery just as the messenger handed the copy to him. He has obviously read it already. He turned it over, saw the inscription on the back and turned the colour of the cover.' (It was a geranium red.) 'He looked furious.'

I felt a sudden tremor of panic. I had been asking for trouble. And though trouble was an essential ingredient in the work I was doing, it was surely stupid to go in search of it. I looked at the journalist, as white-faced as I was. 'What the hell!' I said. 'If I can't present a magazine to Verwoerd without feeling that I may be shot for it, I should go into haberdashery.'

In the end, the tenth issue provoked more comment with its attack on South African Jewry by Rabbi Dr André Ungar, than with the portrait of Verwoerd. Dr Ungar's short career as Rabbi of the Port Elizabeth Progressive Jewish Congregation had almost frightened the wits out of the Jews in the city. Time and again he had devoted his sermons to assaults on government policy. And he had at last been served with a deportation order while preparing himself to leave the country – apparently in disgust at his own congregation – for an appointment in London. His article – entitled 'The Abdication of a Community' – was a crushing indictment of the fears and the assimilated prejudices which kept South African Jewry silent on the racial issue. He maintained that South Africa's 105,000 strong

Jewish community constituted a crucial minority, 'commanding unique possibilities of effective action'. It was markedly
united and coherent, and possessed considerable economic and
political influence 'under the absurd rules of South African
ethnic arithmetic'. Four independently valid and cumulatively
overwhelming considerations required its open opposition to
the whole policy of racial rule. First, the vast bulk of South
African Jewry had either come from Eastern Europe at the
turn of the century, or from Central and Western Europe during the 'thirties, to escape persecution. Secondly, realistic self-
interest would suggest that the community's one chance of
permanent survival in South Africa lay in its acceptance by the
oppressed mass of the population. Thirdly, racial or colour
prejudice was always dangerous to the Jew. It was purely a
matter of time before the edge of discrimination was turned
against minorities merely for the moment' endured. And the
anti-Semitic record of the Nationalist leaders gave little cause
for tranquillity. Finally, Jewish ethics were altogether incom-
patible with race discrimination. Even if it were a hopeless
sacrifice for the Jew to declare the inherent dignity and equality
of all men, ethically and religiously he would still have no
alternative but to do so.

Rabbi Ungar scrutinized his congregants and found them
wanting, not in humanity alone, but in the very Jewishness to
which they so proudly and incessantly laid claim.

'Gentlemen worry about rising labour costs in the board
room and on the golf course and the synagogue entrance hall;
their ladies moan about the unreliability, cheek, unchastity,
clumsiness of servants; spine-tingling stories of violence, riot
and danger in the location pepper up sedately luxurious
dinner parties in the fashionable suburbs. Resigned acceptance
or hearty approval is the prevalent attitude of individual Jews
towards racialism. And the Jews who oppose it and fight
against it, do so not as Jews, because they are Jews – but as
humanitarians, liberals, possibly socialists. Their Jewishness
as such seems to have no bearing at all on their racial align-
ment. That individual Jews vary immensely in their attitudes

is a fact. Whether as Jews they *ought to* be thus divided, is, of course, a very different matter.

' "Render unto Caesar ..." is a Jewishly unacceptable principle. What we give and how we give and why we give unto Caesar are ways of giving (or of refusing to give) unto God. Judaism cannot allow – in any interpretation of the faith – a sharp division between earthly behaviour and heavenward piety. Yet it is commonly thought that Judaism demands ritual conformity in the first place, coupled with dogmatic rigour; a pretty-pretty, almsgiving type of sentimental charity as a secondary requirement: but specific social, economic and political attitudes not at all. And this, of course, is a fatal distortion of the essential message of Jewish tradition.'

Rabbi Ungar's viewpoint was my own, and I vigorously canvassed it in a debate with Dan Jacobson, the novelist, in the pages of the American monthly, *Commentary*. Jacobson maintained that I was denying the South African Jews their essential human character by expecting them to behave with exceptional imagination and self-sacrifice. I claimed – as I claim still today – that the traditions of Jewry, the persecution they had for so many centuries endured and their consequent cries for justice in the dealings of men with each other, fitted them for a singular function. Their history had been exceptional. That seemed reason enough for their conduct to be exceptional also. My own arguments were, of course, secularly based. I could not, as Rabbi Ungar was able to do, appeal to Jewry on the basis of a religious ethic which I did not myself accept. But my acknowledgment of my own Jewishness was a cultural and traditional one, and it was on the cultural and traditional plane that I felt able to make my appeal.

The Green and Sea Point Hebrew Congregation, of which my father and my grandfather had been such lavish members and which I myself had joined as a child, had swollen with the growth of Sea Point itself beyond the resources of the synagogue. At considerable cost, it had built the Weizmann Hall to accommodate the overflow of worshippers at the high festivals and in between provide a centre for cultural and educational

G

activities. One of the largest and best-equipped halls in the city, it was soon hired for concerts and dances by a profitable variety of impresarios and organizations. I booked it for a concert in aid of the Treason Trial Defence Fund.

Teenage white South Africa had just discovered penny-whistle jazz, the music that had emerged from the African shanty towns, in bursts of joy or lament, through thin metal pipes, sometimes only short lengths of curtain rod with crudely gouged holes. It was a wild elusive sound, tempestuous and frail, that had forced itself, in jostling groups of black children, on to the pavements of Johannesburg. The principal exponent, an African in his early twenties called Spokes Mashiyane, was working as a packer in a record company, while his own records were selling to the sons and daughters of one acre plots with swimming pools in Lower Houghton. I offered to pay for Mashiyane's flight from Johannesburg and back, and set my committee to selling several hundred pounds worth of tickets.

Two weeks before the date of the concert, an official of the Green and Sea Point Hebrew Congregation, in charge of the Weizmann Hall reservations, telephoned me. A difficulty had arisen over the booking. Was the audience to be unsegregated? Of course, I replied. A double booking appeared to have been made for the date of the concert. I said that I would hold the authorities of the Weizmann Hall to the booking that they had firmly accepted several weeks before. I had their receipt for the required deposit. A few hours later, the official telephoned again. The synagogue committee had no objection to an un-segregated audience, but would like to make special arrange-ments for segregated lavatories. I said that I was surprised to find the synagogue committee more sensitive than the City Council itself, which had never thought it necessary to have segregated lavatories in the city hall. I had hired the Weizmann Hall with its lavatories distinguished only by their sex. I would keep them that way. The official said that the committee would have to examine the matter. I decided to examine the matter with the committee myself.

I telephoned one of its senior members, a former president

of the synagogue who had for many years been a close friend of my father's. 'I need not remind you,' I said to him, 'that no mention was ever made of segregating the Weizmann Hall, the lavatories or anything else, when the synagogue approached its members, my father included, to pay for building it. I know that my father, for one, would never have provided you with the cost of a brick to build a segregated hall.' There was an embarrassed breathing at the other end of the line. 'We will have to discuss it, Ronald,' he said. 'It is a Jewish communal hall, after all.' 'But one,' I interjected, 'which you are quite happy to hire out to white Baptists or even a conference of the Nationalist Party.' 'There is no question,' he said, 'of refusing you the hall because Natives will be in the audience.' 'I was led to believe otherwise,' I said. 'No,' he hurriedly replied. 'But the concert is for the Treason Trial Fund, and some of us feel that we should not be associated with it.' I felt my eyes prickle with fury and shame. I dug my fingernails into the wood of my desk. 'You can call this blackmail, if you like,' I said. 'I don't care. But if you cancel my booking, I shall call a press conference, and I shall attack the synagogue committee, in public, as cowardly, and dishonest. Money was solicited for the building of a hall to serve the Sea Point congregation. Either you reserve the hall for Jewish functions alone, or you place no restriction upon the hiring of it to others. If you deny the hall to the Treason Trial Defence Fund, because of its political associations, you deny to those on trial for their lives the right of a proper defence. If you deny it, because there will be an unsegregated audience, you are promoting that very race hatred from which Jewry has suffered for centuries. In either case, you will be flouting everything that Judaism means to me, and it is as a Jew that I will publicly denounce you.' 'I see,' he said stiffly. 'I suppose you know what you're doing.' 'Yes,' I said.

The following day he telephoned me and told me that the committee had no objection to my booking, and that the concert might be held as planned. 'Thank you,' I said. 'I'm sure that I have largely you to thank.' He murmured goodbye and put down the receiver. When I met him some months later in the street, he greeted me warily, as one meets an undeclared enemy. I was sorry. He had been a friend of my father's.

The concert itself was a tumultuous success. The hall was packed with whites and blacks sitting together. In the third row from the front, where I had my own seat, a white woman in a full-length ermine sat next to a middle-aged African in a full-length army overcoat. He took a tactile joy in the singing of the young girls we had recruited from Langa to compose the supporting cast, and each time that a particularly well-formed fifteen-year-old appeared on the stage, he emitted a series of loud smacking sounds with his lips, as though he were tasting her. His white neighbour crept ever further into her ermine. After one of the noisiest displays of his appreciation, I caught her eye and smiled broadly. But she just looked protectively towards the two children sitting on her other side and drew the coat more closely around her. An hour later she had taken off her coat – the heat seemed to be rising from the floor in that close-packed hall – and was staring, like her children, open-mouthed at the stage. A few moments before the end of the concert, I rushed outside to watch the building empty itself. On the other side of the road a number of police were waiting, and their faces went through convulsions of astonishment as the doors burst open and the hall disgorged varieties of colour and dress that I don't think Sea Point had ever seen collected in such abundance before. Something like love welled up inside me for that concert audience. I wanted to fling my arms around it and hold it to my face.

In the tenth issue I continued the series on revolution. Michael Harmel, a Johannesburg journalist who was prominent in the Congress of Democrats, disputed the definition of revolution which Professor Brinton had produced and Lewin accepted. Revolution meant a rapid and fundamental change in society, with the displacement of the ruling class, whether there was fighting or not. South Africa itself was colonial in character, with its colonies scattered over metropolitan territory. Such a condition enormously complicated resistance and repression alike. But it revealed how irretrievably South Africa was developing into a unified industrial society. And nowhere in the world had such a society developed without conceding higher living standards and greater political rights to its members than prevailed in the Union. There had been many examples in history where a combination of factors had been compelling enough to make a ruling class submit to urgent and overdue changes rather than drag the people through the agony of civil war.

Dr Edward Roux, University of the Witwatersrand botanist and author of the classic study of non-white resistance in South Africa, *Time Longer than Rope*, gave the debate a new and significant twist.

'It is almost an axiom that any stable form of government can continue only with the consent of the majority. The organs of state power, police, army and so on, are accessory to government, but the most important factor is psychological. Even in a slave state, such as our Western Cape in the eighteenth century, stability depended on the slave accepting his inferior status as something akin to a law of nature.

'I wish to affirm that in South Africa the overwhelming majority of the non-Europeans still accept their second-grade status as inevitable. They believe the white man is "baas" not merely by virtue of the law, the sjambok and the machine gun, but because he is naturally the ruler. This is an illusion, but as long as the illusion remains in the minds of the overwhelming majority, the government's position is invulnerable. To question this belief is something very close to heresy or treason ...

'The static conditions of the old Cape have been replaced by the dynamic industrialism of modern South Africa. In spite of discriminatory and repressive legislation, the African's economic significance and power grow together with his sophistication. His acceptance of the status quo must suffer continued erosion. The final swing over to non-acceptance may be sudden and dramatic and may be triggered off by some event, great or even comparatively trivial, which we at present cannot foresee.'

The Congress leadership increasingly interested itself in the course of the debate, conducting a parallel examination beyond the careful legality of print. Those who had attacked my decision to publish Lewin's article in the first place, confessed to the value of the questions and assessments it had provoked. I asked Professor G. D. H. Cole, novelist, economist, political philosopher and historian, to contribute to the series. It was one of the last articles he wrote. Before I could publish it in the eleventh issue of *Africa South*, April–June 1959, he had died.

In 'The Anatomy of Revolution', he set out to examine the conditions necessary for the overthrow of established authority. Despite the communist faith that socialist revolution was an inexorable necessity, no such successful revolutions had taken place in Western Europe and the United States after the Russian revolution in 1917, simply 'because too few people wanted them, or were even prepared to tolerate them, to make the attempt worthwhile'. On the other hand, revolutions had succeeded in China and recently in Iraq, despite the opposition of the United States, because they had been well led and organized, and still more because the forces marshalled against them had lost too much support to offer any effective resistance. In neither country had the revolution been the work of the industrial proletariat, for the proletariat had been much too undeveloped to assume the initiative. In China, revolution had been based upon a solid peasant movement of discontent. In Iraq, as in Egypt, the army had played the leading role because there had been no one else to play it, though both peasant and industrial worker were ready enough to accept the revolution once it had been successful. Such revolutions might have been suppressed by full-scale Western intervention. But the conquerors would have found it impossible to govern the country afterwards. A backward country could have a successful revolution despite great power hostility, provided that it was united enough not to be governed by quislings from among its own people. But it needed to have, among its revolutionaries, those who possessed not only the capacity to organize the revolution with success, but the ability to take the administration of the country into their own hands afterwards.

Professor Cole finally turned to the special case of peoples ruled by dynasties of alien race, where the loyalty of the armed forces was not open to subversion and the subjects themselves were prevented from possessing arms. Violent revolution was hardly possible for as long as the ruling oligarchy remained united, sufficiently resolved to keep the key positions of influence in its own hands, and ruthless enough to make effective use of its power. Such an oligarchy could retain power indefinitely, provided that it suffered no interference from outside. The single chance of successful revolution lay in the disintegration of government. This might result from a breach in the ranks of the governing élite, or – in the absence of such a breach – if the élite pursued what was, in the objective conditions, an unworkable policy. But revolution would follow the pursuit of an unworkable policy only if such a policy were persisted in when it was clearly failing to work, and the élite clung to it despite its evident failure.

'The best hope in South Africa is not violent revolution, in which the scales would of necessity be weighed very heavily against the Africans, but is a modification of white attitudes following on a realization of the sheer absurdity of what is being attempted at present. In the absence of such a modification black Africa will doubtless in the long run be driven into violent revolt, despite the serious difficulties in its way; but it is not likely to succeed until or unless it can get help from those parts of Africa which have been able to achieve their emancipation without violence.'

Professor Cole had been the first contributor to the series who had clearly pointed to the potential role of independent Africa in South African liberation. In April 1958, Dr Nkrumah had opened in Accra the first conference of eight independent African states – Ethiopia, Ghana, Liberia, Libya, Morocco, the Sudan, Tunisia and the United Arab Republic. Gladly, in the eighth issue of the magazine, July–September 1958, I had published the full text of the conference declaration. It had not been a particularly militant communiqué, but one of its paragraphs could hardly have consoled those members of the South African government who bothered to look at a map of Africa at all.

'We pledge ourselves to apply all our endeavours to avoid being committed to any action which might entangle our countries to the detriment of our interests and freedom; to recognize the right of the African people to independence and self-determination and to take appropriate steps to hasten the realization of this right; and to affirm the right of the Algerian people to independence and self-determination and to exert all possible effort to hasten the realization of their independence; to uproot for ever the evil of racial discrimination in all its forms wherever it may be found ...'

In the eleventh issue, nine months later, we published a report from Catherine Hoskyns, the magazine's observer there, of the first All African Peoples Conference at Accra in December 1958. Over 300 delegates from the trade unions and political parties of 28 African countries, including those already independent, attended. The Conference gave 'its full support to all fighters for freedom in Africa, to all those who resort to peaceful means of non-violence and civil disobedience, as well as to all those who are compelled to retaliate against violence to attain national independence and freedom for the people'. It proposed that independent countries at government level, and others at a personal level, should institute an immediate boycott of South African goods; and that an African Legion should be established 'to protect the freedom of the African peoples'. The African avalanche was audible in Cape Town as no more than a small sliding of stones. But it was audible.

For some months the leaders of the Congress Movement had been discussing a boycott of Nationalist products. They had for long recognized, with the more perceptive of the country's manufacturers and shopkeepers, that the non-whites were possessed, by their sheer numbers, of a vast purchasing power, and that such power, allied with political organization, could profoundly affect the normal patterns of commerce. Some in-

dustrialists had even, on their own initiative, raised the wages
of their non-white employees as a first exercise in public relations across the colour line. One prominent industrialist, of
considerable wealth and hostility to African political advance,
had once lectured to me for an hour after dinner on the stupid-
ity of the government in restraining non-white economic
advance. Higher wages meant higher spending, and higher
spending meant higher profits. His was the capitalist vision
pure, unstained by all the costly complications of prejudice.
But he was exceptional. On the whole, the business community
remained satisfied to make its easy profits from the non-white
population and keep the wages of the workers down to the
minimum level which the government promulgated.

The city of Johannesburg, with its suburbs, has an official
population of 1,037,200.[1] The government of South Africa
calls it white, as the government calls white all of South Africa
outside the scattered cramped 'Native Reserves'. Yet, of
Johannesburg's people, only 375,700 are white, while 594,000
are African, 39,500 are Coloured, and 28,000 are Asiatic. In the
largest white city of South Africa, whites are outnumbered by
non-whites almost two to one.

Of course, only the whites – with the few Coloured and
Asiatics soon to be moved beyond any racial muddle – can in
law own land and trade within the city. The Africans who tend
the tidy gardens of the whites, polish their floors, man the
machines in their factories, deliver their newspapers and milk,
live five and more miles away, hidden on the other side of hills,
behind many bends in the road. Long shuffling lines of green
buses bear them into the city every morning – for the white
city moves only when there are blacks to twitch its limbs – and
then back again, to their swollen townships, at night.

For week after week in early 1957, the buses roared empty
along the roads between the townships and the city, or stood
silent in their garages, safe from fire and stones. The Public
Utility Transport Corporation which owned them, complaining
that its government subsidy could no longer cover its losses,

[1] June 1959 figure.

had suddenly raised the single fare for many routes from four-pence to fivepence. And the Africans in Alexandra Township, nine miles from Johannesburg on the Pretoria road, had refused to board the buses and had walked to their work in the city instead. 'Azikwelwa!' they shouted, 'We will not ride!' and 'Asinamali!' 'We have no money!'. The white-owned newspapers, English and Afrikaans, Nationalist and United Party alike, reported mass intimidation among Africans by political extremists and confidently predicted a speedy collapse of the boycott. But one township after the other – Moroko and Jabavu and Sophiatown, Lady Selborne in Pretoria, Germiston and Edenvale – even those on bus routes unaffected by the increase in fares, joined the long procession down the roads to the white cities, till some 60,000 Africans on the Witwatersrand alone were walking up to 20 miles each day from home and back again. One thousand miles away, in Port Elizabeth, Africans refused to board buses in sympathy and walked the many miles to their work instead.

As the boycott persisted, and both commerce and industry began to suffer its consequences – those who had so far to walk every day were weak at their work and careless of window displays – white South Africa stirred uneasily. More than the green buses, it seemed, would soon stand idle. From 1947 to 1957, the number of whites employed in private manufacturing throughout the country had risen from 129,000 to 202,000, an increase of 57·7%. But the number of Africans employed under them in the same ten years had risen from 200,000 to 367,000, an increase of 83·5%. Already there were almost twice as many Africans as whites engaged in industry. How could industry hope to survive without them?

The white-owned newspapers stopped reporting evidence of intimidation and started instead to sound the depth of that cry 'Asinamali! We have no money!' Suddenly it seemed that Africans could not afford to pay even the eightpence a day that their bus fares had been, let alone the rise to tenpence. Their occasional reluctant wage increases had never kept pace with the bounding cost of living. Most of them were employed in the less skilled grades of the distributive trade, municipal services, the building, engineering and motor industries, and wages in these occupations had averaged just over £11 a month in 1954. Where possible, the wife and older children worked as well, to add some £5 a month to the family income. But a South African Institute of Race Relations survey for the same period had established that an average African family of five in an urban area required £23 10s. 4d. a month in order to maintain minimum standards of health. And since then, the Institute reported at the time of the 1957 boycott, this gap of over £7 a month had substantially increased, with the rise in the cost of living, to the region of £10. The Manager of Pretoria's Non-European Affairs Department stated publicly that most of the workers under his jurisdiction could not pay the increased fares. Over two-thirds of them – unskilled pick-and-shovel workers, whose last wage award had been in 1942 – earned only £9 a month. The old fares, at £10 a year, represented more than one month's wages. The twopence a day increase would raise this to £12. How could they pay? The English-language opposition press demanded a return to the old bus fares, with a larger government subsidy to the Public Utility Transport Corporation. And representatives of commerce and industry hinted at revisions in the wages of unskilled African workers.

The government, however, regarded the boycott as mere defiance of white authority. Soon after parliament convened in January 1957, the Minister of Transport, Mr Ben Schoeman, swung his baton. 'It is quite clear that this is not so much an economic matter; it is a political movement ... There will be no capitulations; the government will not be intimidated. This bus boycott will be broken, and law and order will be maintained ...' Within a few weeks of mass raids, most of them conducted in the chief boycott areas or along the routes travelled by the boycotters, police arrested 14,000 Africans for petty offences. Sympathetic white motorists, who gave lifts to boycotters, were stopped while police, armed with tape measures as well as their batons and guns, carefully measured to ensure that no one sat on less than 15 inches of seat.

Yet, by the middle of March, the boycott had not collapsed. Government intransigence had only succeeded in stiffening its back. Whispers of a 'stay-at-home' by the exhausted Africans issued from the townships to alarm the press. The Johannesburg City Council, in sudden fright, offered to assist in raising a special subsidy, while the Chamber of Commerce proposed a voluntary levy on employers. The Bishop of Johannesburg brought the boycott leaders together with spokesmen of commerce and industry, a fund was launched to cover the cost of a stop-gap subsidy to the bus company, and the buses were at last restored to the routes at the old rate of fourpence a single fare. The boycotters had won.

When the stop-gap subsidy was spent, further funds were found from an additional tax on employers to the Native Services Levy. The fare remained fourpence. But the press soon ceased to concern itself with African poverty. And the spokesmen of commerce and industry grew smug at the benevolence of the boycott settlement. Between 1954 and 1958 wages in the five main fields of unskilled African labour rose an average of 8·3%. The Index of Retail Prices in the same period rose 11·1%.

A constantly expanding slice of South African commerce and industry belongs to Afrikaners who are loyal to the Nationalist Party and zealously contribute to its funds, while displaying an admirable if inconsistent colour blindness in the serving of their customers. Whether anyone in Congress really hoped to bring the government to its knees by an assault on such Afrikaner businessmen, I cannot say. The leaders with whom I discussed a new boycott campaign – against a section of the business community this time – were more concerned to display the economic strength of their followers, as preparation for more fundamental political action. This was to be an organizational, rather than a revolutionary effort. The bus boycott had shown how, on a limited issue, the African worker could be roused to a display of such power that South African commerce and industry would themselves demand the granting of concessions.

If anything like as effective a campaign could be launched against Nationalist business, a new technique of change would have been discovered. From a boycott of Nationalist products, lightning campaigns could be organized against all those sections of the South African business community which did not assist the non-white political movements in their struggle for economic and political advance.

From the outset, I gave my energetic support to the campaign. I flew up to Johannesburg and met those leaders of the Congress Alliance who constituted the joint standing council for the organization of the boycott. And, after consultations with my friends in the African National Congress itself, I helped to launch the whole campaign at a meeting of Cape Town University students on the 23rd of April 1959. For several days before, the campus had been plastered with posters carrying enormous question marks and the words – 'What Next?' – and when I entered the New Science Lecture Theatre in the early afternoon, the hall was packed with almost a thousand students.

There comes a time in the life of a people, I began, when it must say, no more, no further. Just such a time had now arrived in South Africa. All constitutional forms of change, one after the other, had been outlawed, and inevitably new techniques would have to be tried. The decision of the Congress Movement to launch a boycott of Nationalist products was an attempt to marshal the economic power of the non-whites for peaceable change. All South Africans, white and non-white alike, owed it to themselves to see that the attempt succeeded. For the consequences of failure would be terrible and lasting.

My reception was unexpectedly enthusiastic. The critical or antagonistic formed a patently small section of the audience. And the vast majority, while hostile to apartheid, felt helpless to resist it. The parliamentary opposition had proved itself a barren imitation of the government. White movements of protest had either collapsed under government pressure, like the ex-servicemen's Torch Commando, or sustained a silent and

manifestly ineffectual protest like the Black Sash. The Liberal
Party required a passionate commitment without offering any
clear prospect of success. The Congress Movement itself was
too revolutionary, and required a renunciation of all the quiet
racial preconceptions of a lifetime. Here at last, it must have
seemed to them, was a campaign which they could individually
adopt without involving themselves in a programme of revolution. And of revolution they were clearly afraid. I got the
loudest applause when, in reply to an attack on the boycott
from a Nationalist student, I said, 'If you do not want peaceful
change, you will get violent change. But you will get change.
And the choice and the responsibility are yours.' At the end of
the meeting, several dozen students surrounded me to ask for
lists of the boycotted products. I told them that the lists would
be circulated soon. We were consulting with lawyers at the
time over the degree to which we might be held liable for damages in any court case that the boycotted firms might bring.
We expected, in any event, some form of government retribution. And so we planned to keep the compiling and distribution
of boycott lists as anonymous as possible.

The press widely reported my boycott speech and the sudden
secret appearance of boycott lists on the campus a few days
later. I had expected some reaction from the government, perhaps an order banning me from gatherings, though my widely
known differences with the Communist Party seemed likely to
make it embarrassing for the Minister to invoke the Suppression of Communism Act. What I did not expect was what
immediately followed. The day after my boycott speech, the
telephone calls began. At first they were merely spurts of
obscene abuse which turned me sick with bewilderment and
disgust. But then, suddenly, they changed. Soon after I entered
my office in the early morning the telephone would ring, and
one of four distinguishable voices would tell me, coldly and
without elaboration, that I would be killed. It was impossible
not to take the threats seriously. Violence had always lurked in
the corners of South African politics, and had several times
found its victims. My callers themselves boasted an intimidating

organization. They would telephone in the late afternoon to tell me where I had been that day, the times to the minute of my meetings, and the names of my companions, and they would underline the significance of their watch by ending with a reminder that the time and the place of my death were being carefully planned.

I tried to get the telephone calls traced, but the callers were always shrewd enough to make their messages short and ignore my questions or attempts at argument. My suspicions gradually grew that these were not idle cranks, but trained political thugs, either in close and constant touch with the Special Branch or members of the Special Branch themselves. A few days after the threatening calls had begun, the offices of the Food and Canning Workers' Union were wrecked, with £2,000 worth of damage done to furniture and equipment. Along the walls obscene messages had been painted, interspersed with the words 'Ku Klux Klan'. I had held meetings on the boycott in those offices. On the morning that the damage was discovered, I received only one telephone call – a long high laugh.

Half sardonically, I approached the Special Branch for protection and publicly announced it. I applied to the police for a licence to carry a gun. Though there must be few places on earth where whites can obtain licences to carry guns with greater ease than in South Africa, my application was refused. I appealed to the Chief Magistrate of Cape Town. My appeal was rejected. By now, what fear I had, had long been swamped by a surging hatred of my persecutors and my fury at the particular viciousness they had all at once begun to display. They would telephone my sister and threaten to kidnap her two young sons.

One evening I was sitting with my family around the dinner table at 6 Avenue Disandt. We had finished eating and were engaged in some listless discussion. Suddenly there was a loud explosion, and we rushed outside. My motor car was a flight of flame high beyond the telegraph wires. We telephoned the fire brigade, a few streets away; I heard the clang of the engine at once, and then there it was, smothering the flames, before

the car was burnt beyond repair. I briskly congratulated myself on my eccentric thrift, which never permitted me to buy
more than three gallons of petrol at a time. The tank in my car
had been almost empty. We telephoned the police. I remember
how, when they arrived, one of them smiled at me, and I
found myself smiling back. I felt with sudden elusive hysteria
that we were sharing a secret. The police extracted the remains
of a primitive petrol bomb from under the car and idly questioned spectators in the crowd which had collected. They all
appeared well enough acquainted with the series of threats I
had received. After a few questions, they withdrew, and I went
home, over the shrill protests of my family, to sleep that night
at my flat. At eight the following morning, when I returned to
Avenue Disandt for breakfast and to still my family's fears, I
noticed, traced by a finger on the smoked window of the car –
'Poor old Ronnie. Get out of town!' It seemed so juvenile a
message, copied from a schoolboy comic. It could only have
been written after the fire. I wondered if the police had done it.

That morning, my lawyer appealed to the Minister of Justice
himself for my licence to carry a gun, citing as the necessary
new information the attempt to blow up my car. My appeal was
rejected. I informed the press that I would defend myself
against attack, and that if the authorities were unwilling to
provide me with a weapon, I would provide one myself. And I
issued a warning. Those whites who believed that they could
intimidate political opposition by violence might find not only
that their efforts were useless, but that they had instructed their
opponents in a new technique of pressure. The following
morning *Die Burger* devoted its first editorial to the Ku Klux
Klan. After a few sentences of strained scepticism on the
existence of any such terrorist movement, the paper proclaimed
that, if such a movement did indeed exist, it was only doing
Afrikanerdom great damage. It should cease its activities at
once. I don't know whether the members of our local Ku Klux
Klan endowed *Die Burger* with scriptural authority, but certainly, in the months that followed, neither I nor my property
was attacked again. The telephone calls, however, did not for

several weeks diminish, and I armed myself with a borrowed
revolver which I kept within easy reach in a drawer of my desk.
I had only the vaguest idea of how to fire it, but never doubted
that I would use it if ever occasion demanded. I had always
thought of myself as physically squeamish. But for the sort of
people who had set my motor car on fire and were threatening
my family, I had acquired a loathing that left no room for
timidity.

A mass meeting in Sophiatown, Johannesburg, on the
economic boycott and other measures of resistance to Nationalist rule had been organized by the African National Congress
for Union Day, the 31st of May. Congress leaders predicted
an audience reaching 15,000 and more, for Lutuli, who had just
completed his uniquely successful speaking tour of the Western
Cape, during which large numbers of whites had queued for
admission to his meetings, was expected to deliver the opening
address. A few days before the meeting, however, Lutuli was
banished to his village and banned from all gatherings for five
years under the Suppression of Communism Act, while the
meeting itself was banned by the Chief Magistrate of Johannesburg. Congress leaders hurriedly gathered and called instead a
closed delegate conference at the Mahatma Gandhi Hall in the
centre of the city. With a car full of Congress delegates, I
travelled to Johannesburg for the conference, invited to speak
from the platform on the economic boycott.

For some time a publicly silent debate had been raging within
the Congress Movement over its federal composition. I was
sure that the A.N.C. would soon be outlawed. And I believed
that the composition of the Congress Movement, as an alliance
of racially distinct organizations, not only encouraged a
dangerously limited identification, but would inevitably hamper
the creation of any non-racial underground resistance. Ultimately, it was the character of the African National Congress,
the major organization, which mattered. But to the demands,
pressed by an ever-growing number of non-Africans associated
with the Congress Movement, that the A.N.C. accept non-
African members, the organization's leadership returned a

constant refusal. We were told that the rank and file were not
ready for so profound a change in the movement's character.
The ordinary African gave his allegiance to the A.N.C. as his
own organization. To throw it open to members of other races
might be theoretically desirable, but might also erode the
prestige and appeal which the organization possessed among
Africans throughout the country. I was not convinced. If a non-
racial membership was theoretically desirable, then immediate
steps were essential practically to promote it. The A.N.C. did
not have limitless time in which to consider experiment. In its
struggle against race discrimination, it would have to overcome first the discrimination of its own racial membership.
There seemed no way, however, of taking the issue to the rank
and file. The controversy was restricted to the leadership level,
and we were forced to accept the interpretation which the
leaders themselves placed on the mood of their followers.

Outside the Mahatma Gandhi Hall stood a long line of police
fully armed. Inside, some 3,000 delegates had squeezed into a
space sufficient to accommodate with mild discomfort less than
half that number. The audience overflowed the chairs, filled
the aisles and spilt out of the windows and doors into the street
and passages around. I took my seat on the platform near
Oliver Tambo, who as Deputy President-General of the A.N.C.,
was taking the chair in place of Lutuli. A leader of the South
African Indian Congress rose to address the meeting on the
Group Areas Act. It was mid-afternoon, and the heat of the hall
was like the breath of fever in the face. I leant across to Oliver.

'Can I speak on the Group Areas Act?'

He looked puzzled.

'Aren't you speaking on the economic boycott?"

I nodded my head.

'But I'd like to say a few words on Group Areas as well.'

He smiled. 'Of course,' he said.

As the Indian speaker finished and I rose to my feet, I
wanted, with a sudden rush of fear, to escape. I had always been
ambitious. And – it now astonishingly seemed to matter much
more – I had learnt to regard with respect and even love those

leaders of the A.N.C. lining the platform on either side. What I was about to say – my resolution had only taken shape a short while before, watching that quietly tumultuous audience – might not only destroy such political influence as I could hope to have one day in South Africa, but shatter beyond repair the friendships which I had formed with those on the platform. I heard my voice as an echo.

I will not tell you, I said, that group areas are wrong. You know that they are wrong with a deep immediate suffering in which as a white I cannot pretend to share. What my own mind tells me is that all group areas are wrong, whether they are those forced on us by the government or those which have developed, over the years, in our very movements of resistance to racial rule. You can struggle against group areas in many ways. We are here to examine together some of those ways. But one way must, I am sure, inevitably fail – the struggle against group areas in group areas themselves. And we in the African National Congress – for whether I am a member or not, I think of myself as one – are in a group area of our own deciding. We would struggle against segregation with a segregated movement. We would oppose the restriction of the vote to whites by restricting the major opposition movement in this country to blacks. When I have spoken in this way to our leaders here, they have told me that they were willing to throw the A.N.C. open to whites, if only they thought that the ordinary members of Congress would agree. You are the ordinary members of Congress, and so I am asking you to agree. The annual fee for membership of the A.N.C. is half-a-crown. Here is a pound. I am applying for an eight-years' membership. Will you take me?

There was a moment of fragile silence, the most fearful I have ever endured. And then all those seated in the hall, with those packed around them, shouted 'yes'. And applause rose and broke against the platform. I turned to Oliver, gave him my pound, and sat down. Duma Nokwe, the Secretary-General of the A.N.C., leant across and hissed at me, 'You're mischievous.' But there was a thin smile at the corner of his mouth.

Whether or not the Congress leadership would decide to accept white members, remained, I knew, the subject of prolonged debate. But I had taken the issue to the rank and file, and the rank and file had shouted their approval.

The conference continued. As speaker after speaker, from the platform and from the thick of the audience, described the precarious agony of survival for the African under apartheid, the fury gathered, palpable like the taut air before a thunder clap, in the hall. Shortly after nine o'clock that night, the doors at the back suddenly burst open and a file of police – eight uniformed and armed behind four in plain clothes – pushed its way to the platform. A woman in the audience who was speaking of the farm labour system – of her husband who had been arrested because his pass had not been in order and who had never returned from the potato fields of Bethal – stopped, still standing. Those who were sitting rose to their feet. And suddenly the audience began singing 'Somlandela Lutuli' (We stand by Lutuli). I had heard it sung as a political hymn, sadly, softly, a consoling, and I had heard it sung jubilantly, in loud celebration. Now I was hearing it sung, for the first time, as a challenge. The police had reached the platform, and the first of them was talking to Oliver. The audience sang louder, more defiantly, and all at once surged towards the platform. What followed, I remember only in flashes, like the jerks of an old film. We were standing on the platform, singing with the audience, and I was being pushed towards the piano at the side with papers stuffed into my pockets. The singing rose higher. I looked at the police. They would never leave the hall alive. And neither would we. First would come the wild tearing of the twelve policemen, and then a burst of guns at the door. Oliver seized the microphone. 'They have come, these policemen,' he said, 'to search for papers. Let them have what they want. We do not need papers for what we have to do. And they are, these men, after all, only obeying their orders. Let them take their papers and let them go. And let us get on with what we came here to do.'

The surge ceased and the singing, without ceasing, seemed

suddenly to have lost its edge. The police searched the table
and seized several documents. They moved towards me, and I
felt my stuffed pockets, and I backed towards the piano in a
wild hope that I could slip the papers somehow under the lid.
But they suddenly turned away and jumped from the platform
and walked white-faced from the hall. Only after they had gone
did the singing cease. We took our seats, and the conference
continued. Ever since that night I have had a sense of wonder
at the courage and the sharp self-discipline of Africans assembled together. To those who have sneered at African political
movements, frenziedly in fear or with an easy patronage, I have
recounted that night in the Mahatma Gandhi Hall. It was, in
the splendour of a people's defiance, and the control of a chosen
leader's quiet voice, for me the peak of political experience in
South Africa.

A meeting of the joint boycott council of the Congress Alliance, which I attended in Johannesburg soon afterwards, had
decided on a nation-wide distribution of boycott lists on the
13th of June. Every effort was made to ensure that the date was
known only to a few of the essential regional organizers. On the
night of the 12th of June, I collected a few of the students
from the university who had offered their help and whom I
believed I could trust, and gave them several thousand leaflets –
printed secretly in the offices of a trade union – to push through
the letter boxes of selected white suburbs. A local leader of the
African National Congress, Joe Morolong, a member of the
South African Coloured People's Organization, Alex La Guma,
and I, drove with the bulk of the pamphlets – in the Vauxhall
I had borrowed from my mother while my own car was being
repaired – to Langa and Nyanga, the two main African areas on
the outskirts of the city. We were leaving Nyanga when I saw,
reflected in my driving mirror, the headlights of a car following
and rapidly gaining on us. I put on speed. I was certain that
our pursuers were the police. But the faster I went, the faster
the car followed behind, gaining on me all the time. I slowed
down and stopped just as it swung in front to push me off the
road. Within a few moments a second car drove up, and from

the two, twelve police – four of them in plain clothes – jumped to surround us. 'Big fishes, nê?' one of them said and grinned. I recognized Captain van der Westhuizen, local head of the Special Branch, a tall twitchy man, and his plump customary companion, Sergeant Sauerman, author of a pallid Afrikaans novel and much the most intelligent of those in the force I had met.

'What are you doing here?' asked van der Westhuizen.

'Why must I answer your questions?' I asked.

'Do you know that this is Nyanga?' asked Sauerman. 'Have you got the necessary permit? You know you need a permit to enter a Native area?'

I looked at him as blandly as I could.

'Are we in a Native area?' I asked. 'I don't remember passing any fence or notice.'

It was feeble, of course, but it was all I had.

'We are going to search the car,' van der Westhuizen said, 'and you as well.'

I handed him the revolver in my pocket.

'This is all you will find, and a few pamphlets.'

I looked at Joe and Alex. It would not be as easy for them. ' I want to phone my lawyer,' I said to van der Westhuizen. And I added with emphasis, 'He will act for all three of us.' Van der Westhuizen stared at me and said nothing.

As we were being driven to the Philippi police station near by, I looked at my watch. It was a few minutes past ten o'clock. My two companions had been placed one in each of the police cars, and Captain van der Westhuizen accompanied Sauerman and me in the Vauxhall.

'What are you charging me with?' I asked van der Westhuizen.

'We are not charging you, yet,' Sauerman said.

'You will allow me, of course, to contact my lawyer.'

'In good time.'

When we arrived at the police station, I looked for Joe and Alex, but they had apparently been taken into other rooms. It was for them alone that I felt any real unease. I knew that my colour and my profession would secure me for the moment from all but polite if persistent questioning and perhaps minor charges. Having recovered from the agitation of my arrest, I was prepared to sit back and enjoy my first single encounter with the police. Some of them, I remained convinced, had been at least party to the weeks of anonymous persecution before. I had not considered the possibility of arrest when setting out for Nyanga. I supposed that someone in Congress – for Congress, like any revolutionary movement, was busy with spies – had disclosed the date of the boycott list distribution to the Special Branch. But now that I found myself in their hands, I intended to make myself as useless to them – and as irritating – as possible. It wasn't difficult. Even Sauerman, the most astute of them, travelled to his incriminating questions by a clearly sign-posted road. It needed no unusual intelligence to lead him on and then, suddenly, turn him aside or simply stop dead. Every now and then I demanded to see my lawyer. It was the prospect of what might happen in the non-white section of the police station that kept jerking my nerves. Too many non-white prisoners had been beaten up – or just suffered heart attacks – during questioning by the police. Every now and then I would interrupt the questioning to ask where they were, to suggest that I be allowed to call my lawyer on their behalf, only to underline that I was concerned about them and to hint that I would regard their experiences as my own.

After three hours of questioning, towards the end of which I found it increasingly difficult not to giggle, partly I suppose from sheer exhaustion, partly from relief at the failure of my questioners to secure any admission at all which might embarrass me, Sauerman suddenly rose and asked me to accompany him.

'You may telephone your lawyer,' he said.

'Thank you,' I replied, as acidly as I could. 'Are you charging me yet?'

Sauerman stared at me. 'There's still plenty of time,' he said lightly.

I phoned my lawyer in full hearing of the police, and told him that I had refused to answer any questions which I regarded as incriminating. He asked me whether I wanted him to come, and I said that it didn't seem necessary. I just wanted to know how best I should conduct myself until I was charged. He suggested that I refuse to answer any questions at all, and get in touch with him again later in the morning, after I had been charged. He would speak to van der Westhuizen himself. Before handing on the receiver, I asked him to phone the press and tell them of my arrest, and of Joe's and Alex's as well. A yelp of protest came from van der Westhuizen. I handed the receiver to him. Then Sauerman asked me to follow him. We went to the Vauxhall, I got into the driver's seat, and waited for him to speak.

'Just drive to your office,' he said.

'I haven't got the key to the front door of the building,' I replied, for the first time fearful as I wondered whether there was anything left in my files which could seriously incriminate me or any members of the Congress Movement. I remembered going through them two weeks before and destroying several letters, but perhaps there was something I had missed. I suddenly thought of a letter I had received that morning from Congress headquarters in Johannesburg. It still lay in a crumpled ball at the bottom of the waste-paper basket, waiting for collection by the office cleaner in the early morning.

'Someone must have the key to the building,' Sauerman said. 'We had better go and get it. No one is entering your office until we have been through it.'

'There is an agent of some sort who lives in Sea Point. Perhaps we can get the key from him,' I said.

'Good,' he replied. 'I'll tell the others to meet us there. What's the address?'

I gave it to him, and after whispering to van der Westhuizen, who had just loped from the station and stood louring over the car, he told me to drive there. On the way he became garrulous and even wheedling. He spoke about a son of his who had 'advanced' ideas, and about his job. 'It's a job like any other, I suppose. I work for them today. Perhaps, who knows,

I'll be working for you to-morrow,' and he grinned at me. 'Would you let me keep my job?'

'I doubt very much,' I replied, 'whether I will ever have much say in the matter. Those who have, might consider you disqualified by the zeal you show in serving your present employers.'

'Zeal?' he said. 'I give the best of myself to everything I do. If I were working for you, you would ask for nothing less.'

It was almost two in the morning when I parked outside the Sea Point flat of the agent who had the office next to mine. It was not the first time I had called on him for his key. I had to ring the bell for several minutes before he appeared, white-faced, at the door.

'I'm sorry,' I said, 'I have been arrested, and the police want to search my office. May I have your key to the building?'

He looked at me furiously.

'How can you wake me up at this time of the night?' he shouted. 'Couldn't it wait until the morning?'

I felt myself see-sawing between laughter and outrage. His display of violated dignity was backed by bedraggled blue-and-yellow striped pyjamas.

'Do you really think,' I shouted back, 'that I wake people up at this time of night for fun? If you want the police to wait until the morning, you can tell them so yourself.'

I pointed to the large police car which had just driven up behind the Vauxhall.

He looked at it, gulped, and disappeared down the hall, to return a moment later with the key.

'Thank you,' I said, 'I'll return it as soon as I can.'

We drove to my office, and I sat on the desk watching van der Westhuizen and Sauerman search through my files while the other policemen, having measured the size of the room with their eyes, crowded outside. Once or twice Sauerman dipped his hand into the waste-paper basket, but searched no further. After half an hour, he turned to me and said that we could go. All he had taken were a few typescripts of articles, most of which had already been published in the magazine. I told him this, but it seemed to make no difference. We drove to my flat, where they searched for almost an hour, but found nothing that they wanted. My library disappointed them. My political books were persuasively respectable – I had disposed of the dubious ones months before – and the Special Branch was not interested in literature.

I got into the Vauxhall with Sauerman again, we drove at his suggestion for coffee to a hot-dog stand on the parade, and then back to the Philippi police station. Again he questioned me, and at last, some time after six, he charged me with possessing a revolver without a proper licence and with entering a Native area without a permit. Joe and Alex were then brought up from the cells, and were charged with having entered Nyanga illegally.

A young policeman approached me with the pen and watch, money and cheque book that he had taken from me when I had first arrived at the station. 'You have a lot of money in your bank,' he said. 'Your cheque book says £1,650.'

'If you look carefully,' I said, 'you will see a minus sign in front of the figure. That's not money, that's an overdraft.'

I don't think he believed me. I paid the bail for the three of us, and asked whether we could go.

'Why not?' said Sauerman.

CHAPTER SIX

REVOLUTION IS NOW

IN January 1959, after an Emergency Action Conference of the Nyasaland African Congress, disturbances had broken out in various parts of the territory. On the 24th of February, Southern Rhodesian troops had been dispatched by the Federal government into Nyasaland, and some 250 Congress officials and supporters had been arrested. Tension had risen still further, and on the 3rd of March the Governor had declared a State of Emergency, banned the Nyasaland African Congress altogether, and arrested Dr Hastings Banda, its leader, who was flown to imprisonment in Southern Rhodesia. The Federation of Rhodesia and Nyasaland, which had been imposed in August 1953 by the British government on the hostile African majorities of all three constituent territories, was erupting into rebellion and repression. The Governor of Northern Rhodesia banned the restive Zambia African National Congress, while Sir Edgar Whitehead, Prime Minister of Southern Rhodesia, used the Nyasaland and Northern Rhodesia disturbances as an excuse to declare a State of Emergency in his own territory, proscribe its principal African organization, the African National Congress, detain 495 of his political opponents, and 'tighten up security legislation'.

I decided to devote most of the twelfth issue – I was involved in the last stages of its production at the time of my arrest – to the crisis in Central Africa. Kanyama Chiume, then a member of the Nyasaland Legislative Council and Publicity Secretary of the banned Nyasaland African Congress – he is now Minister of Education in the territory – wrote on Nyasaland. Kenneth Kaunda, President of the banned Zambia African National Congress, smuggled out to me from his place of rustication an article on the political crisis in Northern Rhodesia. Joshua Nkomo, President of the banned Southern Rhodesian African National Congress, who had escaped arrest by being abroad when the State of Emergency was declared, wrote on conditions in Southern Rhodesia, and Moses Makone, who had never been a member of any African political movement at all, described his arrest and the 38 days he had spent in prison by mistake. Garfield Todd, the former Prime Minister of Southern Rhodesia, granted a long interview to a representative of the magazine, and made clear his hostility to the trend of events in the Federation, while Barbara Castle, M.P., wrote on 'Labour and Central Africa', expressing the British Labour Party's profound concern at developments in the Federation and stating her belief that Nyasaland should be permitted to secede if it wished to do so. Frank Barton, former Editor of the *Central African Post*, contributed a study of the Federal Prime Minister – I entitled it 'Portrait of a Failure' – in which he carefully examined the structure of the Welensky myth.

'Certainly a part of his success had been due to his treatment of, and thus his treatment by, the Rhodesian press. He is on first-name terms with dozens of Rhodesian, South African and English newspapermen. He has cultivated their friendship until it is a model of what the relationship of a politician on the make and the press should be – always "good for a quote", always "ready to play ball". When his car breaks down on the way from Government House and he accepts a lift from an unknowing motor-cyclist, he makes sure that this "human interest" tit-bit finds its way into the eager hands of the reporters; when a flustered airport manager produces a cup of tea for him during a terminal building press conference, the busy eyebrows will rise, and Welensky will inquire about "tea for the gentlemen of the press?" When none can be produced at short notice, he purses his lips and gently refuses to drink his own.

'A great deal of his success, and the thing that may hasten his downfall, is the over-fine art he has developed of being all things to all men. To the Afrikaner he will recall his Afrikaans mother; to the ultra-Britisher, England becomes "home" for him; to the European trade unionist he is "one of you"; he even tried to tell the Africans of turbulent Nyasaland that he was "as much an African as you". It did not go down very well.

'For his relations with the Africans, there is little to be said. The simple truth is that, born and bred in the country though he is, he understands them no better than he does the Eskimos. Only lately has the truth slowly broken upon him that he cannot carry them with him on the same tide of oratory, bluff and charm that won and keeps for him the bulk of European support.'

My own editorial was a letter to Welensky peaceably entitled 'Dear Sir Roy'. I asked him to consider the accomplishments of the six years during which the policy of racial 'partnership' had been pursued by the Federal government.

'Nyasaland survives in the Federation today as occupied territory, its allegiance as sure and as lasting as the guard at your detention camps and your army of occupation can forcibly ensure ... No settler in Nyasaland has been killed; though underneath the interminable explanation that you have piled high upon them, lie the bodies of fifty Africans shot by your security forces.

'Your associates in Southern Rhodesia have followed their leader and thrown themselves head over heels into a riot of repression ... Having outlawed the Congress Movement and detained its leaders, they have busied themselves in disfiguring the statute book with the most repressive measures that have ever mocked the principles of parliamentary rule. Outdoing even the Nationalists in mutilating the rule of law, the governing party you control has provided itself with powers of arbitrary arrest and made the most elementary African opposition into a criminal offence.

'If its objects were to terrorize African sentiment into submission and break the hold that the Congress has upon African allegiance, it has failed ludicrously in both. For far from stilling African hostility, it has inflamed it; while by arresting moderates and radicals alike, it has offered its opponents the obduracy

of extremes and united them on the rack of Congress martyr-
dom. Above all, by preventing the Africans from organizing
themselves peacefully for change, it has left only the avenue of
civil disobedience open to opposition, and stimulated the very
violence against which it now pretends that it was obliged to
protect itself. When even boycott is banned as a political
weapon, revolution remains the only recourse left the oppressed. Can that be what you and your accomplices actually
want?'

In the twelfth issue too, Joe Matthews, former President of
the African National Congress Youth League and now one of
the most significant younger theorists in the Congress Movement, took the symposium on revolution one stage further. He
maintained that racialism need not in itself be the main vehicle
of revolution, and that history contained examples enough of
whites who had fought one another 'under the compelling
pressure of economic forces, despite the presence of a huge depressed non-white group in the same country'. He emphasized
the frustrations of the African middle class, which lacked the
main incentive of its counterparts elsewhere, the investment of
accumulated capital in land and property. Finally he pointed to
the dangers as well as the advantages of an indigenous tyranny.

An imperial power generally possessed a secure home base.
Any difficulties in colonial rule did not result in direct disturbances at home, for the enemy – the colonial people themselves – lived at a distance. The Algerian war, for example, was
financed by the French from a relatively undisturbed economy
in France itself. In South Africa, however, the situation was
altogether different. A single integrated economy, dependent
on the labour of what might be called the colonial people, had
been erected, while the metropolitan power possessed no base
from which operations could be conducted in relative security.

'And that is the nightmare of the strategists of white supremacy. One can almost see the general staff of apartheid arguing
in favour of the creation of secure white bases in which there
are no Africans present; which do not depend on the Africans
for labour; which are not part of a mixed society. Is not this

perhaps the real reason for the suggested Balkanization of South Africa into white and black areas, despite the clearly fantastic nature of the whole concept?'

Over one article in the twelfth issue, I engaged in a long wrangle with my lawyer. At my request, Stanley Uys had written a contemptuous article on the enlarged Senate, constituted in 1955 by the Strijdom government to acquire its two-thirds parliamentary majority and so remove the Coloured voters from the common roll. It had, however, been retained long after its original purpose had been served, and its vast Nationalist membership had been instrumental in electing Dr Verwoerd to the premiership – 'a noteworthy, but not notable, function', as Uys described it. In his cartoon for the twelfth issue David Marais had drawn a picture of an enormous Dr Verwoerd, accompanied by tiers of diminutive Verwoerds, smiling in approval at a speech by one of their number. It was a cruelly valid caricature of the Senate, and the article provided ample documentation.

'No tour of the Houses of Parliament is complete without a visit to the famous enlarged Senate. The guide escorts his party to the public gallery and they peep down into the Chamber. He explains that there has been a big change. In the old Senate – the one which expired with the passing of the Senate Act in 1955 – the 30 Government Members used to sit on one side and the 18 Opposition Members on the other. Now the Government has 78 Members, and they stretch up one length of the Chamber and down the other, leaving only a tiny corner on the President's left for the remnants of the Opposition – 12 men clinging on valiantly, like the man in the cartoon dangling over a precipice and clutching at a stem of edelweiss.

'The first meeting of the enlarged Senate in January 1956 was a gala occasion. One of the newcomers was Senator Louis Weichardt, former leader of the Greyshirt movement in South Africa. "The Greyshirts," he explained "were liquidated for something far superior to take their place." This tribute, presumably, was directed at the Nationalist Party of which he had now become a respected spokesman. Another newcomer was

Senator Jan Grobler, one-time member of the Nazi-type "New Order", started during the war years by Oswald Pirow (now prosecuting in the treason trial).

'The enlarged Senate costs £220,000 a year. At the last full-length session (lasting nearly six months), 4 Government Senators made no speeches at all, 7 made only one speech each, and 8 made only 2 speeches each. One Senator, beginning "I would like to congratulate the Minister ..." spoke about 600 words in 7 minutes, and nothing else for the rest of the session. He could calculate his emoluments at £3 the spoken word, or £285 the speaking minute. Commenting on an increase of £400 in the free trunk-line telephone calls made by Senators, the *Cape Times* said: "This raises the query whether some Senators perhaps talk more on the long-distance telephone than they do on the floor of the House"...

'The term of office of the enlarged Senate expires next year, and agitation for its reform is starting up again. Next year, too, the four Senators representing Africans will be abolished under the mis-named "Promotion of Bantu Self-Government Bill". This will reduce the Opposition in the Senate to eight – all United Party Senators from Natal.

'The United Party, therefore, has a remedy in its hands. If the Government fails to abolish the enlarged Senate next year, it can walk out and leave this grotesque institution to the Nationalists.'

My lawyer rightly held the whole tone of the article to be provocative. He took particular exception to the title – 'The Senate Farce' – and suggested that it might be changed so as to make somewhat less probable any intervention by parliament in the protection of its dignity. For once, I refused altogether to listen. The enlarged Senate was a farce, and my recent experiences had encouraged me in my resolution to say so.

After discussion with my friends in Congress, I decided to fight the charges of the police against me instead of pleading guilty and paying the small fines involved. Though my possession of a fire-arm without a proper licence was a serious offence, the circumstances under which I had borrowed it were such that no court seemed likely to prescribe more than a nominal penalty. But the press of South Africa – including the Congress-supporting weekly *New Age* – had not published the names of the Nationalist products on the boycott list, for fear of being sued for damages. If I could somehow insert the list into the proceedings of the court – copies of it had after all been seized by the police on the night of my arrest – its publication would at once become privileged and immune to any legal action by the boycotted concerns. In defence of the fire-arm charge, I possessed a signed statement from the Executor of the Estate to which the revolver belonged, specifying in terms of the law the period for which he had lent it to me. To the location charge, I maintained that I did not know I had been in Nyanga, that the notice boards at the entrance to the location were illegible at night, and that I had no recollection of having seen them.

The case immediately caught the attention of the press, which gave considerable space to my defence and cross-examination in court. To all suggestions from the Prosecutor that I could not have missed the Nyanga notice boards, I replied that it had been a moonless night and that at no stage had the beam from the headlights of my car fallen on them. A visit to the area on the following day had revealed the boards as set some distance from the road, and the lettering on them as cramped, small, and difficult to read even by daylight.

'Are you blind or only half blind?' the Prosecutor eventually shouted at me.

'No, just colour blind,' I said.

For a moment he stood staring at me in silence, and then suggested an adjournment of the case.

When we resumed some three weeks later, on the 17th of July, he began by questioning me closely on my colour blindness, and I experienced the nastiest moment of the trial. I had been too clever by half, and I was now forced to admit that I was not literally colour blind, just politically. But I continued to maintain that I had not seen the notice boards at the entrance. I hadn't. It would have needed a magnesium flare to read them on a dark night, I declared.

The Prosecutor turned with pardonable impatience to the fire-arm charge and soon made clear that he doubted my whole defence. The certificate of loan, he suspected, had been signed and acquired after my arrest. He asked me why I had not produced the certificate during my detention, and I replied that I had not wished to endanger the man who had lent me the revolver. I had felt it proper to consult him before disclosing his name. The Prosecutor asked how, in terms of the law, I could conceivably endanger anyone by borrowing a revolver from him. I was astounded. Government intimidation of its political opponents was so accepted a feature of Nationalist rule that I had never for a moment, in all the preparation of my case, assumed that it would be called into question by the Crown. It had been inexcusably stupid of me. He pressed me to give examples of those intimidated for their political beliefs and actions. I cited my own case, with the weeks of assiduous persecution by the local Ku Klux Klan, and declared that I feared similar treatment for someone who had gone to the lengths of providing me with a revolver to defend myself. How, the Prosecutor measuredly asked, could the Ku Klux Klan know what I said or showed to members of the police force? For a moment I thought of saying 'because the police and the Ku Klux Klan are the same!' But I knew that it would sound absurd – what proof could I offer? – and I saw that I was trapped. 'The government itself would find ways of making life difficult for whomever had lent me the revolver,' I replied. He pressed me again for examples of government intimidation. What specific cases could I give the court?

Moving through my memory was like searching a cluttered attic in which I stumbled over all the objects I did not want. Suddenly I remembered Leah, who had once gone to a musical evening at the home of a well-known political opponent of the government and had later been told by a student – with advertised access to the Special Branch – where she had been, with whom, when, at what time she had arrived and what time left.

Prosecutor: 'You have said that people were intimidated. How was this woman intimidated?'

'To have your name taken and to have been watched seems to me in a civilized society intimidation enough.'

He asked for further instances. I replied that I could remember none just then, but that I would be able to produce dozens if I were given access to newspaper files. It was such instances that had made me wary of involving anyone else with the police.

Prosecutor: 'But that is only what you have read about?'

'I believe the world is round because I have read about it.'

He asked whether I had been scared by the authorities before my arrest at Nyanga.

'I am not scared of the authorities *now*,' I replied. I was angry at last, and my assurance was returning.

Prosecutor: 'Why did you take a fire-arm to the location?'

'I took it with me because I had been threatened and my car had been blown up.'

The magistrate adjourned the case with an announcement that he would himself inspect the notices at the two official entrances to Nyanga. Before we set out, on the night of July the 22nd, I handed to him a signed affidavit listing eight crude examples of government intimidation, all of which had been widely reported in the press and with which I had consequently been acquainted at the time of my arrest. They had all taken place in the four years since my return from studying in America and included bannings and the refusal of passports, the interrogation and search of men and women – none of any political prominence – who had somehow excited the attentions of the Special Branch.

The magistrate, who came with me in the Vauxhall, while my lawyer followed with members of the Special Branch in another car, asked me to drive into Nyanga. Some hundred yards after we had entered the location, he asked me when we would be approaching the notice boards.

'We have just passed them,' I said triumphantly.

'Drive back to them,' he said shortly.

We drove back and he proceeded to measure them with a ruler and shine his torch on the cramped lettering.

I was convinced that I would now, after all, win the case. But whether I won or not, now seemed unimportant. My counsel, in a shrewdly conducted examination of me, had led me to describe the circumstances of my arrest and the leaflets that the police had seized from my car. He had then asked me to describe the contents of the leaflets, and I had quoted the list of Nationalist products against which the boycott had been called. The next issue of *New Age* had carried the list, in unavoidable black type, to its almost 30,000 purchasers. My counsel too, a close friend who was to die soon afterwards during an operation on his leaking heart, had used the occasion of the case to launch a vigorous onslaught on the whole system of residential segregation. The locations were not concentration camps or leper colonies, he cried. They were simply suburbs in which Africans lived. Why should anyone be prevented from entering them?

On the 28th of July we assembled for the magistrate's verdict. My lawyers were confident that, however unpersuasive my defence, I would be given the benefit of the doubt. But when the magistrate began reading his verdict, faltering over the long words, the reassurance dropped from their faces. It sounded as though it had been written by one of the more strident propagandists in the State Information Office. It was not a judgment, it was a torrent of abuse. Never, said the magistrate, had a smoother or more practised liar appeared before him in the many years of his experience. My whole defence had been a concoction of untruths. He rang as many changes on this theme as he could and then announced that he saw no alternative but to fine me £2 on the location charge and £10 for possessing a fire-arm without a licence. My counsel leapt to his feet and asked for permission to appeal.

The case subsequently went to the Supreme Court, but the judge, referring to it as the *cause célèbre*, upheld the magistrate's verdict on a point of law – without further comment on the character of the defence.

The government, however, did not hold its retribution until the conclusion of the case. One day, during the trial in the magistrate's court, I was sitting in my office when I heard a knock at the door.

'Come in!' I yelled, and the door opened to a tall, sunburnt man with a clenched face, who – I immediately suspected – was a member of the local Ku Klux Klan.

'What do you want?' I said angrily, my hand stretching towards the knife that I now kept in my office desk since the police had seized my revolver.

'I am the Chief Immigration Officer,' he said.

'Prove it,' I demanded.

From under his arm he took a khaki-coloured file, bulging with press cuttings, on which my name was printed in large ink capitals. From it, he drew a letter, which he handed to me. It was from the Minister of the Interior, informing me that I was to surrender my passport immediately to the Chief Immigration Officer at Cape Town. I was stunned. I had expected any number of things, but somehow not this. My passport had remained for me a secret pledge, like a pantry crammed with tinned goods in the event of sudden calamity.

'I don't carry it on me,' I said quietly.

'Of course.' He nodded. 'I will come here at ten o'clock tomorrow morning. Please see that you have it with you then.' And he left.

The following morning, at three minutes past ten, he arrived at the office, and I handed my passport to him. He looked embarrassed. 'I am only a civil servant,' he mumbled. 'I sometimes have to do things that I'd rather not.' I smiled. 'Of course,' I said.

Another gate clanged shut in my mind. Well, I thought, that about does it, there is nothing more they are likely to throw at me. After the Ku Klux Klan, the arrest, and now the taking of my passport, the range of retribution has shrunk.

A few days before the magistrate delivered his verdict, Captain van der Westhuizen visited me at my office and handed me a letter from the Minister of Justice. It informed me curtly that

I had been banned in terms of the Suppression of Communism Act of 1950 from all gatherings in the Union of South Africa and South West Africa for a period of five years.

'Anything else?' I asked van der Westhuizen.

He shrugged his shoulders and left.

I don't suppose that I had ever really believed that this would happen to me. Other people, with long records of political dissent, the leaders of the Congress Alliance and those who had once been prominent in the Communist Party, received such notices. I knew that the word 'gathering' meant a meeting of any two or more people for any common object, and I realized – with a gape of bewilderment – what that letter from the Minister would mean for me. Not for five years, at least, would I be able to meet legally with even one friend to discuss a political campaign or exchange political opinions. Each time that I discussed with a regular contributor to the magazine the organization of a forthcoming number, I would be breaking the law and risking several years in prison. I would have to resign even from the Treason Trial Defence Fund, since meetings of the Treasurer's Committee were undeniable gatherings in terms of the law. I would, at least publicly, be silenced. The sheer blatant fraud, the cowardice, of using the Suppression of Communism Act against me, despite my public record of antagonism to the Communist Party, infuriated me. If I was to be punished, I wanted to be punished for what I had done and what I believed.

Slowly, however, some small consolation, and with it a resolve, took shape. The banning notice I had received might serve to stir awake at last those independent progressive opponents of the government who slumbered securely while blacks or white communists were persecuted. And I would flout the ban whenever I thought it safe or necessary to do so. I would continue to organize the raising of money for the defence of the treason trialists and I would continue to work with the Congress Movement in its campaigns, though furtively now and with a well-rehearsed script of evasion. I had always been frank in my dissent. The government could succeed in clothing my dissent in deceit. But my dissent itself was now more vital than ever.

Protests to the government poured in from the Congress for Cultural Freedom abroad, with its well-stocked armoury of respectable intellectuals. Many of the magazine's foreign sponsors publicly expressed their disgust. And the *Cape Times*, in its long leading editorial of July the 29th, expressed the mood of the most cautious liberal opinion within South Africa itself.

'The importance in principle of the banning of Ronald Segal is that Segal is not a communist, has not been a communist, and it is not even alleged that he is a communist. The evidence available from his writings tends to establish the contrary – that he is a doctrinaire liberal whose dislike of regimentation and enthusiasm for civil and individual liberty are such that he is as opposed to communism as to any other form of authoritarianism. The curb which has been put on his liberty is a purely executive action taken in terms of a statute which a civilized legislature was persuaded to enact because it was persuaded that the combating of communism required the delegation of arbitrary powers to the executive. The Communist Act makes the Minister the prosecutor, judge and jury in the trial of an individual; the proceedings throughout are in complete secrecy; there is no provision for appeal and no indictment; the accused is given no indication of the evidence against him and no opportunity to present a defence. No civilized country in peace-time and in its senses would give powers like these to a politician unless the purpose was to deal with the evil of communism. Hence the importance of the fact that it is *not* alleged that Segal is a communist.

'The Communist Act did not declare that it is a crime to edit *Africa South*. It did not define as a crime the collection of funds for the treason trial, and there is as yet no law which makes a boycott a criminal offence. It is not a crime to believe that men were born equal in the sight of God and that a policy of racial repression is a short-cut to political suicide in a multi-racial community. There may well be people who believe that these things should be crimes, but the point is that, at the moment of writing, they are not. Yet Segal has been made the victim of punitive executive action by the process of asserting that what he says and does "encourages" communism.

'In one sense it can be argued that the expression of sentiments of liberty, equality and fraternity "encourages" communism. But what, in this sense, does not "encourage" communism? By anyone with a sufficiently closed mind, "encouragement" can be read into anything which weakens the hold of Nationalist authoritarianism on this unhappy country. Communism can be "encouraged", in the Nationalist sense, by an Archbishop who wants to see the doctrines of Christianity translated into political practice, by a newspaper which reports that the world at large hates unjust discrimination on grounds of colour, by a politician who asserts that the only course of sanity is government with the consent of the governed. This was the point at which Hitler's Germany arrived. The "Red danger" was Hitler's greatest asset, and the crime of encouraging communism was simply defined – it was anything which opposed Nazism or which Hitler did not like. The action against Segal is important because it indicates that we are arriving at the same point. He has committed no crime, he is not a communist, and his "encouragement of communism" is indistinguishable from vigorous political opposition to the policies of the Nationalists.

'If the Nationalists believe that men like Segal are a menace to peace and good government, let them pass legislation making it a crime to express the robustly liberal views of *Africa South*, to champion the cause of students whose passports have been refused or to organize boycotts. But it becomes political persecution and political oppression to use the machinery of the Communist Act against a man who can be accused of encouraging communism only by stretching language to include every effective critic of the present Nationalist regime. Just a few short years ago, when Nationalists were defending the Communist Act as a means to deal with communists, critics expressed the fear that the day would arrive when the Act would be used against political opponents who were not communists. That day has arrived.'

At my request, my lawyer wrote immediately to the Minister of Justice, demanding to know his reasons for issuing the ban against me. We entertained, of course, small hope of a reply. The Minister's discretion under the Suppression of Communism Act was, as the *Cape Times* leader stated, absolute. There was no recourse to the courts from any banning notice he might issue, and he was not obliged to provide any reasons at all for his decision. Indeed, to our knowledge, he had never done so. We were accordingly astonished when, at the end of August, we received from him a reply, running to five foolscap pages of single space typing, outlining the reasons behind his decision to ban me. From September 1956 to June 1959, he maintained, I had taken 'an active part in agitation and propaganda', and had 'encouraged the overthrowing of the State by means of revolution'. 'This agitation, propaganda and conduct,' he claimed, 'are similar to the methods advocated by known Communist leaders such as Marx and Lenin, and may, therefore, further the achievement of certain objects of communism.'

In support of these extraordinary allegations, he quoted extracts from the articles on revolution which had appeared in *Africa South*, and extracts from a speech on the Congress boycott which I had delivered a few months before to students at the University of the Witwatersrand. I at once gave the letter to the press, commenting that the articles in *Africa South* to which the Minister had taken such offence were political analyses, many of them written by scholars of repute, and that it was a serious matter for the whole press of the country if an editor could be personally banned for publishing such material. The extracts from the boycott speech were garbled and illiterate; indeed, the government agent who had attended the meeting had as little knowledge of spelling as of syntax, and his report bore as little resemblance to the manner of my speech as to the matter. I challenged the Minister, if he thought he could substantiate his allegations, to bring me before the courts and prosecute me for treason.

Meanwhile I prepared for the thirteenth issue of the magazine.

In it, under the title 'Revolution is Now', I made my own editorial contribution to the symposium on revolution. I could hardly, after all, be banned more than once, and my passport had already been withdrawn.

With parliament reduced to the functions and status of a government gazette, I maintained, and all constitutional opposition restricted to the futilities that a race-frenzied electorate would allow, change itself had become finally inseparable from revolution. Yet those who talked most of an explosion, were least able to define the form that such an explosion might successfully take. In a society where revolt walked always in the shadow of massacre, a Bastille-storming type of upheaval was unlikely to occur and unlikely to achieve any fundamental change if it did. It was far more rewarding to examine the functions of government, and the way that they were rapidly decomposing in South Africa, if the prospect of revolution was not to remain a mere mystique.

For a government could exist just as long as it was capable of governing, as long as it fulfilled its fundamental function of maintaining law and order. While it did so, society could be coerced into sustaining it, because the alternative was that very lawlessness, with its sacrifice of life and property, that government existed to prevent. It was when a government ceased to be capable of governing that society was forced to find an alternative in order to survive, and it submitted to revolution as the only escape from chaos.

It was in the context of such a definition that revolution in South Africa could be seen as a pulsating reality. The 1957 Report of the South African Commissioner of Police had just been published, and I compared its figures for crime and prosecution with those in the report of London's Police Commissioner. The metropolitan area of London, with a population of more than 8,000,000 and all the complex conflicts of a cosmopolitan culture, had registered 30,097 arrests during 1957, or an average of 82 arrests a day. During the same year, 1,525,612 people had been committed for trial in South Africa, and of these 1,448,582 had been convicted. Each day of the year, there-

fore, some 4,200 South Africans were arrested and tried, out of
a population of 14,500,000; each year, one out of every ten
inhabitants – women and children included – was convicted of
a crime.

Even more significant were the figures for crimes of violence.
During 1957, there had been 11 convictions for murder in the
metropolitan area of London. The number of convictions for
murder in South Africa had risen from 390 in 1953 to 798 in
1957. (Australia, with a population of 9,000,000, had some 30
convictions a year; and New Zealand, with a population of
2,200,000, only 4.) Where London in 1957 had registered 96
cases of criminal violence resulting in death, including all
deaths directly caused by dangerous driving, South Africa during the same year had recorded 4,654, of which 1,992 had been
murders. Some 12 people, it seemed, died every day of the year
in South Africa as a result of violence. And of these, 5 were
murdered.

Even the police had succumbed to the general decay. In
1958, some 2·77% of South Africa's white police force of
12,000 men had been convicted of crimes; in 1957, the latest
year for which figures were then available, 10 cases of miscon-
duct had been registered within the force of metropolitan
London, or ·06% of a total of 16,345 men. Between the years
1946 and 1948, 223 policemen had been charged with crimes,
and 174 convicted. Between 1956 and 1958, the number
charged had risen to 1,263, of whom 840 had been convicted.

Yet revolution, I admitted, remained for the most part a
shadow in the mind. Men did not throw bombs into crowded
cafés, and rioting was largely restricted to the isolated African
areas beyond the hill or across the river. The country was still
an overseas safe-deposit box. But there had been a change, there
was a twitch at the corner of the eyes. Congress campaigns
gathered headlines where hardly a handful of years before they
had been sedulously spiked. The government bought 80
armoured cars from Britain to protect the police in the pursuit
of their duties. Durban's black slums smouldered with men
and women driven over the edge of despair. Boycotts inside

the country, and of all South African goods by hostile governments and individuals abroad, unnerved the economy. And,
within Afrikanerdom, the legislators were being elbowed out
of the way by the thugs. White terrorism had already begun,
as secret societies sprang up to sustain white supremacy.

It could go on like this, getting just a little worse each day,
for a few years more. And then it could not go on any longer.
For no one, white or black, would be able to endure it. Five
murders a day. Then ten? Then twenty? Nearly five thousand
deaths by violence every year. Then ten thousand? Then
twenty? How much lawlessness could a society sustain?

'It is temptingly easy to think of revolution in sudden terms,
a storming and a surrender, lightning in the streets. But revolution is slow and persistent, a wearing away of resistance to
the point of snap. Revolution is now.'

African resentment exploded in Natal during June 1959.
Two months before, Native Administration officials had begun
clearing Cato Manor, a slum of cardboard and rusted-tin shanties in which some 80,000 of Durban's Africans lived. Those
without proper documents, those who had not served one employer continuously for ten years or lived in the area without
interruption for fifteen years, found themselves subject to endorsement out of Durban altogether, with their only alternative a retreat to the starvation of the Reserves or a pitiful wage
on the white farms. And even those entitled to live and work in
Durban were being issued with orders to remove, under the
Group Areas Act, further from the city, to a far more distant
African township called Kwa Mashu. Cato Manor, like Windermere, was a slum; but, like Windermere, it was a thin
crumbling ledge of humanity as well. It was near to the city,
and the cost of transport to work was already more than the
average weekly income of £2 5s. could safely encompass. As it
was, 95% of the Africans in the city of Durban were reported
by the *Natal Mercury* to be living well below the breadline. The
extra 10d. a day in bus fares which would result from any move
to distant Kwa Mashu would drive them even deeper into the
want which drained their lives.

Riots in South Africa often have tiny fuses. It is the last frustration which explodes the whole heap beneath it. Suddenly Cato Manor rebelled, because the City Council's demolition workers, in the course of enforcing the mass removals to Kwa Mashu, were destroying the illegal beer stills. And it was by brewing and selling beer, that the women of Cato Manor swelled their small family incomes. On Wednesday, the 17th of June, the women sent a deputation to the Native Administration officials, demanding that all forced removals and the demolition of their homes cease at once and that the Council's own beer halls, which made an annual profit of £107,000, should be closed. The officials formally rejected both demands, and the police dispersed women who were picketing the Cato Manor beer hall. On the following day, several thousand women gathered outside the beer hall and were ordered to disperse by the police. When they refused to do so, the police opened fire and fell upon them with flaying batons. Cato Manor, and other African townships in the area, burst into flame. Thirty buildings, including three churches, valued at £250,000 were burnt by rioters. Some 70,000 dossiers, compiled by Native Administration officials to organize the mass removals, were destroyed. In the repression that followed, one white policeman was officially reported as shot, four Africans killed and twenty-four wounded. Unofficial figures were a great deal higher.

For the thirteenth issue I commissioned Myrna Blumberg, a South African correspondent of the London *Daily Herald*, who was later arrested and detained during the 1960 State of Emergency, to publish an account of the Durban riots and analyse their cause. The picture she drew of white reaction was blisteringly accurate.

'In the glass house that was my hotel, stridently chic with artificial pools and rockeries in the hall, not one holiday reservation was cancelled because of the riots. Lounging in the well-sprung beds, the sun-tanned holiday-makers, mostly from Johannesburg, had their eight-course breakfasts sent up on trays carried by non-white waiters as usual.

'A large, round businessman with a pink smile who generously gave me a lift from the airport to save me time, blinked in bewilderment at my interest. "But what are three thousand crazy kaffir girls going to do?" he asked. "I'll tell you when *I'll* call it serious. I'll call it serious when my girl brings my morning tea in late."

'He guffawed and waved his plump hands in the air. But he could not give me any direction for getting to the tin terror of Cato Manor. He had never seen the place.'

Conditions were even worse for Africans in the white rural areas than in the festering black slums of Durban and the other cities. South African farmers were generally inefficient and dependent for any profit at all on the cut costs of unskilled African labour. The second world war had created boom conditions for agricultural products, and during the past twenty years white farmers had increased the area they cultivated from 6·8 to over 10 million morgen, out of their total land holding of 102 million morgen. But this increase had only led, despite some mechanization, to ever-growing demands for unskilled labour. And this labour itself became ever more difficult to obtain as the war-stimulated development of industry drew Africans into the towns. Between 1936 and 1957, while South Africa's total non-white population had increased by 48%, its urban non-white population had bounded by 119%, from 1,843,000 to 4,040,000.

The farmers, however, had not met the challenge of regular working hours and higher wages which the towns offered, by significantly raising the conditions of African farm labourers. Government statistics revealed that in 1954 the average monthly income in cash and kind of a male farm labourer had been only 74 shillings, excluding free 'accommodation', while a subsequent survey by the South African Institute of Race Relations had assessed the average income for an African family of six in the white rural areas as £9 a month in cash and kind.

For the thirteenth issue of *Africa South* I commissioned James Fairbairn, South African correspondent of the British

New Statesman, to examine conditions on the white farms. And in an article, which he entitled 'The New Serfdom', he analysed the degree to which government policy was creating an enslaved rural labouring force, compelled to accept whatever conditions the white farmers felt ready to offer it, or starve.

Cato Manor or Windermere might be little more than traps of hunger and disease. But it was easy to see why the Africans in the white rural areas regarded them still as an escape.

'It has become almost impossible for farm workers or their families to settle in the towns. In theory, a farm worker may move from one farm to another. But, since 1952, matters have been so arranged that, in effect, no African farm labourer can leave his work without his employer's consent. No one may now employ an African over 16 years of age without his producing a reference book, which must be endorsed every month and in which the fact and date of discharge must be entered. To employ an African whose previous employer has not released him in this way is an offence. If a farmer refuses to accept a labourer's notice and refuses to enter a discharge in his book, there is nothing the labourer can do about it. If he leaves without an endorsement, he becomes a deserter, commits an offence, and cannot look for work on neighbouring farms. And even if his *baas* lets him go, he can only get another job as a farm labourer in the area or, if he is lucky enough to have a stake there, risk the starvation in the Reserves. The towns are closed to him; and in effect, he and his children and his children's children can be nothing but farm labourers, untouched by outlandish ideas such as minimum wages or maximum hours of work. Their lives are completely dependent on the paternalistic whims of their white *baas*, who may, if he wishes, forbid them religious and social gatherings, beer-brewing and drinking, and bar their children from school.

'Naturally, the realization of this new serfdom depends on the effectiveness of the white State's administrative machine, and here, as elsewhere, tyranny is being tempered by inefficiency. This and economic realities no doubt account for the fact that, while the years 1951–7 saw the Union's total African population increase by 14%, they increased its urban African population by 42% and the African population of "white" farms by only 17½% (from 2,120,000 to 2,500,000).

'The increasing measure of success which Nationalist farm labour policy is meeting with, however, may be judged by the fact that the number of adult male labourers increased by 19% (from 629,000 to 750,000). These latter figures indicate that the Nationalists are succeeding dramatically in reducing the number of squatters and labour-tenants.'

Of course, however much the South African government might have deplored such energy, the rest of Africa was not standing still, and I tried as far as possible to mirror its movement in the magazine. When the Rev. Claude de Mestral had written on the Belgian Congo in the third issue of *Africa South*, April–June 1957, he had portrayed a paternalism hardly disturbed by the nationalist upheaval throughout Asia and elsewhere in Africa, or the indigenous political movements beginning to flex their muscles in the Congo itself. Events since then had moved with startling speed. On the 4th of January 1959 there had been violent rioting in Leopoldville when 30,000 unemployed workers had marched in protest through the city, and the administration had announced territorial and communal elections for December of that year. In the event, this concession was to be considered inadequate by the new Congolese nationalist leaders, who were to insist upon – and, at the end of June 1960, receive – their independence. In the thirteenth issue of *Africa South*, I published the first in a series of three articles on the Congo by Colin Legum, African correspondent of the London *Observer*, who assessed the developments leading to independence and would subsequently detail the events that followed it, through the revolt of the Force Publique, the secession of Katanga, and the creation of a United Nations presence in the country.

The face of French West and Equatorial Africa, where some 25 million people inhabited an area of 7 million square kilometres, was also changing fast. In September 1958 General de Gaulle, newly brought to power as the President of the fifth

French Republic, had offered the black African colonies of France a free choice, by referendum, between complete independence and autonomy within a refashioned French Community. Guinea, by a vote of 1,136,000 to 57,000, had chosen complete independence, while the remaining eleven – The Central African Republic, the Congo Republic (Brazzaville), Dahomey, Gabon, the Ivory Coast, Mauritania, Niger, Senegal, Soudan (later the Republic of Mali), Tchad and Upper Volta – had for the moment chosen the Community. Leaders like Gabriel d'Arboussier of Senegal were speaking of a vast new coalescence of African states, the vision of a united continent.

'I am willing to forecast that within ten years from now we shall have come together to found a great new federal state, bilingual in French and English, that will include Ghana and Nigeria as well as our own West Africa. Not a unitary state … but a federation of federations, a loosely organized but highly progressive and modern society of 50 or 60 million African people.'

Such events and ideas gave uneasy dreams to those still deep in a colonial slumber.

The Congress campaign to boycott Nationalist products in South Africa had moved, with the encouragement of the Congress leadership, and the assistance of organizations like the All African Peoples Conference, into an international boycott of all South African goods. Jamaica had severed all commerce with South Africa, and the Trade Union Congress of Ghana had promised action as well. It seemed a promising enough beginning. Soon consumer boycotts would spread even through Europe, while the independent states of Africa itself would take administrative action to cut South African trade. In 1958 Ghana's imports from South Africa were worth £1,500,000; by 1961 they would shrink to £10,000. Nigeria's imports from South Africa in the same period would dwindle from £751,000 to £95,000; Sierra Leone's, from £164,000 to £69,000.

In August 1959 Julius Nyerere, President of the Tanganyika African National Union and soon to be Prime Minister of yet another independent African state, wrote to *Africa South* in warm support of the boycott.

'When I was a schoolboy, a friend of mine took me to the tailor one day and had me measured for a pair of shorts. We were great friends. His was mine and mine was his. He knew I needed a pair of shorts very badly. A few days later I got my pair of shorts, well made, fitting perfectly. I was proud of myself and proud of my friend. But it was not long before I discovered how my friend had obtained the money with which he had bought that pair of shorts for me. I returned it to him immediately. I could not disapprove of the manner in which the money had been obtained and still enjoy what the money had bought for me.

'It is this same principle which makes me now support the boycotting of South African goods. We in Africa hate the policies of the South African government. We abhor the semi-slave conditions under which our brothers and sisters in South Africa live, work and produce the goods we buy. We pass resolutions against the hideous system and keep hoping that the United Nations and the governments of the whole world will one day put pressure on the South African government to treat its non-European peoples as human beings.

'But these resolutions and prayers to the United Nations are not enough in themselves. Governments and democratic organizations grind very slowly. Individuals do not have to. The question then is what an individual can do to influence the South African government towards a human treatment of its non-white citizens.

'Can we honestly condemn a system and at the same time employ it to produce goods which we buy, and then enjoy with a clear conscience? Surely the customers of a business do more to keep it going than its shareholders. We who buy South African goods do more to support the system than the Nationalist government or Nationalist industrialists.

'Each one of us can remove his individual prop to the South African system by refusing to buy South African goods. There are millions of people in the world who support the South

African government in this way, and who can remove their support by the boycott. I feel it is only in this way that we can give meaning to our abhorrence of the system, and give encouragement to sympathetic governments of the world to act ...'

A few days before the letter was published in the thirteenth issue of the magazine, another letter had, piquantly, appeared in the *Cape Argus*. A more than usually imaginative supporter of white supremacy had written to propose that the South African government approach well-known moderates like Nyerere and, with offers of assistance in the economic development of their own territories, enlist their support against the extremism of the boycott.

Resistance in Natal had not been shattered by police violence. Far beyond Durban, in the rural areas, women demonstrated against government policy by destroying dipping tanks and sending tumultuous deputations to government officials. They set fire to sugar plantations, and the white population began to arm itself. By the 21st of August more than 10,000 women had been involved in disturbances, and 624 Africans had been sentenced to a total of 168 years' imprisonment and/or fines totalling £7,130. Soon afterwards 365 women were arrested at Ixopo alone, convicted and sentenced each to a fine of £35 or four months imprisonment – a total of 122 years' imprisonment or fines of £12,810.

The deportation from Durban of women not legally entitled to live there had helped to spread disaffection and political consciousness into the more remote areas; but the resentments covered the whole spectrum of government policy, from Bantu education to compulsory land resettlement schemes, from increased taxation to the cruelty of the pass laws. As the Director of the Bantu Administration Department in Durban himself admitted, however, the crucial issue was poverty. 'The basic and ultimate reason is an economic one – the poverty of the urban Bantu; the discrepancy between his earning capacity and his cost of living; his inability to meet the demands of modern times in a city modelled on the Western way of life;

his inability even to meet the barest necessity of life, to feed, clothe, educate and house himself and his family.' From an official charged with putting into effect government policy, this was a damaging admission indeed.

I invited Professor Leo Kuper, Dean of the Faculty of Social Science at the University of Natal and author of 'Passive Resistance in South Africa', to contribute his analysis of developments in Natal to the fourteenth issue of the magazine, January–March 1960. He drew especial attention to the growing participation of women in African resistance and measured its significance.

'The involvement of the women has meant the deeper involvement of the men. They are embittered by baton charges against the women, by their arrest and imprisonment. They are shamed by the militant role of the women, by the imputation that they are allowing them to fight their battles because police action will be less violent against women than against men. But above all, the woman represents the home. During the Cato Manor disturbances, the women sang, "You touch women, you touch grinding stones". The militancy of the women threatens the family hearth.

'In consequence political consciousness had been heightened among the Zulu people, a remarkable development given the general political backwardness of the population of Natal, both white and non-white. Some attempt was made to fasten responsibility on the African National Congress. This is a conventional allegation. Any disturbance must be due to Congress or Communists or both, and the allegation has the function of deflecting analysis away from the ideologies of the government. Congress disclaimed responsibility – I have no doubt personally that the demonstrations were largely spontaneous – and immediately sought to restrain violence. It has now set itself the task of guiding the new political consciousness in constructive non-violent action along the lines of Congress policy. The task is made all the more difficult by the introduction of the raw inexperienced cadres of the women, and the deeper emotional involvements of the men.'

While non-white resistance was increasingly taking a violent shape, the government was constantly expanding its tyranny. In the early years of Nationalist rule, the press and the courts had circumscribed government terror. But now the Nationalists were preparing legislation to deal at last with the press, and they had consistently over the years been moving towards the complete captivity of the courts. Dr Verwoerd himself, while Minister of Native Affairs, had said, 'I have had experience of judicial people and heaven help me if they ever have anything important to decide.' He was rapidly ensuring that such judicial decisions as had to be taken – and he was all the while extending the area of executive authority – would be taken by his servants alone. It was, of course, imprudent to publish criticism of the judiciary. Even those judges still left who were personally hostile to the Nationalists remained zealous in defending their dignity, and I had tried during the years of publishing *Africa South*, as far as was consonant with frank political criticism, not to risk imprisonment for contempt of court. The time had now arrived, however, when I felt it dishonest to preserve silence on the judiciary any longer. I approached Leslie Rubin, who represented the Africans of the Cape Province in the Senate and who was himself a Doctor of Laws, to write an article for the fourteenth issue on the state of the judiciary. He readily agreed, and we decided to entitle it 'Nationalist Contempt of Court'. He quoted numerous statements by Cabinet Ministers and other leaders of the Nationalist Party in criticism of the judiciary and in confirmation of their resolution to make it subservient. And he showed how the government was ignoring the principle of seniority in choosing and promoting judges.

'The Hon. Mr Justice Botha was appointed Judge-President of the Orange Free State Provincial Division 22 months after he had been appointed to the Bench, and at a time when he was junior to most of his colleagues on the Bench and to 28 other puisne judges in the country. Among recent appointments to the Appellate Division, one is junior to 15, another to 16, and a third to 23 puisne judges in the country. The present Chief

Justice, the Hon. Mr Justice Steyn, who had been law adviser
to various government departments, was appointed to the
Bench in the Transvaal (in the face of vigorous protests by the
Transvaal Bar) in 1951, and to the Appellate Division in 1955.
He is junior to 2 Judges of Appeal, and in judicial experience
to 17 of the 59 judges in South Africa. His appointment as
Chief Justice overlooked Appeal Judges Schreiner (17 years at
the Bar, appointed to the Bench in 1937 and to the Appellate
Division in 1945, who acted as Chief Justice) and Hoexter
(called to the Bar in 1918, appointed to the Bench in 1938, and
to the Appellate Division in 1949). The Hon. Mr Justice Beyers
was appointed to the Bench of the Cape Provincial Division in
1955, and to the Appellate Division in 1958. In 1959 he returned
to the Cape Provincial Division as Judge-President of a court
which includes 3 judges senior to him in judicial experience.'

Ever since the Nationalists had gained power in 1948, South
Africa had survived in a state of suspended terror. The
mechanism of tyranny had been developed with patience and
care – in the self-perpetuaton of Nationalist rule through electoral delimitation and disfranchisement, in the punishments
with which the law had been loaded against any effective forms
of opposition, in the functions and powers with which an
obsequious parliament had dressed officialdom and, particularly, the police. Political opponents were banned and
banished without trial; the security police pried everywhere,
listening and scribbling, pursuing and interrogating, with all the
bland insolence of their inviolable dossiers; passports and permits were seized or refused without reason or appeal. Yet, on
the crudest comparison with consummate terrors, like Nazi
Germany or contemporary Portugal, the press and the courts
in South Africa had protected the law from persistent and open
outrage. Political antagonists had not just disappeared, while
their families endured exemplary victimization; trial in public
court had remained the prerequisite of imprisonment and
execution. The law might have been defaced beyond recognition, but it was still standing. Whatever one's judgment
of the treason trial, its interminable proceedings and the

vagrancy of the prosecution, the accused had not simply been rounded up and shot, or shovelled secretly into concentration camps.

Now the judiciary and the press – the two surviving safeguards of civil rights – were finally being undermined. The Deputy Minister of the Interior announced the government's intention to introduce internal censorship in accordance with the report of the Commission of Enquiry into Undesirable Publications. And the Minister of Justice threatened legislation to ease the retirement of recalcitrant judges.

Despite ceaseless appeals by the Congress leadership for calm, violence continued to rack the rural areas of Natal. But the only Nationalist reply to violence was greater violence, and the growing reply of its victims was more violence still. South Africa was moving towards a collision of terrors with self-accelerating speed.

While the government had entrenched itself in power, the United Party had been wandering in bewilderment through the wilderness of defeat. Unable to rival the Nationalists in the ruthless promotion of white supremacy, it had shown itself resolute only in its refusal to provide a principled alternative. Patiently it had waited for the Nationalists to split, or for the electorate to turn in a sudden upheaval of despair against the government. But why those in possession of power should sacrifice themselves to division, or why a white electorate should ever turn in despair from a government that was giving it precisely what it had itself demanded, the leaders of the United Party were unable to discover or explain. In consequence they had presented to the electorate a display of craven ambiguity, assaulting in debate the more brutal measures of racial repression and then meekly trooping to the government side as soon as the vote was called. Their reward had been their crushing defeat in the general election of 1953, and five years later a surge towards the government so strong that almost two-thirds of the seats in the House of Assembly had fallen before it.

Increasingly the small liberal wing of the party had agitated

for a change of policy. Opposition by mimicry had been discarded by the electorate; the presentation of some real alternative to apartheid could hardly meet with a more ignominious
rejection and might well lure the electorate at last; and, in any
event, the United Party had a duty to provide the country with
a policy of escape from racial clash. The right wing, however,
under the leadership of Douglas Mitchell, Chairman of the
United Party in the stronghold of Natal, interpreted defeat
quite differently. The voters had discarded the opposition because they distrusted the mischievous liberals in it. Victory
could only lie with those who promised most persuasively to
keep white supremacy secure. And now Dr Verwoerd himself
was providing the opposition with a real opportunity to outbid
the Nationalists in intransigence. The government's creation of
small scattered Bantu homelands, in pursuit of the long heralded objective of territorial segregation, could be attacked as
endangering the integrity of South Africa and the whole traditional structure of white rule. The liberals would be forced to
withdraw either from the party or from their own liberal positions, and the opposition could then approach the electorate
as safely purged, a pledge to retain the racial rule which the
government itself was so irresponsibly risking with its Bantu-
stan experiments.

When the annual congress of the United Party met at Bloemfontein on the 11th of August 1959, the right wing proved to
have massed the overwhelming majority of delegates behind it.
Careless of its own undertaking in 1936 to purchase up to 7
million morgen of land for African occupation in return for the
removal of African male voters in the Cape from the common
roll, the party decided to oppose all further acquisition of such
land if it were to be used in swelling the government's Bantu-
stans. Twelve M.P.s, almost a quarter of its parliamentary
strength, resigned from the party, one to sit in the Assembly as
an independent, the other eleven to form in November, at a
conference in Johannesburg, the Progressive Party. Dr Jan
Steytler, M.P., formerly leader of the United Party in the Cape
and soon to become parliamentary leader of the Progressives,

issued a statement to explain his own resignation and that of his colleagues.

'We believe the time has come when white people should stop taking important decisions affecting non-white people without proper regard as to how the latter think and feel. Since the Bloemfontein congress we have, in fact, consulted a number of responsible Natives and we have found that they deplore in the strongest terms this decision taken at congress. They most certainly regard it as a breach of faith on the part of the white man. It is our view that South Africa cannot afford political stratagems of this kind, which destroy the trust and respect of the Native people in the guardianship of the white man ... We have come to the conclusion that the temper of the Bloemfontein congress showed a complete unwillingness on the part of most delegates to face up to the challenge of contemporary events here and in Africa. The impression we have is of a party congress reluctant to move with the times, unwilling even to interpret its own principles in a forward-looking manner. From the tone of congress we believe that many delegates want to fight the Nationalists with the weapons of race fear and race hatred.'

The tone of the statement itself, with its deferential reference to the 'guardianship of the white man' and its careful allusion to 'responsible Natives', disclosed a design that smacked a great deal more of the paternalist than the progressive. At first, the press did not take the break-away too seriously. It seemed improbable that any new political grouping could make significant inroads upon the monopoly of white opposition held by the United Party. And then Harry Oppenheimer, South Africa's premier millionaire, Chairman of the massive Anglo-American Corporation and De Beers, which dominate the country's gold and diamond production, announced that he was resigning from the United Party, since he felt himself to be 'in general sympathy with the Progressive group'. Though he did not formally adhere to the new party, it was widely rumoured that he had promised it his financial support. Influential figures in industry and commerce stirred, shook themselves, and padded after him. The large-circulation English-language newspapers, till then assiduously and even abjectly loyal to the United Party, began to note its inadequacies; several openly welcomed the Progressive Party as an alternative opposition. On few occasions had the prestige and power of the Oppenheimer name been more dramatically displayed.

The Johannesburg conference of the Progressive Party in November proclaimed as its objective a policy for the peaceful and prosperous co-existence of the different racial groups. It voted for the repeal of several basic apartheid laws, including the Population Registration Act (which compels every citizen to carry a racial identity card), the Group Areas Act, the Extension of University Education Act (which expelled non-whites from the mixed universities and established tribal colleges for Africans), and the Immorality Act. It called for the abolition of the pass system and the dropping of industrial colour bars. It advocated trade union rights for skilled and semi-skilled non-whites, and it proposed, doubtless with a calculating eye on the Oppenheimer mines, trade union facilities for unskilled non-whites 'under government supervision'. Finally, it established a Commission of Experts under Advocate Donald Molteno, a former African representative in the House of Assembly, to recommend a programme of constitutional reforms. Harry Oppenheimer himself agreed to join the Commission.

Most leaders of the Congress Alliance, however, for whom the mining empires and the government had always seemed indistinguishable oppressions, remained unimpressed. They saw no reason why the birth of the Progressive Party should promise them an escape from white supremacy. If anything, it fortified their disillusionment with parliamentary politics. The United Party, purged of its liberals, was now a uniform reaction. And the Progressive Party, with its opulent appearance of reform, sought power from an electorate that cared only for the preservation of its privileges. How could such a party hope to arrive at government? And if, fantastically, it did, what then? Such were just stirrings on the surface. In the deeps, the tumult of a united non-white resistance had still to form. For African and Indian had not yet merged their differences completely, while the one and a half million Coloured were still, inertly, appealing for white compassion.

On Wednesday, the 28th of October 1959, at Paarl, the centre of the Western Cape's fruit and vineyard belt, Mrs Elizabeth Mafekeng was served with a notice, signed by the Minister for Bantu Administration, banishing her to a place called Southey in the hot wasteland of the North-West, hundreds of miles away. There had been no trial, and no conviction, and there was no appeal against the order. She was given 12 days in which to prepare for her going, to say goodbye to the home she had lived in for 32 years, her husband and 10 of her 11 children, perhaps for ever. Her youngest child, a daughter two months old, was permitted to accompany her to the little cluster of huts that constituted South Africa's first concentration camp for women. The indictment against her was crushing. She was President of the African Food and Canning Workers' Union, and Vice-President of the Women's League of the African National Congress. In 1955 she had gone, as the South African delegate, to an International Food Workers' Conference in Bulgaria. She had also travelled to China, to Sweden and to Britain. She had participated in the 1952 defiance campaign, and she had marched to Pretoria in order to protest against the extension of the pass laws to women. On the 2nd of October 1959, she had been arrested after leading a demonstration in Paarl against the pass laws, but the charge had been dismissed in court.

As an active member of Congress, Mrs Mafekeng knew what she would find in Southey. For there were other such camps for those who had been banished before her – a dozen huts on the bare, baked veld, with only the sun and the flat earth for 50 or more miles around. One exile had written from his new home on the Glen Red Farm near Vryburg in the North-West Cape: 'I am placed in a tin house with no windows and only one big door, a house that is very cold in winter and very hot in summer. I have received no grant from the government that I may live. I am in a land of thorns and sand only.' Mrs Mafekeng was being treated with greater generosity. The government promised to pay her £2 a month for her needs. She would not be permitted to move without official permission.

Writing in the fifteenth issue of *Africa South*, April–June 1960, Myrna Blumberg reported the conversation that she had had over the telephone with the Native Commissioner in Vryburg, who was to be in charge of Mrs Mafekeng's welfare. 'This is a cattle farm with the ... ah ... vegetation of the district. She will have two rooms furnished, of course, very simply. The nearest families are about 100 yards away, European engineers on the farm. She could work as ... ah ... a domestic servant, in one of their houses.'

On Friday, the 6th of November, 3 days before Mrs Mafekeng had to leave for Southey, groups of African and Coloured workers began to gather outside her small white terraced cottage in Paarl. By Monday morning there were some 3,000 of them standing in the road, waiting. Throughout the day they waited. Mrs Mafekeng did not appear. The crowd grew, and suddenly, with the coming of night, its resentment burst into riot. For three hours it engaged in open battle with the police. It stoned and overturned cars, attacked and wrecked a nearby white-owned shop. Paarl hospital that night treated 8 non-whites and 2 whites for injuries; one non-white later died. On the following night violence broke out again. Again the crowd clashed with the police, and left its injured behind it. But the government had sent reinforcements backed by Saracen armoured cars from Cape Town, and peace was soon restored to the smug oak-lined streets of Paarl. Meanwhile, Mrs Mafekeng had eluded the grasp of the police and, with her baby in her arms, had slipped from the back door of her house and been driven across country and over the border into the British Protectorate of Basutoland. Dr Verwoerd commented that the British government could 'have all the Mafekengs'. And Mr Mafekeng replied: 'I am not willing to be dumped with my children in the bush of Basutoland. People are not to be moved around like cattle. I have worked here for 24 years for the same firm. What I want is my wife back. We were legally married in church, yet the government removes her from me and the children without law. I came home from work and found her gone. She had run away to escape the government, and she couldn't even say goodbye to me.'

Cape Town, usually so confident in the docility of its Coloured population and its record of quiet race relations, was profoundly shaken. The rioting at Paarl, less than 40 miles away, had been overwhelmingly Coloured. It was disturbing enough that the working Coloured population should be showing signs of deep political discontent. Even more disturbing was that such discontent should have centred around the figure of an African trade unionist. The *Cape Times* editorial of November 11th condemned the rioting. But it continued: 'Violence is only roused in conditions of violence, where feelings are running high because of real or fancied grievances.

'The basic point to remember is that Mrs Mafekeng has been flung out of the home where she has lived for over 30 years because of some secret police reports and upon the nod of a Minister. At the stroke of an official pen she has been deprived of practically every right that makes life worth living to most human beings. Down the ages human beings have been reacting violently to just this kind of treatment, and fighting to have it removed from the conduct of governments ...

'Clashes between the unfortunate police, who have to meet the consequences of government policy, and the non-white masses, who are infuriated by it, are becoming monotonously regular. There have been 105 major clashes of this order since 1948, and the rate seems to be increasing, for 33 of them occurred in the past two years. We are going deeper and deeper into a blood-tinged bog of racial troubles – and the government shows only a crass determination to go in deeper still.'

The Cape Nationalist newspaper, *Die Burger*, reacted rather differently. 'The next time people have to be banished, they must not be given time to organize protests ...'

I had begun to write on South Africa for publications

abroad. To Britain's *New Statesman* of February 28th, 1959, I contributed a long supplement on 'The Creeping Tragedy of South Africa', which told the story of the 1957 bus boycott, traced its causes in the poverty of the best-paid Africans, and detailed the principal laws of white supremacy. I assessed the potential of non-white resistance and concluded that the Congress Movement, still operating in a neon world of semilegality, was unprepared for any showdown with the government, but would doubtless be equipped soon enough by being driven underground.

For the *Spectator* of November 6th, I wrote the story of Mrs Mafekeng's banishment, and of other banishments, like that of Chief Mopeli, which had taken place in the past ten years and which had escaped public attention altogether.

In 1950 the Africans of the Witzieshoek Reserve in the Orange Free State had rebelled against government seizure of their cattle in one of those 'agricultural betterment' schemes which leave the Africans even poorer than they find them and so force ever-larger numbers into migrant labour on the white farms or down the white mines. Chief Mopeli, ruler of the rebellious tribe, had been arrested, tried and sentenced to one year's imprisonment in Johannesburg's Fort. But he had served his sentence unbent, and on the day of his release the government had banished him to Bothaspruit, in the wastes of the Eastern Transvaal. In 1958, still defiant, he had been banished again, to Frenchdale, in the semi-desert of the Northern Cape, near the Bechuanaland border.

I maintained that the whole civilized world bore some responsibility for these banishments by the idleness of its antagonism to apartheid. And I suggested that the British people in particular should ask themselves whether the Commonwealth had not become a vast moral connivance, upon the shoulders of which the South African government could risk its postures in safety.

I could not address meetings in South Africa any more. I could not travel abroad to address meetings there. But I could write my loathing of the South African government and its multiplying cruelties. Never before had *Africa South* seemed so vital to me. In its pages, and in the pages of a few magazines abroad, I could speak in spite of my ban.

The image of South Africa abroad was increasingly distasteful. This in itself, of course, did not unduly distress that section of the world's business community with interests in the country. Capital has never displayed too tender a conscience over unjustly governed societies – provided that, like South Africa, the returns on investment have been sufficiently consoling. The continual increase in violence that marked Nationalist control of South Africa, however, was adding insecurity to distaste. Foreign investors showed a growing reluctance to gamble on the country's future and were withdrawing capital at an alarming rate. Clearly, the opposition business community in South Africa itself, whether United Party or Progressive, would welcome a change of government – but not a change so considerable as to transfer power from white into non-white hands, and no change at all if the only conditions for it involved substantial economic sacrifice.

And so the South African Foundation was launched – an association of dutiful government and white opposition businessmen, with wide and influential representation from the press, to lift the face of South Africa abroad. Among its members was Anton Rupert, Afrikanerdom's most successful industrialist, whose great trek into tobacco had unfurled the flags of the *volk* as far afield as Canada and England; and Sir Francis de Guingand, a high-ranking officer during the second world war who now cultivated a profitable South African retirement among the orchards of British big business. Adding a trans-Atlantic flavour was Mr Charles Engelhard, the American platinum millionaire, whom gold promised, Verwoerd willing, to make even richer. And the presence in the Foundation of Harry Oppenheimer provided the final disenchantment for those few non-white leaders who had hoped for some sudden salvation from the birth of the Progressive Party.

In my leader for the fifteenth issue, entitled 'Foundation

Cream', I questioned the activities of the foreign investors involved, and drew what I believed to be the logical conclusion
of the alliance between Progressive Party and Foundation.

Mr Charles Engelhard himself was hanging his assets from the
neck of white supremacy, to fall in the basket if the head should
ever have to roll. And the choice was not solely his. He was a
citizen of the United States, acting as a self-employed public
relations officer for the government of a foreign country to
which the vast majority of its citizens were irreconcilably opposed. It seemed reasonable to ask what facilities the State
Department would be likely to afford an American millionaire
who devoted his energy and assets to confirming in power the
present Hungarian regime. His conduct undoubtedly endeared
him, together with his country, to the Nationalist government.
It was speedily, however, making the non-whites suspicious
of the precise part that foreign investors, with the countries
that housed them, were playing in the perpetuation of white
supremacy.

Mr Oppenheimer's membership of the Foundation had
different implications. For he was not only a public supporter
of the new Progressive Party, he was commonly reputed to be its
pocket. Whether or not his cheque book gave him complete
control over the party's policy would have to remain the province of an enlightened speculation; but his influence would be
popularly measured as paramount, and non-white South
Africa would judge the Progressives accordingly. Loyalty to
the South African government abroad and support for the aspirations of the non-white peoples were increasingly exclusive
of each other; and whoever addressed himself to the first would
soon enough find himself repudiated by the partisans of the
other.

The road to white–black co-operation in the fashioning of
South African democracy might have many detours; but the
South African Foundation, as at present paved, was unlikely
to be one of them.

'The new beauty parlour, we know, has many proprietors
and even more willy-nilly associates; but its clientele is of

necessity limited to only one paying customer. And she, un-
happily, is old as well as ugly. One wonders for how long she
can stand the strain of being made over with quite so much
industry. Too scanty a treatment is unlikely to do much for
her looks, but too energetic an overhaul runs the risk of reducing her to collapse. We do not doubt that the proprietors are
clever at their work; we merely think it prudent to ask them
whether they are fully aware of the gamble they are taking.
When their one client dies, as die she must one day – doubtless
the sooner for her frenzied attempts at rejuvenation – will there
be time and opportunity left to find another? And if the company goes into a final forced liquidation, are the proprietors
and their associates likely to escape the effects of its insol-
vency? The search for beauty, we are told, ennobles and rewards. The attempt to disguise ugliness instead promises to
prove not only degrading but costly.'

More than ever I saw the pure pursuit of money as degrading. I had no reason to suppose that millionaires like Engelhard and Oppenheimer were not decent human beings in their
conduct towards their families and friends. It was even possible
that they gave lavishly of their resources to assist a multitude
of good works in secret; their public benefactions were certainly not notable. But they seemed content enough not only
to accumulate such resources, through the vicious organization
of South African society, but even, when that organization
came under serious attack, to excuse and help protect it from
destruction. And they were not unusual in that. The extent of
their resources alone selected them for comment. How many
equally decent, even rather more than usually kind human
beings –some few of them in the lounge of 6 Avenue Disandt –
had I not heard excusing the measures employed by the South
African government to shatter non-white political campaigns.
They were doubtless considerate of their own servants and
even sometimes strongly affected by a paragraph in the papers
which described some particular personal suffering of apartheid. They could always be counted upon for a small dona-
tion towards the running costs of a crèche for African babies.

I

But militantly mounted campaigns of non-white resistance threatened to drain their pockets, and it was in their pockets, like some certificate for a high-yielding equity, that they kept their consciences.

When first I returned from the United States to start *Africa South*, and sold my preference shares in Greatermans Stores, I joined briefly in the feverish national gamble on the 'Kaffir' market. Of course, I did so for the most pardonable of motives. If the capital I possessed was inadequate to finance the magazine, I would swell it by shrewd speculation. Whenever I could spare a half-hour or so, I would rush guiltily across to the office of my stockbroker and watch the ticker-tape jerking out the relapses or recoveries of the day. And soon I found myself wondering: if the political front would only remain quiet for another month, till the results of the bore-hole in that rich area were announced, I would be able perhaps to pay for another issue of the magazine. I sold all my gold shares, at a slight on balance loss, and stripped my allegiance to the bone.

I remember still how the rich and renowned progressive, who had given valuable and even courageous service in the cause of more comfortable race relations, exploded to me once in sheer exasperation at the stupidities of the Nationalist government. 'If they would only allow a small propertied black middle class. It would be the strongest barrier of all against revolution.'

In London, Paris and New York, as in Johannesburg, Cape Town and Durban, the decent human beings scan the fluctuations of their shares in South African mines and industry, and pray – or work – against non-white rebellion until they can extricate their own money. If only the political front will remain quiet, and they can retrieve their investments, with a small profit perhaps … The Foundation has done its job well. In part through its influential diligence, the prestige of Dr Verwoerd and his government, within white South Africa and abroad, stands higher today than it has ever done. Foreign capital, which scurried from the country year after year, is beginning to return. Large British, French and American firms, with growing West German and Japanese participation, are building factories and oil refineries, contracting for the output of mines, acquiring shares in South Africa's easy prosperity. White rule seems so much more secure than first impressions – or malicious reports – once pictured it. And, of course, this replenished confidence overseas serves to make white rule even more secure. It matters little, after all, how money is made, provided that it is made.

The Commission of Experts set up by the Progressives to discover a franchise policy on which to campaign, issued its report in November 1960, to advocate two voters' rolls. It proposed a standard 4 level of schooling and an income of £360 a year as qualifications for the common roll; the special roll, open to all adults, would elect only 10% of parliament. This, however, was a majority, not a unanimous proposal. A minority report signed by Dr Zac de Beer, the Progressive Party's Executive Chairman, and by Harry Oppenheimer, advocated instead a common roll qualification of £360 in income a year and a standard 6 level of schooling. It was not altogether surprising that, at a subsequent party conference to discuss the report, it should have been the minority report which was accepted. *Contact*, the liberal fortnightly, strongly criticized this franchise policy, on the grounds that it would exclude 98% of the country's non-white population from effective participation in government. It calculated that only 130,000 non-whites, out of an adult non-white population of some eight million, would be placed on the common roll. It concluded – and it was difficult to deny its logic – that the programme of the new party was rooted in the dogma of white supremacy.

Throughout 1959 events moved swiftly towards a massive racial clash. I began to write a political fantasy around the Johannesburg boycott of 1957; but, inevitably, it turned into a study of attempted revolution. Skipping mischievously through African folk-lore is the tiny figure of the tokolosh, a sort of African Puck to whom responsibility is ascribed for anything from an accident with the washing to a sexual misadventure. The tokolosh, in his wry gaiety and resilience. seemed to me an obvious symbol for the will of the African to

survive and surmount the assaults of white domination. Yet
the mood of the country itself during that year dictated the
development of the story. Out of the bus boycott, and with the
presiding presence of the tokolosh, African resistance turned to
a general strike. Police tore through the township, where a mass
meeting of Africans was being held, and left the dead and the
injured twisted behind them. The strike continued, and white
industry and commerce ground helplessly to a stop. And then,
adding to the hunger and want already big in the township,
the summer floods broke the back of African resistance. Turning away from the tokolosh, and their trust in themselves, the
Africans of the township walked, this time in defeat, to their
work in the white city. The events which were to shake white
South Africa for a short while from its complacency were only
a few months away; in the weeks that I spent in writing
'The Tokolosh', they seemed inescapably imminent.

In 1954 the South African Department of Native Affairs
had assumed absolute control over the administration of Africans in the international trust territory of South West Africa.
In just one more challenge to the authority of the United
Nations, the South African government decided that the inhabitants of the old location in Windhoek, the capital, should
move to a new township, Katutura, at a safer distance from the
white areas. The Africans refused to move. The rents in Katutura would be substantially higher than in the old location, and
the distance at which it was situated from their places of work
would compel the Africans to meet transport costs that
their wages were far too low already to permit. In any event,
they rejected the whole basis of the planned mass removal.
They believed that they enjoyed a right to the land which they
occupied, that to deprive them of it would violate the whole
spirit in which the mandate of South West Africa was supposed to be administered.

During 1958 and 1959, officials of the Windhoek town council and of the South African government made several fruitless
attempts at persuading the Africans to move. On the 1st of
November 1959 the local authorities began evaluating the

houses in the Damara section of the location, in preparation for a forced removal of the inhabitants. On the 4th of December the Administrator of South West Africa refused even to meet a protest deputation. And on the 10th of December eleven Africans were killed and 50 more injured, 32 of them seriously, in clashes between the police and the inhabitants of the location.

The United Nations stirred. On the 18th of December its Committee on South West Africa resolved to cable the South African government.

'The Committee conveys to you its gravest concern over the recent regrettable incidents in Windhoek, resulting in the loss of life and bodily injury of many residents of the location. The Committee urgently requests the mandatory power to desist immediately from this deplorable use of force and from proceeding further with the enforced removal of the residents to the new site at Katutura. The Committee considers these actions of the mandatory power to be in complete disregard of human rights and dignity.'

On the 21st of December the Committee passed a resolution similar in wording to its cable and dispatched it both to the South African government and to the General Assembly of the United Nations. Another resolution drew the attention of the Secretary-General to the situation in the territory. The independent African states sent an urgent appeal to the Secretary-General for his intervention. In the weeks that followed, it seemed increasingly probable that the United Nations would be forced to consider some action over the deteriorating situation in South West Africa. And then South Africa itself erupted into racial violence on the 21st of March 1960, in the African township of Sharpeville near the steel city of Vereeniging.

CHAPTER SEVEN

EXILE

IN 1946 Dr A. B. Xuma, then President-General of the African National Congress, entered into an agreement with Dr Y. M. Dadoo, then President of the Transvaal Indian Congress, and Dr G. M. Naicker, President of the Natal Indian Congress, by which the African and Indian political movements would work together on all issues of common concern in the struggle against white domination. This agreement was confirmed at the annual conference of the African National Congress in the same year, and formed the basis for the joint African–Indian defiance campaign of 1952.

In 1953 the white Congress of Democrats and the South African Coloured People's Organization were founded, and soon both were campaigning in close association with the African and Indian Congresses. Then, on the 26th of June 1955, at Kliptown in the Transvaal, some 3,000 delegates of all races, in the main representing the Indian and urban African masses, adopted the Freedom Charter, as the political basis of a Congress Alliance, with a National Consultative Committee to co-ordinate the activities of the five constituent organizations – the African National Congress, the South African Indian Congress, the South African Coloured People's Organization, the Congress of Democrats, and the South African Congress of Trade Unions. The Preamble to the Charter stressed the inter-racial character of the movement.

We, the people of South Africa, declare for all our country and the world to know –

That South Africa belongs to all who live in it, black and white, and that no government can justly claim authority unless it is based on the will of all the people:

That our people have been robbed of their birth-right to land, liberty and peace by a form of government founded on injustice and inequality:

That our country will never be prosperous or free until all our people live in brotherhood, enjoying equal rights and opportunities:

That only a democratic state, based on the will of all the people, can secure to all their birth-right without distinction of colour, race, sex or belief:

And therefore, we, the people of South Africa, black and white together – equals, countrymen and brothers – adopt this Freedom Charter. And we pledge ourselves to strive together, sparing nothing of our strength and courage, until the democratic changes here set out have been won.

The Charter then detailed the specific aspirations of the Alliance, in terms little different from those of the Universal Declaration of Human Rights, and concluded with the dedication –

'These freedoms we will fight for, side by side, throughout our lives, until we have won our liberty.'

From early in 1957, a group within the African National Congress began agitating for more militant resistance to the government and an end to the inter-racial alliance of the Freedom Charter. Calling themselves Africanists, the dissidents were most vociferous in the Transvaal, where they collected round a periodical, *The Africanist*, edited by Robert Mangaliso Sobukwe, an Assistant in Bantu Languages at the University of the Witwatersrand. Increasingly they assailed the A.N.C. leadership for participating in an alliance which 'watered down African nationalism', and relying largely on the personal following of Josias Madzunya, whose passionate black racialism had acquired some small popular allegiance in the African townships of Johannesburg, they aimed at displacing the leadership of the Transvaal A.N.C. altogether.

In March 1958 a National Workers' Conference was held at

the African township of Newclare in Johannesburg to call a
national stay-at-home for the week of the 1958 general election,
in protest against the travesty of democratic franchise which
the poll would represent. Delegates to the conference had been
specially elected throughout the country, and though the mass
came, of course, from the A.N.C., all the constituent organizations of the Congress Alliance were represented. I had travelled
up from Cape Town by car with three African and two white
delegates and had arrived in Johannesburg on Friday afternoon, the day before the conference was due to be held. On
Saturday it rained, with the fitful pelting of a Transvaal
summer, and when we arrived at Congress Square in Newclare,
we found only the cruising cars of the Special Branch and a
few furtive flags. The conference had been postponed until the
Sunday.

At ten o'clock on the following morning, under a hot blue
sky, we drove into a tumultuous Newclare. The whole township glittered with the noise and movement of a festival, and
long lines of shuffling, dancing Africans, dressed in the green,
gold and black that are the Congress colours, and flourishing
Congress banners, posters and flags, were moving through the
streets to the already crowded dust brown square. I felt again
that sudden surge of complete emotional commitment, that
flow of elation and triumph which had swept me before at
demonstrations of African resistance. Here, despite the threats
of strong government action which had diligently been reported in the press, despite the confusion of the last-minute
postponement, despite the sullen Special Branch radio cars and
armed police around the square, was a demonstration of joy,
of a great glad resilience far more formidable, it seemed to me,
than any outburst of resentment or fury could be. In the
snatches of song by pulsating groups of women, in the very
silences of the expectant old men from far-off rural areas, there
sounded a rhythm of challenge.

Before parking the car I drove around the square and saw,
on a little hill overlooking the crowd, a large group of khaki-
clothed police with Sten guns in their hands and a throbbing

radio car. I waited for the anger which had always washed me before at the sight of this force, straining for the sudden quick command to fall upon the women with their songs and their flags, the children with their cheap sweets, the earnest gesticulating huddles of young men near the platform. But I felt instead the celebration of the crowd below. And I didn't care.

Taking my seat at the press table, I waited for the meeting to begin. Behind me was a rusted lorry on which the speakers sat, and in front, on the other side of a long table at which members of the Special Branch scribbled in their notebooks, was the murmuring crowd, 10,000 people and more by now, constantly swollen by further streams from the streets around. The speeches began, and half listening, I watched Colonel Spengler, head of the Special Branch, as he sat scowling no more than two yards away. Suddenly he picked up a powerful pair of binoculars and trained them on me. I don't suppose there is anything on earth more disconcerting than to be stared at from a distance of two yards by huge blue discs at the end of a pair of binoculars. I began to itch all over, to speculate crazily on what his reaction would be if I suddenly got up, walked towards him, and snatched the binoculars from his face. The blue discs did not move, and though I turned several times to watch the speakers, the discs were always there, staring at me, when I looked back. Then I smiled, nudged the reporters on either side of me, pointed obviously at the binoculars, and Colonel Spengler scowled, turned round, and trained his large blue discs on the crowd behind him.

It was in the early afternoon, when a young African woman was assailing the pass laws, her voice rising and wheeling through the air, that a song started somewhere at the back of the crowd. Suddenly there was a circle of dancing women, holding their pass books in their hands and singing 'Li ea chisoa li pasa' (The passes are being burnt). It was the song of the women of Winburg, in the Orange Free State, who had burnt their passes in 1956 and gone in their defiant hundreds to prison. The crowd rose murmuring to its feet, and the journalists climbed excitedly on to the table. One of the women struck a match and held it up to her pass-book. And I saw Spengler stretch out his hand to the field telephone in front of him. In that moment, everything seemed all at once to stand still. Pass burning was an attack on the law at its weakest joint and, knowing this, the police had always reacted to it with fury. I imagined them on the little hill near by, lifting their Sten guns and shooting at us in one splutter of rage after the other, while we scurried helplessly to escape. And the crowd itself, brooding over the persistent wrongs which the speaker had cited, was clearly uncowed, waiting as well for the command that would unleash its own power. Two more matches were lit, and the women danced their passes tantalizingly over the flames. And then the woman at the microphone shouted above the rising murmur of the crowd at the song itself. This was not the time to give the police the excuse for which they longed. See, how they waited, how they wanted it. A time would come for burning the passes, all of them, one day, but not now. The women at the back paused in their song and sat down, and the crowd turned with a low murmur towards the platform again. I saw Spengler drop his hand from the field telephone, and I felt a strange mingling of relief and dejection.

The conference continued, but flat now, its effervescence gone. Only at the end, in the dusk, when the delegates voted their resolution, did the crowd rouse itself to the glad tumult of the beginning. On the 16th of April, white South Africa would troop to the polls in the ceremony of its general election. From Monday the 14th, the beginning of election week, the Africans, Indians and Coloured, with the sprinkling of whites who supported them, would join in a national stay-at-home, to ballot by abstention.

The Prime Minister, then the dying J. G. Strijdom, threatened retaliation 'with the full might of the state'. Leaders of the United Party, fearful of being outstripped in the race of repression, noisily called upon the government to take firm action against Congress. The police force, and then the army, were called into readiness against the threat of a general strike, and newspapers, ranging from the Nationalist and

United Party dailies down to the docile 'Bantu Press', predicted failure, a savage reaction to any success, and the
discomfiture of all subversives. In the cities, employers threatened mass dismissals, and in the Reserves, the puppet chiefs of
the Native Affairs Department twitched to the fingers of Dr
Verwoerd. The momentum of arrests in the townships, for an
endless series of technical offences, rapidly increased. Then all
at once Madzunya and Potlako Leballo, on behalf of the
Africanists, condemned the stay-at-home. Overnight they were
hailed in the press as 'the most responsible and powerful
Native leaders'. Both were immediately expelled from the
A.N.C. by the National Executive. An open break between
Africanists and Congress became inevitable.

The strike failed, not spectacularly, but effectively all the
same, for demonstrations of resistance in South Africa cannot
afford to go halfway, and at the end of the first day it was
officially abandoned by the A.N.C. Only in Johannesburg and
the surrounding industrial areas, in Port Elizabeth and in
Durban, did substantial sections of the non-white working
population stay at home, and then not in the overwhelming
numbers that might have drawn in the reluctant during the
succeeding days. At the Transvaal Conference of the A.N.C. in
Orlando that November, Madzunya, despite his expulsion,
announced himself as a candidate for the post of Provincial
President. Finding themselves hopelessly outnumbered, however, the Africanists withdrew from the conference altogether,
and, on the 2nd of November, announced their secession from
the A.N.C. 'We are,' they declared, 'launching out openly as
the custodians of the African National Congress policy as it
was formulated in 1912, and pursued up to the time of the
Congress Alliance.' The press jubilantly reported the decision
as a 'major split' in Congress. The A.N.C. national conference
in December displayed a united confidence in its leadership,
the Freedom Charter, and the whole inter-racial Congress
Alliance, and news of the Africanists disappeared from
the press.

Congress had split before over its alliance with progressive

organizations of other racial groups. In 1950, a band of dissidents led by Selope-Thema had been expelled for their
attacks on co-operation with the South African Indian Congress and, having formed themselves into a new movement
called the African National Congress National Minded Bloc,
had assailed the A.N.C. leaders as 'paid agents of the Indian
merchants'. Towards the end of his life, Selope-Thema had
joined Moral Rearmament. The Bantu National Congress of
Mr Bhengu had called for a 'purified Bantu movement' and
the rejection of all ties with Indian and other racial groups.
Within a week Bhengu had announced a following of 2 million
and promised to represent the country's Africans at UNO.
Shortly afterwards he was tried and convicted of a non-
political offence, and his organization disintegrated. The
Supreme Council of African Organizations had possessed indefinite aims but a certain strategy: it had consistently attacked
all A.N.C. campaigns and called upon Africans to renounce the
'Indian-directed' Congress Alliance. It had also disappeared.

While white South Africa was celebrating the arrival of Van
Riebeeck at the Cape in 1652 with a long week-end of outdoor
distractions, from the 4th to the 6th of April 1959, the Africanists held their inaugural conference in Orlando. Josias Madzunya himself failed to gain a place on the National Executive,
in a rejection more of his wildcat personality than of his
policies. The thick-set black-bearded man, closely wrapped in
his khaki army overcoat, accepted his repudiation by the
movement which he had helped to establish and appointed
himself its 'watch-dog'. Potlako Leballo was elected General
Secretary, and Robert Mangaliso Sobukwe, the National
President.

Sobukwe delivered a long theoretical disquisition to the conference at its opening session, but his example was not too
rigorously followed. Three clergymen decorated the platform,
and in prayers and addresses they attacked 'the hooligans of
Europe who killed our God and have never been convicted',
while cheers greeted the salute to 'a black man, Simon of
Arabia, who carried Jesus from the Cross'. A post-conference

article in *The World*, white-owned but strangely sympathetic to the new political grouping, discussed the formation of an African national church, which 'would play a leading role in Africanist affairs, just as the Dutch Reformed Church did in Nationalist Party affairs'. Delegates noisily assailed the influence of communists over the A.N.C. and the corrupting effects of the alliance with Indian, Coloured and white.

I had never had a moment's sympathy with the aims and activities of the Africanists. Their whole movement was inspired by a black hysteria which might have possessed its brief emotional compensations, but which took no account of the degree to which modern South Africa – despite all that white governments could do – had become a racially integrated society. The anti-Indian bigotry, which reverberated through so many Africanist articles and speeches, had reached its flaming climax years before in the 1949 Durban riots, when Africans, in an explosion of hatred and despair, had turned from the well-protected whites to the helpless Indians of the city, killing and burning. Yet South Africa's Indians were as economically depressed and politically subjugated as the Africans. Below the thin, almost transparent crust of the professional and merchant middle class, lay the mass of Indian workers, cutting sugar cane with their children, for pennies a day, in the heavy heat of the Natal plantations, or working in the hotels and factories of Durban. To associate them with the oppressors instead of the oppressed was morbid and cruel, and stupid. From the mass of their half million citizens had come constant and overwhelming support for resistance to white supremacy. From their leaders, in the main members of the small middle class, had come money for Congress campaigns and the necessary leaven of political sophistication and experience. The whole doctrine of civil disobedience had been evolved by Gandhi, in the early years of the twentieth century – he had led the first passive resistance campaign in 1906, against the threatened extension of the pass laws to Indians – and it was Gandhi himself who had founded the Natal Indian Congress, in 1894.

The anti-Indian prejudices of the Africanists mirrored only a suicidal race exclusiveness. If Africans could not co-operate with Indians in resistance to white supremacy, how much less could they co-operate with the Coloured, or the dissident whites? And how was it possible to conceive a successful revolution in a highly complex industrial society, where one-third of the total population – 3 million whites, 1,500,000 Coloured and 500,000 Indians – were indiscriminately banished from African aspirations? It was not enough, as the leaders of the Congress Alliance realized, to promote a revolution. It was just as vital to keep society alive once revolution had re-shaped it. I had my own criticism of Congress, and I had increasingly voiced it in public. I believed passionately that the Congress Alliance should be replaced by one movement, to which members of all races in South Africa could belong. Yet I recognized it as the best material for change that we had, indeed as the only mould for the recasting of South Africa. And I was unashamedly partisan. The pages of *Africa South* were at all times open to the Congress leaders, and my personal association with Congress campaigns left no possible doubt of my allegiance.

I was accordingly astonished when I received an article on Africanist policy by Peter Nkutsoeu Raboroko, Secretary for Education in the National Executive Committee of the Pan Africanist Congress. As a statement of the Africanist case, in extravagant detail, by a senior member of the organization, it filled me with distaste and foreboding. Could such views conceivably attract any real popular following? And if they could, did we not face the dangers of a black supremacy every bit as bad as the white which it had arisen to fight? My first reaction was to return the article without comment. But I knew that *Africa South* would fail in its function as a front against apartheid if I denied the Pan Africanist Congress access to its pages. The Africanists existed, and one couldn't make them disappear by ignoring their ideas. Yet I could hardly believe that such racial hysterics represented the measured viewpoint of the P.A.C., and I wrote to Sobukwe, suggesting this and proposing that he contribute an article himself. In a tone of high irritation, he replied that the article by Raboroko had been written with the full knowledge and collaboration of the National Executive and that it fully expressed the P.A.C. viewpoint. He complained that *Africa South* had been rigidly partisan in its support of the A.N.C., and he insisted, in all justice, that I give the P.A.C. as well an opportunity to address itself to the international audience which the magazine commanded. That was that. I published the article – entitled 'The Africanist Case' – in the April–June 1960 issue, together with a reply from Duma Nokwe, Secretary-General of the A.N.C.

Maintaining that the A.N.C. had deserted its original objectives by adopting the Freedom Charter and forming an alliance with movements of other racial groups, Raboroko dubbed the A.N.C. 'the Charterist Congress' and assailed it as 'a union of exploiters and the exploited'. Its members stood 'exposed as the self-confessed lackeys and flunkeys of the white ruling class and the Indian merchant class'.

'The gravamen of the Africanist charge against the Charterists, therefore, is that they have betrayed the material interests of the African people. They have sacrificed these interests upon the political altar of an ungodly alliance, an alliance of slave-owner, slave-driver and slave. The ostensible object of this alliance is the destruction of slavery and the freeing of the slave, and yet the real motive is the perpetuation of that slavery under a new guise. The Kliptown Charter, erroneously called the Freedom Charter, offers a classic illustration of the essentials of Charterism.

' "And, therefore, we the people of South Africa," proclaims the ultimate clause, "black and white together – equals, countrymen and brothers – adopt this Freedom Charter ..."

'To them master and slave – the exploiter and the exploited, the oppressor and the oppressed, the degrader and the degraded – are all equals. To them indigenous African nationals and immigrant European foreign nationals – the dispossessed and their dispossessors, the victims and their robbers – are all countrymen. For them the progressive and the reactionary –

the African subject and his foreign overlord, the African nationalist and the colonialist or white supremacist, the liberationist and the collaborationist – are all brothers.'

At the December 1959 national conference of the A.N.C. in Durban, delegates overwhelmingly voted to begin a decisive struggle against the pass laws on the 31st of March 1960. The Pan Africanist Congress attacked the decision as aimed at mere alleviation, and rather inconsistently launched its own courtesy campaign in which its members would demand proper treatment at shops or take their custom elsewhere. Instructions scurried to A.N.C. branches all over the country, and by February 1960 the massive machinery of Congress was moving towards another collision with the government. Endlessly we debated its possibilities. Would it catch popular fire, like the defiance campaign of 1952, or the paralysing stay-at-home on the 26th of June 1957?

Then suddenly, on Saturday, the 19th of March 1960, Sobukwe announced at a press conference that he would launch a Pan Africanist Congress anti-pass campaign on the following Monday, when he and his followers would leave their passes at home and, brandishing the slogan 'no defence, no bail, no fines', would surrender themselves peacefully for arrest at police stations throughout the country. I remember reading the news with furious impatience. Sobukwe was deliberately jumping the gun. Of course, the campaign would fail, because the P.A.C. commanded little support in the country. But inevitably the A.N.C. would be forced to postpone its own campaign for several weeks, perhaps months, or launch it in an aftermath of dejection and bewilderment.

I was sitting in my office on the morning of Monday, the 21st of March, restlessly reading through a pile of submitted typescripts, when the telephone rang.

'Have you heard about Nyanga?'

'No.'

'Two thousand or more, queuing at the Philippi police station for arrest. And crowds at Langa too. The police are almost submerged. They're arresting one by one.'

'I'll be over in a minute.'

I remember slowly getting up from my chair, arranging the papers on my desk, slowly closing the door of my office behind me. I'd been wrong. Whatever its support in the rest of the country, the P.A.C. had gained a clutch on Cape Town, the one urban area where Congress organization and influence had always been so infirm.

As I walked up Plein Street, past the busy bazaars, and into the hot quiet of Barrack Street to the offices of *New Age*, I thought how we had always said wryly, half to excuse ourselves, that Cape Town would learn the news of successful revolution by telegram from Pretoria. Yet here were Cape Town's Africans in sudden revolt, while the rest of the country seemed to stretch sullen and inert, and not in revolt against white rule alone, but, from behind their own barricades of race, against the whole policy of inter-racial resistance. Of course, there were reasons. Uniquely in Cape Town, the Africans composed a small minority, not only of the total population, but even of the major non-white portion. Some 65,000 strong, they were less than a quarter as numerous as the city's almost 300,000 whites, less than one-fifth as numerous as the city's almost 400,000 Coloured. Here they could not see, as they saw so starkly everywhere in Johannesburg and its satellite cities, the promise of survival and ultimate victory in the sheer pressure of their numbers. Even their right to live in Cape Town at all was disputed, and the government had already announced, under the Eiselen Scheme, its intention to remove them altogether from the Western Cape, which could then be turned into an ethnic labour monopoly of the Coloured. I had always measured Africanism as a manifestation of despair, and the city's Africans, threatened with expulsion from their concrete 'bachelor' barracks and their rusted tin and boxwood shanties to the slow starvation of the Reserves, had cause enough for their despair.

The P.A.C. campaign had fallen flat on its face in the pivotal areas of Johannesburg, Durban and Port Elizabeth. Sobukwe himself had surrendered at the Orlando police station with a

mere 50 supporters. Only at Sharpeville, the African location
which fed with its labour the steel town of Vereeniging some
40 miles from Johannesburg, had a mass meeting gathered in
response to the P.A.C.'s call. Here there had been 'trouble' –
that word which in South Africa covers everything from a
street skirmish to a riot – and there were rumours, not yet confirmed, of police shooting and several casualties.

I had no heart for the pile of typescripts on the desk in my
office, the blousy short stories, the laced-in articles, which
reduced so much human horror to sentiment or statistical
tables. I had a rapid lunch and wandered up to the House of
Assembly.

There was a twitching of nerves as the members stood for the
muttered prayer and took their seats. Black South Africa had
once again forced a way into the dry disputes of the all white
Assembly, at its most comfortable when discussing irrigation
and transport or listening to the Minister of External Affairs
assail the outside world. I can remember nothing of the debate
except the intervention of a Nationalist back-bench member
from the Vereeniging area, who complained with deep emotion
that, when riots broke out, only one African was killed. He
need not have lamented so soon. By nightfall, the mounting
figures for the dead of the Sharpeville shootings seemed to
promise a record.

I was at my mother's home that night when a journalist from
the *Cape Times* telephoned to tell me of the Langa riot. Some
8,000 Africans had collected in the main square of the location
towards dusk for a meeting of peaceful protest. Suddenly the
police had started firing. The Africans had fled from the square,
and then, from roofs and shadows, had hurled rocks and
bottles at the police. Rioting had broken out, and soon many
buildings were on fire. The Coloured driver of the *Cape Times*
car was beaten to death, and the car itself burnt. By the morning, 3 Africans had been killed and 30 injured by police
bullets, and 7 buildings, including 2 schools, destroyed.

In the newspapers of the 22nd, the scale of the trouble at
Sharpeville was at last measured. Sixty-eight men, women and

children had been killed, and over 200 injured. Later, largely on evidence carefully collected by the Bishop of Johannesburg and his lawyers, it was established that the peaceful protest meeting of 5,000 people had been fired upon, suddenly and without warning, by the police. The Africans had scattered and fled, but the police had continued firing at them. At the inquiry which followed, doctors who had examined the dead and wounded gave evidence that some 75% of them had been shot in the back.

During that week, with almost all the Africans in Cape Town on strike, with sudden black crowds of protest at police stations, sudden black movement through the streets, it was possible to believe that revolution had begun. The city seemed to be in a state of siege, and it was easy to forget for a moment the armed might of the state, which had merely glinted at Sharpeville and Langa, and imagine instead a wave of non-white fury, rising and breaking across the country. The international reaction to the Sharpeville shootings staggered white opinion. Reports of huge angry demonstrations in Britain, even in the political distances of Scandinavia, roared from the front pages of the newspapers. The government seemed stunned, not by the shootings themselves, but by the singular protests that they had stirred abroad. Why, after all, were the Sharpeville shootings any different from the others? That the Nationalists, and the Smuts government before them, had ordered? I felt a momentary pang of impatience myself. They had got away with so much for so long. They were almost entitled to count a little longer upon the bland, polite indifference of the outside world.

It is strange, now that the P.A.C. seems to be languishing as a significant political force inside South Africa, its leaders squabbling among themselves within the country and without, that we should have felt at the time, despite our passionate partisanship, that Congress and its aspirations were in headlong flight. We had always been isolated in Cape Town from the mainstream of resistance politics, and our isolation as always distorted our focus. That Wednesday Brian Bunting visited

Nyanga and was ordered, by a group of young P.A.C. toughs, to take his white face and white paper away at once. I was furious. I had often hotly disagreed with Brian, privately and in print. Over international affairs, New Age and Africa South had frequently collided. New Age had invariably supported Soviet policy and conduct; Africa South had specifically assailed Soviet intervention in Hungary, and many editorials had attacked the moral manipulations of East and West alike. Yet New Age itself, under Brian's direction, had been invaluable to the Congress Movement, reporting its activities, conveying its case, circulating news to the most remote rural areas. Despite constant police persecution of its agents, it reached a readership of more than 100,000 – many copies travelled a whole township street before falling to pieces – and so provided the Congress Alliance with the one mass organ of publicity it had. Brian himself had been 'named' as a communist, and banned from all public gatherings under the Suppression of Communism Act, while his wife, Sonia, had been arrested in December 1956 for high treason. If ever whites had enlisted in the ranks of resistance to white rule, leaving behind them in consequence all the privileges and protections of their colour, the Buntings were among them. I remember still how their youngest child would stare at them, as though they would suddenly vanish under his eyes. That they should have been rejected, with all they had given and all they could do, merely because they were white, by those men in Nyanga, seemed the final disfigurement of the society which we wished one day to shape in South Africa.

I sat at my office desk on Thursday afternoon, in a frenzy of frustration. The day before, Lutuli had called for a stay-at-home Day of Mourning, in memory of the Sharpeville and Langa dead, on Monday the 28th of March. But it seemed an inadequate demonstration at such a time. While the rest of black South Africa stirred uneasily, waiting for a Congress call to bring it to its feet, Sharpeville and Cape Town's African areas were already flourishing their defiance in the government's face, at P.A.C. command. In Langa and Nyanga bands of young Africanists roamed the streets, threatening Congress leaders, a revolutionary police. And factory after factory shut down, deserted by its always before so docile black labour force. 'What is happening?' a crumpled manufacturer, who had occasionally given me small donations for the Treason Fund, shouted at me. 'Why all at once?' I shrugged my shoulders.

Though my telephone was carefully tapped, not to speak of the telephone in the national headquarters of the A.N.C., I put through a call to Oliver Tambo, A.N.C. Deputy President-General, in Johannesburg. In retrospect, the conversation seems just to have skirted the absurd. I felt that I was whispering into the ear of the Special Branch all the time, and though I had desperately ceased to care about the consequences for myself, I knew how vital it was that Oliver should say nothing on the telephone that might be of subsequent value to the police. At the same time, I wildly wanted some reassurance that Congress would seize the initiative from the P.A.C. as soon as possible and hurl the weight of its organization against the government. I said that the P.A.C. seemed in complete control of Cape Town, and that it was certain to fill any political vacuum elsewhere that Congress by its inaction would produce. Was a democratic union of races to disappear from resistance politics altogether? Oliver tried to soothe me with delicate assurances, and though I was no more clearly informed of Congress intentions at the end of the conversation than I had been at the beginning, I had caught a mood and I put down the telephone with a surge of relief.

On the Friday afternoon, at four o'clock, the telephone rang, and a voice which I did not recognize asked me to come at once to the offices of a trade union a few hundred yards away. I wondered for a moment whether it was the Special Branch setting a trap, then shrugged off the possibility, bounded down the stairs and ran to my appointment. I was shown into a small room and found Oliver there, sitting alone at a table. He had taken the morning plane from Johannesburg. After we had warmly greeted each other, we sat down and talked. We were only dimly conscious of the risk that we were running.

Our discussion was in clear defiance of the five year ban with which we had both been served under the Suppression of Communism Act. The city was teeming with police, and it would have been stupid to suppose that both of us had escaped being trailed. Oliver told me of the Congress plans for mass pass burnings – Lutuli would burn his own pass that Saturday – and the national strike. The P.A.C. might hold Vereeniging and Cape Town, but Congress would rouse Port Elizabeth and East London, Durban and Bloemfontein, Johannesburg and Pretoria and the smaller cities of the Reef. We were discussing the support that the call might yet collect in the Western Cape when an African woman opened the door and announced, with quiet politeness, as though inviting us to tea, that members of the Special Branch were searching the large office next door. Oliver and I looked questioningly at each other.

'Can they see the top of the stairs from next door?' I asked her.

'I don't think so,' she said in her still unruffled voice, 'they are busy looking at the files.'

Oliver and I stood up slowly, and, like two pantomime comics imitating ballerinas, tiptoed out of the office and down the stairs. When we reached the landing of the third floor and saw that we had not been followed, we dropped back on to our heels and clattered down the remaining three flights of stairs into the street outside. And there the late edition of the evening paper fired the news at us – the government intended introducing legislation at once to outlaw the A.N.C. and P.A.C. alike.

Walking down to the Parade as fast as we could without running – the sight of the two of us pelting through the streets together would soon enough have drawn a crowd – we reached my car and set off for the home of a friend at Camps Bay in noisy disregard of the speed limit.

As we drove over Kloof Nek, along the road that twisted down to the sea, we discussed the A.N.C. Executive decision that Oliver should leave the country if the organization were

ever banned, so that one leader at least would remain free to
speak openly the aspirations of his people and conduct any
international campaign for their relief. I suggested that I drive
him to Johannesburg that night, and from there into Bechuanaland. Basutoland was much nearer, and we could get there,
skirting Bloemfontein, by the following morning, but Basutoland was entirely surrounded by South African territory. It
was a refuge, not a road to the outside world. Swaziland was
sandwiched between South Africa and Portuguese Mozam-
bique, and Salazar's police would be as predatory as Verwoerd's. Only Bechuanaland promised some chance of escape,
through the Federation of Rhodesia and Nyasaland in the
north, to Tanganyika and the relative safety of a United Nations
Trust Territory, still under British mandate but far enough in
its progress to self-government.

At the home of my Camps Bay friends, we made our plans,
with a blanket carefully wrapped around the telephone and a
whisky to take the sudden exhaustion from behind my eyes.
At dusk I abandoned Oliver to a quick dinner and drove to my
mother's house, where the announcement that I was leaving
for Bechuanaland that night was greeted by my family with
pained delight. They seemed to suppose that I was going for
good – in the tactical retreat from arrest that all had advised
with increasing passion since Sharpeville – and I did not con-
tradict them. I had not for a moment considered leaving South
Africa for longer than was necessary to take Oliver to safety.
I had encouraged that resistance to the government which I
hoped would rear itself high in Monday's general strike and
the promised pass burnings, and withdrawal seemed like
desertion. But every one of the 1,200 miles to the frontier
carried the chance of arrest. The police seemed poised for a
sudden swoop on all those whom they considered subversive.
If it was any consolation for my family to believe that at least
I would be out of South Africa once and for all at the end, the
deception was pardonable. There would be time enough when
I returned to argue about why I had done so.

We searched through the library and the garage, but could

find no road map of Southern Africa. And so, while my family emptied its purses and pockets for my journey, my mother's young Coloured driver Joseph drove down the road to the garage we always used, to fill the petrol tank of the car and buy a map. I had decided to take my mother's Vauxhall rather than my own Chrysler, which I supposed was better known to the Special Branch. But at the garage, I later learnt, a member of the Special Branch, off-duty, was chatting with the proprietor. When Joseph asked for a map of Southern Africa, the Special Branch policeman grumbled to himself:

'I wonder what Ronald Segal wants with a road map.'

'That isn't Ronald Segal's car,' said the proprietor. 'It's his mother's.'

'I don't care whose bloody car it is,' said the policeman. 'That was the car we arrested him in at Nyanga.'

He seemed to hesitate, then shrugged his shoulders and talked of something else. Perhaps he was tired that night.

My sister had meanwhile gone to my flat and hurriedly packed a suitcase. Her mind could hardly have been on her work – we had grown very close to each other in the past few years – for the assortment of clothes that I later found myself with in Bechuanaland contrasted curiously with the baked dust all about me – two bathing costumes, and enough thick woollen jerseys for an expedition into the Antarctic. I crammed a solicitous supper down my throat, and armed against the night with sandwiches and a thermos flask of scalding coffee, I set off in the Vauxhall. Having collected Oliver, I wrapped him in Josph's white coat – it was several sizes too large – so that he might look like my driver. An African driven by a white would cause comment enough in the small towns at which we would have to stop for petrol. The driver's white coat gave to Oliver the reassurance of a uniform, the unsuspicious servitude of the black.

I hope that I shall never spend another night like that again. We drove the thousand miles to Johannesburg – with a brief stop at Kimberley in fruitless search of Dr Letele, the A.N.C. leader there – at over 80 miles an hour, expecting to be stopped at every small police station we were forced to pass. At last, in the early afternoon, we reached Johannesburg. I drove to the home of a friend, and Oliver went off with feverish instructions to return no later than 9 o'clock that night. I had just enough energy left to brush my teeth, take off my clothes, and creep into bed. I slept until evening.

Of course, Oliver did not arrive at nine o'clock. My affection for him, it seems to me, must always have been strong; it has persistently survived his assaults on my relatively rigid sense of time. When he had not arrived by half past ten, I began to pace the floor. He had almost certainly been arrested, but I could hardly have telephoned the police to make sure. At eleven o'clock he arrived with his wife, Adelaide, and even the friendly recriminations I had stored up for him, I postponed when I looked at her face. They said goodbye to each other, and we set off for Bechuanaland.

I had anticipated trouble at the frontier, a South African police post or a group of stern and demanding British officials behind a formidable barrier. We had even thought of abandoning the car two miles from the frontier, and crossing into Bechuanaland on foot at some distance from the road. But we decided to take our chance and encountered only an African policeman, accompanied by what looked like an outsize visitor's book. We wrote in our names, drove to the nearest town, Lobatsi, some six miles away, parked the car outside the dark and locked hotel at half past three in the morning, and slept till dawn. We then went in search of the District Commissioner, a fresh-faced young man with a library of Book Club choices, and announced Oliver's intention to seek asylum. The District Commissioner was sympathetic but non-committal. I gathered that in this haven from apartheid, where Britain had hung its civilizing flags, there was only one hotel, and that it accepted only whites. I expressed my disgust, with what must have seemed to the earnest official a singular breach of taste under the circumstances, and was told that Oliver could stay at the Resident Commissioner's, some three miles from the town, in a building for visiting Chiefs.

After a lunch of biscuits and fruit, which we bought at a trading store and then ate in the car, I drove Oliver to the deserted hostel – the Chiefs were all apparently in between visits – and, after a short dispute with him over my inveterate imprudence, set off for Johannesburg. I remember wondering to myself, as I drove through the dust across the border, through the Zeerust Reserve and on to the shimmering tar of the road back to the city, whether I would ever see Oliver again. The response to the strike call had been overwhelming, and when I reached the home of my friend again that evening, I learned how Johannesburg had resounded during the day, its streets and pavements still, with the eyes waiting at the windows. The following day I prepared to return to Cape Town, and in the evening met friends of mine on the A.N.C. National Executive. As we sat around our furtive drinks behind the close drawn curtains, discussing the pass burnings, an extended strike, the reassumed initiative of Congress, now forced underground, I remember interrupting wryly – 'The next time we meet, I suppose, will be in detention.' We said goodbye to each other, with measured lightness, and after supper, I went straight to bed, with my suitcase ready packed for the journey home.

My friend woke me just after seven in the morning.

'It's just come over the radio. There were mass arrests throughout the country last night. A State of Emergency has been declared. You had better go while you can.' I jumped out of bed and ran downstairs to the telephone. It had come at last then, I thought, the swoop that we had so long awaited, without ever seeing it close, the loud knock on the door in the early morning, the order to dress, the drive to the police station, and the stay – for how long? for years? – in prison or the special concentration camp. I telephoned Ruth First and heard her voice at the other end of the line with a tremble of relief. She at least had not been arrested. But Advocate Joe Slovo, her husband, had been – and Walter Sisulu, and Duma Nokwe, and the Chief himself, and how many more? I had to see Ruth at once. She explained she had to be at the Magistrate's Court that morning for a test case on a *habeas corpus* application for Joe's release. The State of Emergency might not, after all, have been legally declared.[1] The government was increasingly contemptuous of detail. With flashes of Edgar Allan Poe's *Purloined Letter* in my mind, I said that I would meet her outside the Magistrate's Court at half past ten. If the police were looking for me, they would hardly expect to find me there of all places.

For two hours that morning I wandered restlessly through the house, trying to make up my mind whether I should return to Cape Town or cross the border again into Bechuanaland. Under the State of Emergency, *Africa South* might well be banned altogether or effectively smothered under countless restrictions. I might serve some purpose by publishing abroad and smuggling copies of the magazine into South Africa, by assisting Oliver in the campaign for U.N. intervention. I knew that the overseas press would attend to South Africa now, in the spectacle of crisis, but that their focus would soon enough shift. Yet I felt that to leave now was a desertion, and that I would find my exile sour and shameful as no imprisonment would be. And I wondered, too, whether flight would not put an end, beyond return, to any real chance I might have of helping to shape a new South Africa. I don't suppose that I shall ever know why I suddenly decided that I would leave. It was certainly in part a belief that I could be of service to Congress abroad, that *Africa South* should survive. In part as well it was the nagging knowledge that I had given my family trouble enough, and that if I stayed I would inevitably give them more. Perhaps, in the end, the pride of prison just meant less than the sourness of exile.

At half past ten I was at the Magistrate's Court, leaning against one of the pillars at the entrance while members of the Special Branch passed by, one after the other, without noticing me. At quarter past eleven, Ruth had not yet arrived, or had

[1] With characteristic muddle, the government had flown the wrong gazette to Johannesburg. The Court released the arrested, who were held until the right gazette arrived, when they were formally arrested again.

entered the building by another way, and missed me. I felt the
sweat trickle down my cheek. I walked once round the building, got into my car, and drove the two hundred or so miles
back across the border into Bechuanaland.

At the Chiefs' hostel, Oliver, dressed in trousers and vest,
was sitting on a chair in the sun, with the building white and
empty behind him and the sporadic creaking of a few crickets
in the otherwise silent dust and grass around. He saw me and
smiled. Then I told him the news, with the names of those I
knew had been arrested. We set off for the post office at the
edge of the town. I had brought £100 with me – a Johannesburg Sunday newspaper later adjusted the figure to £5,000 –
and Oliver sent a cable to the Secretary-General of the United
Nations, requesting facilities to appear before the Security
Council, while I cabled Rosalynde Ainslie, the representative of
Africa South in London, to see what chance there was of our
getting travel documents from Britain or one of the African
states. Then we drove down to the hotel.

We walked through the gate and were approaching the steps
to the entrance, when a pasty-faced thick-set man detached himself from a group of young whites at the bar and bounded down
the steps towards us. We stopped, and when he reached us he
pushed Oliver in the chest with his open hand several times.

'Get out. We don't want your sort here.'

'Wait a minute,' I said, getting between him and Oliver, and
beginning to shake uncontrollably with rage. 'Who the hell do
you think you are?'

'We don't want him here,' he shouted. 'And we don't want
you either! Run somewhere else.'

I looked at his drinking pals on the veranda, clustered at the
bar as though seeking their own asylum among the bottles, and
staring down at us with safe dislike. I had a quick vision of a
brawl there, in the gathering dusk of the hotel garden, before
the crowd of Africans collecting in the street outside. I began to
shout also, at the men around the bar as much as at him.

'Bechuanaland doesn't belong to you yet. And we will go
where we please here. Understand? And if you try and stop us,

any of you, I'll have you dragged through every court in this territory. Do you hear?'

We stood staring at each other. Then suddenly one of the crowd on the veranda ran down the steps and hustled our assailant away towards the building of bedrooms on the left. I turned to Oliver.

'You want to leave?'

'Yes,' he said.

I drove him back to the hostel, and we arranged to meet again on the following morning. Then I returned to the hotel.

The proprietor said how sorry he was that he could only put me up for that night, but that all his rooms were booked. And then the telephone in the public box just inside the entrance of the hotel suddenly rang. Someone called out that I was wanted, and I went to the phone. It was a journalist from a Johannesburg newspaper.

'Mr Segal?'

'Yes.'

'So you are in Lobatsi?'

'Obviously.'

'Do you intend staying there?'

'I have no idea.'

'Where will you be going?'

'I don't know.'

'Is Oliver Tambo with you?'

'No.'

'Did you leave South Africa together?'

'I'm not sure that any of this is your business.'

'May we phone you again?'

'You will, anyway.'

'Thank you very much, Mr Segal. We will be phoning you again.'

I put down the receiver, and the phone rang again immediately.

'A trunk call for Mr Segal. Ronald Segal. Is he there?'

'Yes, speaking.'

It was a Bulawayo journalist this time. Was I planning to

enter the Federation? I had no idea. Yes, he could get in touch with me again. And I put down the receiver. I could think only of that short scene in the garden of the hotel, and why I had left South Africa at all. There at least I knew what to expect. If I brawled, if I hated and was hurt, even if I was in prison, it was my home. Here I was alone. I longed for my mother and sister, the reassurance of their closeness. And suddenly I missed my whole family, aunts and uncles, cousins and nephews, all of them so casually for so long waved, as a distracting buzz of demands, away from my mind. I hadn't cried since I had been at school, more than ten years before, but as I sat in the dining-room, alone at a corner table, stirring the soup in the thick plain white plate, I bit into my lower lip to keep myself from crying. I thought of asking the District Commissioner to let me live with Oliver in the Chiefs' hostel. And then my pride reared away from it. No one was going to drive me out of that hotel, or out of the town, as no one had driven me from school ever, until I was ready to go.

The proprietor came up to the table and told me that the Divisional Commissioner wished to see me. I found him in the entrance of the hotel, and we went to sit on the bench in the small dark quadrangle formed by the bedrooms.

'I was very sorry to hear of the trouble this afternoon. I hope you will forget it. The man was ... ah ... not quite himself. It won't happen again.'

'I can't speak for Oliver Tambo. If it had been me that hooligan had hit, I would be charging him now with assault. And I don't care whether he was drunk or not. I don't think that kind of bullying should be answered with a private reprimand and then politely forgotten. But that's Oliver's business. I can only say for myself that I didn't expect to find, in a British administered protectorate, an atmosphere so reminiscent of a farming back-water in the Transvaal.'

The Divisional Commissioner's voice stiffened.

'I can give you my firm assurance that nothing like this will happen again. There will be no problem over accommodating you in the hotel. You may stay as long as you please. I have spoken to the proprietor. The man who interfered with Mr Tambo has been told that if he does anything similar again, we will be forced to reconsider his residence in the territory. I have asked him to apologize to you.'

I shied away from the embarrassment of having that pasty-faced man bluster his excuses in my face.

'There is no need for him to apologize to me. If he apologizes to anyone, it should be to Oliver Tambo. And I am sure Oliver will regard it as an adequate apology that he should be treated in this territory like an ordinary human being, with a level of culture, it seems to me, conspicuously lacking among the white settlers here.'

'I am sure he will have nothing to complain of, and I hope we can now regard the matter as closed.' He paused. 'I hear that the newspapers have been getting at you?'

He looked at me uncertainly. Of course, Oliver and I were training a sudden spotlight on the territory, and one which was shining into all the neglected corners. What nuisances we must have seemed to him. Had I been in his place, I doubt if I could have concealed my irritation under so firm a crust of courtesy. As I returned to the dining-room I made up my mind that I would use our 'spectacle' value to secure first our refuge and then a speedy escape. I was subsequently criticized for publicizing our condition so much. But Lobatsi was swarming with white South Africans from the farms and mines in the southern part of the protectorate, and even had they been apathetic – which I had increasing reason to discover that they were not – I had proved to my own disturbing satisfaction how easy it was to slip across the border and back again. Our discretion would only have assisted those who were endlessly conspiring to kidnap us. Britain was still doubtless a power in the world, but her Special Branch, slouching lugubriously at the bar of the hotel, promised a precarious protection. I preferred to make my own preparations for a diplomatic incident.

Some weeks later, five Africans were reported to have sought asylum in Bechuanaland and to have been directed to the office of the Resident Commissioner in Makeking, across the frontier in South African territory. There they had been arrested by the South African police. More than a year later, with, one would have thought, the rights of asylum in the Protectorates undeniably established, Anderson Ganyile, the refugee Congress leader from Pondoland, was kidnapped, together with two political associates, by South African police who had slipped across the border into Basutoland. Imprisoned for some five months, he was only released, with a hollow apology, after strenuous public protests and, presumably, secret demands by the British government.

We had to leave Bechuanaland soon. Neither of us was of the slightest use to anybody where we were. We had chosen not to go to jail, and in our different ways each of us would have to prove to himself the value of his choice. Oliver never spoke about it – Congress had, after all, instructed him to leave – but I knew that he, too, felt his escape as a desertion.

I decided against telling the press about that afternoon's incident – but not because I wanted to save the British administration in Bechuanaland from any embarrassment. It seemed to me that the territory would have been more contented and secure, and certainly far more advanced in resources and government – its development in both was equally primitive – had only enough embarrassment been caused the British administration before. But I did not want to provide at that moment a single apostle of apartheid with the satisfaction of knowing that over the border, under British rule, the Deputy President-General of the African National Congress had first been refused accommodation, and then assaulted, in a hotel, because he was black.

The next day Eric Louw announced in the House of Assembly that two of the most dangerous agitators, Oliver Tambo and Ronald Segal, had escaped, and were preparing to give evidence at the United Nations. His remarks were widely reported in the press, and my stay in Bechuanaland turned suddenly into a siege. During the late afternoon and evening, whites from the district around would gather in the bar and lounge of the hotel and either stare at me, with silent hatred, as the embodiment of all subversion, or engage me in argument which soon enough degenerated into threats and abuse. Every now and then a member of the Bechuanaland administration would call at the hotel to ask me if I had any complaints, but since I could hardly demand the deportation of the whole white community, and would quite literally have faced death rather than the humiliation of a personal bodyguard, I invariably if temperately expressed my satisfaction, and gratitude, for the inquiries. At times I could take no more and would push past the sullen groups, the shouted questions, walk quickly to my bedroom, lock the door and fling myself on the bed with a book. The trading shop at the bottom of the road near the railway line sold a variety of paper-backs, all brightly covered and monotonously dreary inside. I consumed an average of three a day, till my diet of artificial violence made the real violence threatening me seem fictional and inept. Sometimes, with a mischievous curiosity, I would go into the bar as the radio brayed the news and listen while snide political commentaries were fired at my head by the inmates.

One night a group of Afrikaners from the mines near by, with their wives and children, entered the lounge of the hotel and crowded around the table next to mine. Their spokesman, a youngish man with half his hair and none of his upper front teeth, invited me over for a drink. Because he did so with what seemed to me a challenge, I accepted. Was I going to the United Nations, he asked. The newspapers said so. I answered that I would certainly go, if I thought it would help rescue South Africa from those who were disfiguring and would one day destroy her. It was pompous enough, but its candour apparently appealed to him, and he set out laboriously to explain to me how like children the Natives really were. His wife, a slovenly woman with a loose two-year-old in her lap, cut him short. 'It's you who's destroying the country, you and those others who make trouble with the kaffirs. They don't want anything themselves. They are happy with what they's got, but you come along and tell them this and that, and then they start wanting they don't know what. You leave the kaffirs alone, or you just watch out.'

K

There was a murmur of agreement round the table. Her husband looked at me. 'Now I don't care what you think you ought to do,' he said slowly. 'But I'm telling you this. Don't you think you're going to the United Nations, because you're not. Do what you like, but don't think that we will let you go there and make trouble. We'll kill you before you go. I promise you that.'

Another mumble rose from the table. I got up.

'You invited me for a drink, not to hear yourselves tell me what you hope to do to me.'

'Don't go,' he barked, 'we're not finished with you yet.'

'But I'm finished with you,' I said quietly, and without looking back to see whether they were following me – I didn't want to know – I walked carefully to my bedroom, locked the door, and picked up one of the paper-backs by the bed. I must have read for an hour before I realized that I had read the book before, and, flinging it away, I switched off the light and went to sleep.

One evening, I returned to my room and found a parcel on my bed, with a short note from a family acquaintance who had been in Cape Town, seen my mother and been induced to drop a small package – 'nothing much!' – at the hotel in Lobatsi on his way by car to Southern Rhodesia. I wondered briefly whether it was really from my mother or a shrewdly wrapped bomb, then decided that I was reading too many paper-backs, and opened it. There were grapes and figs inside, and a hazelnut cake, and two packets of *matzos*. Of course, it was Passover, and my mother was reminding me, with the thought that perhaps it might be a companion for me. I felt a wild longing for my home again – the lawn with the pine trees around, and the dining-room table with the silver candle-sticks gleaming in the light – and I knew that I would never see it again. And I lay on the bed and howled, with my face in the pillow, nakedly, as I had not done for years.

On the 9th of April, ten days after my arrival in Bechuanaland, I got back to the hotel in the late afternoon – Oliver and I had driven aimlessly for hours – to a murmur of excitement in the lounge. As I entered, the room fell silent. I walked up to the proprietor and asked him what had happened.

'Dr Verwoerd has been shot,' he said.

'Was he killed?' I asked. I had often thought, when will it happen? And now that it had, it seemed weird and frightening, like headlines in the morning paper that flying saucers had landed.

'They haven't said so yet,' he said. 'Just shot.'

I went straight to my room, astonished by all the implications. I wondered whether the assassin had been an Indian, and I shuddered from the revenge that white South Africa would take. Then I went to the bar to hear the news bulletins, was startled and relieved to hear that Verwoerd had been shot by a white farmer at the Transvaal Agricultural Show, and drove at once to the Chiefs' hostel to tell Oliver. When I returned, the Afrikaner miner and his family, with their friends, were sitting in the hotel lounge. He got up and walked over to me. Slowly he said, 'If Dr Verwoerd dies, I'm telling you, we will beat you up till you can never stand on your legs again. That's all.' And he turned and walked back to his seat.

That night the District Commissioner told me casually that he had heard rumours of a plot to kidnap me and take me back across the border, but that there seemed very little in them, and that the administration was anyway on its guard. I stifled a desire to tell him just how little that reassured me, and thanked him instead. Somehow it didn't seem to matter any more. As I had discovered during those weeks of persecution by the Ku Klux Klan in Cape Town, fear can stretch only so far, and then it snaps. To hell, I thought, to hell with them all.

On the following day, Frene Ginwala, who was representing *Africa South* in East Africa, telephoned to tell me that there was a chance the Indian government would issue Oliver and myself with travel documents, while a letter from Rosalynde Ainslie arrived with news that the Ghana government was taking steps to provide us with passports. But the days dragged by, without more news, one burning empty sky after the other. I loathed Lobatsi. I felt that if I didn't leave at once, I would spend the rest of my life in that sullen town, besieged by the sun and the hot dust all around, with the only relief that short hot walk down the street to the railway-line and back.

When one night a reporter from a Johannesburg newspaper telephoned me for his regular questioning, I said that I was leaving. I would try and cross into Rhodesia. And if I was arrested there, and returned to South Africa? It needed no courage, I replied, to prefer prison in South Africa to an endless asylum in Bechuanaland. In South Africa, I would be home. The reporter was lavish in his thanks; he had a story from me at last.

Straight afterwards I sat alone at a table in the lounge, drinking one whisky after the other till I felt I would fall asleep without having to wade through another of those paper-backs by my bed.

The next morning, the telephone hardly stopped ringing. Was I really going to cross into Rhodesia? There were rumours that I had been offered travel documents. By Ghana? India? I said that I had no documents at all, but believed that one government or other might issue them to me. In any event, I doubted whether Sir Roy Welensky had the right in law to refuse me transit if I were bound for Britain. I was leaving one part of British territory for another, through what was still territory under the ultimate control of the British government.

I did not believe that Welensky could afford to seize us and then bundle us back into the arms of the South African government. I knew that he might arrest us, but I thought that even if he did, we would soon become politically so hot to hold that he would drop us over the frontier into Tanganyika. Certainly, whatever he did, he would have to do openly, since we were entering the Federation in the shrill glare of the press. There could be no furtive shove into the back of a car, no unaccountable reappearance in South Africa. I had discussed it over and over again with Oliver, and we had on balance agreed upon the risk. And so, on the following day, it must have been some three weeks after my arrival, we climbed into the Vauxhall just after dawn and drove along the red dust of Bechuanaland's main road, bouncing and sliding, to Francistown, some 55 miles from the Rhodesian border.

We arrived in the late afternoon, registered with the District Commissioner, and found accommodation once more in racial separation – Oliver with an African clergyman on the outskirts of the small town, I at the main hotel, whose proprietor turned out to have met my father many years before. The atmosphere seemed to me little different from Lobatsi, though its English accent was less adulterated, and I made up my mind to attempt the frontier the next day. After supper the hotel proprietor cornered me and, with growing bewilderment, questioned me on my politics. He had clearly supposed that my opinions were misrepresented by the press, since such provocation would have been most unsuitable for a son of my father. After an hour of exposition, he quietly remarked that I looked very much like the rest of my family, and courteously withdrew. I went to bed, and soon after breakfast picked up Oliver, and set off for Rhodesia.

We must have travelled halfway when a cloud of dust rushed from the distance towards us, giving out a long and anguished wail. In a moment a large American car had shot past and screamed to a stop somewhere behind. I slowed down and, when I saw my brother emerge from the other car, stopped altogether.

Thirteen years older than I, Cyril had seen little of me during my childhood, had joined the army at the outbreak of war, and then settled in Bulawayo, Southern Rhodesia, soon after the Nationalists had come to power in South Africa. A consistently successful businessman, with cautiously liberal views, he found my political opinions extravagant and my character exotic. On the occasions we had met since my return from America, we had disputed but never quarrelled, and our relationship, however strained, retained a strong sediment of feeling from the self-protective family attachment which we both possessed. I was much the more impatient and casual. Since the death of my father, Cyril had assumed an insatiable sense of responsibility for his family, and though I found it irritating myself, I knew

that many relatives, at varying stages of remove, had cause
enough to be thankful for it. Now he was exercising, required
or not, his sense of responsibility towards me. He had approached a friend of his in the Southern Rhodesian government, who had sounded Federal intentions and reported that no
guarantee was possible against my arrest. If I were found in the
Federation without proper papers, I would face the possibility
of deportation home on any request for my extradition from
the South African authorities. Cyril had accordingly set out to
warn me against barging my way into Rhodesia, and to suggest
that instead I settle in Francistown. He would find work for me
with a business associate of his in the territory and, after six
months, I would be entitled to apply for status as a permanent
resident and so acquire British papers. The prospect of six
months in Francistown flashed through my mind, and I blinked
with disbelief.

Cyril climbed into the Vauxhall, and there we sat, the three
of us, disputing, with Oliver and he in makeshift alliance
against my impetuousness. In the end it was Oliver who
decided, for although I was prepared to challenge Welensky's
attitude – I almost wanted to see what would happen if he
arrested us – I realized that I had no right to risk Oliver's use-
fulness as well. And so I agreed at last to return to Francistown
and reassess the situation there. A chance still existed that within the next few days we would be presented with papers by a
sympathetic government. If I lost patience, I could then cross
the border on my own, while Oliver remained behind if he
wished. I turned the car round and drove back into Francistown.
Cyril returned to Rhodesia and was met at the border by
journalists and a group of uncommonly vigilant officials, who
searched every inch of his car.

In Francistown too, staying with the inevitable Indian trading family, was Dr Yusuf Dadoo, former President of the South
African Indian Congress and one of the formidable figures in
the political struggle of the previous twenty years. Having
qualified in medicine at Edinburgh in 1936, he had returned to
South Africa and flung himself into progressive politics, head-

ing a rank and file rebellion against the moderate leadership of the Indian Congress Movement. In 1940 he had served four months' imprisonment with hard labour for having called upon non-whites not to join the South African armed forces, unless guaranteed equality with whites in salary and service. Then, participating in the 1946 Indian passive resistance campaign, he had suffered three separate terms of imprisonment, ranging from 3 to 6 months, and been fined as well for having incited African mine-workers to strike. In 1946 too, he had been elected at last President of the Transvaal Indian Congress, and this change in leadership had immediately resulted in the Xuma–Dadoo–Naicker Pact, which forged a front of common African–Indian resistance to white supremacy. In 1948 he had been elected President of the South African Indian Congress, and had held the office until 1952, when he had been banned under the Suppression of Communism Act, and forbidden to hold any executive position in the South African Indian Congress or any other of 40 specified progressive organizations.

On the night of March 29th, a friend had woken him to tell him that the police were poised for mass political arrests. He had driven out of Johannesburg some two hours before the police had swooped on his home, and had crossed the border into Bechuanaland. There, several days after Oliver and I had arrived, we had heard from him that he was staying with an Indian trader in Lobatsi. We had spent some time together, but he had found his own way to Francistown, having made up his mind against chancing the Rhodesian frontier with us. Oliver had, of course, worked much with him in the past. I had not. But I grew enormously fond of him in the hours of common escape we spent together. He seemed nothing like his reputation. I found him genial rather than sharp, neither rigid nor rancorous, gentle and jolly and shyly unascetic. I had expected, from what I knew of his career, someone thin, wiry, passionate, calculating. His almost chubby face, with the large pipe for ever hanging from it, astonished and then warmed me to a quick affection.

The night of my return to Francistown was among the most

gloomy I have ever spent. Alone in the bar of the hotel, I contemplated six months behind a counter while I waited for my Bechuanaland residence. I decided to wait for a few days, and then leave, whether I had papers or not. I kept pointlessly worrying about the next issue of the magazine, the contributors I might salvage from South Africa, the problems of publication abroad. Had my subscription lists been seized by the police? And if they had been, would the receipt books at least have been overlooked? They were at my flat, and the Special Branch had found its first visit there unrewarding. Oliver was safe in Bechuanaland, and with Yusuf there to help. The Afro-Asian states would sooner or later get him documents for his appearance at the United Nations. I could not expect to be included in any such international invitation. And I did not have the emotional control to remain much longer in Bechuanaland. My stay there seemed so irrelevant. In prison, I felt that at least I would be serving some purpose. The number and character of the imprisoned were in themselves challenges to the government. Abroad I would be participating in a campaign of ever more necessary propaganda. But every day in Bechuanaland was a dreary waste.

At ten o'clock that night I was called away from the bar by two members of the Bechuanaland administration. They had evidence of a plot to kidnap me, but insufficient to take what they regarded as suitable precautions. They therefore suggested that I accompany them to the administrative headquarters and spend the night there. I was their responsibility, one of them said with great earnestness, and they could not take risks with my safety. I told them that there had been similar plots in Lobatsi, but that nothing had ever come of them, and I asked them whether they had any special reason to take this one seriously. They replied that of course they could not be certain, but that they believed it to have been promoted by men of significant resources. I looked at them, and saw that they meant what they said. I was to give no alarm by leaving the hotel openly, they proposed. They would drive round the corner down a side-street and wait while I packed my case by torchlight. And, of course, they themselves would later explain to the proprietor. I smiled, at the thought of his surprise. What would my father have said? With my case silently deposited in the back of the car, we drove to the administrative offices and sat round a table in the otherwise dark and deserted building, talking – I seem to remember – of nothing more consequential than the climate.

Suddenly the telephone rang. It was Frene Ginwala from Salisbury. She had rung the office of the District Commissioner in the hope that someone would be there, even at night, and could tell her where to find me, and the call had been circuited through the switchboard to the room where I had taken my temporary refuge.

'The Indian government has issued you and Oliver and Yusuf with papers. A plane will be landing with them at six o'clock tomorrow morning in Palapye.'

'Good God, where's Palapye?'

'I don't know, somewhere in the middle. You should be able to get there tonight.'

'Why not Francistown?'

'The airstrip there is controlled by the Witwatersrand Native Labour Association, and they have refused any landing permission.'

'Who runs Bechuanaland?'

'They do, it seems, or parts of it.'

'Where's the plane coming from?'

'Salisbury.'

'I see.'

'It's a private aircraft and can only do a six-hundred-mile leap at a time. You will have to land in Blantyre.'

'Blantyre?'

'We don't know yet whether the Federal government will accept the Indian documents, but those I have spoken to seem to think that it's worth the try. From Blantyre you can reach Dar es Salaam in one flight. I'll be there to meet you.'

'I'll round up Oliver and Yusuf and we will leave at once.'

'Have you any photographs? You'll want one of each of you.'

'Oliver and I have, and Yusuf is sure to have brought one with him.'

'One thing more. Try and get to the strip early, so that you can clear it of any large stones. The pilot says that otherwise it may be difficult to land.'

'I'll put Yusuf to work.'

'I'll see you in Dar es Salaam.'

The two officials had already heard too much of the conversation for me to pretend any inconsequence. I told them the whole plan, and they seemed only too anxious to help in disembarrassing their jurisdiction of our presence. They thought I could get to Palapye within four hours of reasonable driving – it was about halfway southwards to Lobatsi – and offered to accompany me in collecting Yusuf and Oliver before seeing us all off the premises. If there was going to be any kidnapping, they transparently hoped that it would take place outside their district.

The drive to Palapye was terrifying, and I think that all three of us have seared in our memories, for years to come, its turns and twists and quick swaying stops. Half the cattle in Bechuanaland seemed to have sought the dormitory of the road by nightfall, and lay there, around corners and in hollows, staring up at the on-coming car with drowsy indifference. The headlights would suddenly catch the glint of their eyes, or the looming bulk of a body; I would jump on the brakes, and the car would slither to a stop in the deep dust, inches from their shapes. Then, stirred at last by the lights and the rage of my hooter, they would slowly rise, give a glare of disgust, and lumber lowing off the road. On one occasion I stopped the car so near to one large family that the mudguard touched the muzzle of a mountainous form, which stood stock still and abused me for several minutes. At last, turning its head away in sullen satisfaction, it walked several hundred yards down the road in front of us, with swinging behind, before swerving into the bush.

It was dawn when we arrived at Palapye, and I thought we would be able to find the airstrip at once. I did not expect a concrete terminal, with lines of lights and an entrance of advertising posters. But I supposed that there would be a simple signpost. After driving for more than an hour in vigorous circles, till my watch showed six o'clock, I drove right into the huddle of houses that constituted the town and up to the only garage. The proprietor must have noticed the number plate of the car and drawn uncomfortable conclusions, for his manner manifestly soured. He agreed to take storage of the car, which I said we would leave at the airstrip and which would later be collected by someone from South Africa, but his directions to the airstrip itself were indistinct and decorated with challenging suggestions that we contact the police. Oliver and Yusuf were dubious, but I saw myself driving day after day for the rest of my life in fruitless search of a vanished airstrip in the middle of the Bechuanaland bush, and I settled the argument by driving straight to the police station. An African policeman offered to show us the way, and we drove at last, with a carload of white officials close behind us, on to what he called the airstrip and what seemed to me just another stretch of ordinary, Bechuanaland earth. Wryly I told Oliver and Yusuf to start picking up the stones while I parked the car, and we had started off-loading the luggage when a thin mumble made us look up at the sky and the sudden speck of a plane.

Within a few minutes the pilot had landed, and we were settling ourselves inside the plane with furtive glances at the single propeller. We looked at each other and gulped. The pilot handed me an envelope with our Indian travel documents inside. They were not impressive. I recall mine as having read bleakly – THIS IS TO CERTIFY THAT RONALD MICHAEL SEGAL HAS EXPRESSED A WISH TO TRAVEL TO INDIA. WE SEE NO REASON TO DOUBT HIS STATEMENT. There was then space for a photograph, and beyond, the stamp of the Indian Trade Commissioner in Salisbury. We examined our new passports. They did not inspire confidence in us. And what they would do to the Federal authorities, didn't bear thinking about. Still, they were the only ones we had, and I felt a gush of gratitude to the Indian government for having provided us with them. Yusuf looked at me questioningly.

'Have we any glue?'

'For the photographs?'

'Yes.'

I asked the pilot, but the plane apparently had no use for glue.

'We will have to use pins,' I said.

'They aren't going to look very official,' Oliver suggested.

'They don't look very official now,' I replied.

Carefully we pinned our photographs to the documents and signed our names beneath. Then we buckled ourselves in, and told the pilot that we were ready. The plane taxied down the airstrip – I wondered very briefly about the stones – and then we rose into the sky. For the next few hours Yusuf and I plodded a concentrated route through some shabby months-old American magazines – I had resolutely steered Oliver to the front seat next to the pilot – while the plane every now and then plummeted and soared in sudden response to what the pilot consolingly called air currents. Every now and then I peeped through the window at the thick green growth far below, and speedily turned the back of my mind on the single engine. My brother Maurice, who had flown bombers during the war, had once told me that the two dangerous stages in a flight were the take-off and the landing. We had clearly taken off, I comforted myself, and the landing seemed infinitely distant. Then suddenly the pilot turned round to say that we were approaching the airport at Blantyre, and we all stiffened with foreboding. If Welensky intended to arrest us, his police would be gathered on the tarmac. None of us supposed that the Rhodesian government could conceivably be unaware of the passengers whom the chartered plane was carrying.

We were right. An impressive portion of Nyasaland's police were at the airport. But they apparently constituted an exhibit, for we were ushered straight through to immigration and customs. The Chief Immigration Officer regarded our documents with distaste.

"Why are the photographs pinned on?' he asked.

I stared at him.

'Perhaps,' I said, 'the Indian government issues them that way. This is how we received them.'

'It's very unusual.'

'I don't doubt it,' I replied.

He looked at me appraisingly, and then said:

'We will have to keep them, of course, and I will get in touch with you.'

'Thank you.'

As we left customs, we were approached and warmly welcomed by Philip Howard, Managing Director of the London and Blantyre Company, the Nyasaland branch of Booker Brothers. He invited us to his home for lunch and proposed that we spend the night with him, and then continue our journey early on the following morning. We happily agreed and followed him outside to his car, where his lovely Anglo-Indian wife was waiting. With an easy charm, she chatted us out of our tension, till we began to ply her and her husband with questions about Nyasaland. Their house was some distance from Blantyre, in a great profusion of green, billowing around to the limits of the sky. After lunch we went to our rooms and slept, to be woken for a light afternoon tea on the porch, with the green slowly deepening in the disappearing light. Suddenly the telephone rang. Philip Howard went to answer it and returned a few moments later.

'It's for you,' he said to me. 'The Immigration Office.'

We looked at each other without a word, and trooped into the hall.

'Yes? Ronald Segal here.'

'Mr Segal, this is the Immigration Office. I am afraid that your papers are not in order. We have checked with Salisbury.'

This is it, I thought, and my face must have shown it, for I saw the reflection of my quick fear in the faces around me. I tightened my voice.

'Then you had better check with Salisbury again. The papers were issued by the Indian government. And any complaint that you have about them, you should make to India's accredited representative in Salisbury. It is a matter for the Indian and Federal governments to sort out, not for us.'

His voice took on a cautious note.

'We are in constant touch with Salisbury. I just thought that you would want to be kept informed.'

Not so easily, I thought.

'Am I to understand then that we are all of us under arrest? Because if we are, I feel that the press should be kept informed of it as well.'

'No, no,' he said emphatically. 'There is no question of that. It's just that we cannot return your documents until we are satisfied with them.' He paused. 'I am afraid that you cannot leave with them.'

I saw a line of light under the door.

'I see. Does that mean that we cannot leave without them?'

'We cannot stop you,' he said. 'If you wish to leave without them, that's your business.'

'Thank you. We will be at the airport tomorrow morning at half past six. And you can stop us from going only by arresting us.'

I was later to learn that during that same day in Blantyre the South African government had applied to the Chief Magistrate for our immediate extradition, on the grounds that we had committed a criminal offence in terms of South African law by leaving the country without passports. The Chief Magistrate had ruled against the application on a delicate technicality. We had not reached Nyasaland from South Africa, but from Bechuanaland, and it was not an offence to leave Bechuanaland without a passport.

That night a group of young Nyasaland politicians, including Aleke Banda, Secretary-General of the Malawi Congress Party, together with three clergymen, one of them a Church of Scotland missionary with strong radical attachments, gathered at the Howard house. Dr Hastings Banda had been released from prison in Southern Rhodesia at the beginning of the month, and the Malawi nationalists were in a state of anxious elation. The British government had clearly retreated from its policy of repression. No one, of course, was prepared to predict the immediate prospects. Yet underneath the uncertainty was the confidence that Nyasaland would emerge, soon, from the control of Salisbury into independence. The timing of federal dissolution was disputed; the inevitability was now admitted, and enjoyed.

By arrangement with the pilot, we reached the airport at six o'clock and ate our breakfast next door to a table of alert if cheerful members of the local security police, with whom Philip Howard appeared to be on terms of bantering acquaintance. At last the pilot came to tell us that he was ready, and we walked on to the tarmac and climbed into the plane. As we strapped ourselves into our seats, the seconds seemed to separate into infinitely slow poundings of the heart. Then we taxied down the runway and were airborne. Barely an hour later the pilot turned round and smiled.

'We are in Tanganyika now.'

I looked at Oliver, and we shook hands. And then all at once I felt it, the sense of irretrievable retreat.

My exile had begun.

CHAPTER EIGHT

A VIEW BEYOND

THAT white supremacy, the subjugation of twelve million people by three million in South Africa, can survive indefinitely, few if any sane people believe. Even the leaders of the Nationalist Party, with the cataracts of power coating their eyes, sense the possibilities of defeat and prepare only for postponement. They do not belittle the force at their disposal. And they, better than anyone else, have measured their readiness to use it. They have a powerful army and air force, and they can rely absolutely on the allegiance of both to their common colour. Almost the entire white population would, in a crisis, rally round them. They are substantially increasing their military strength; the 1962 budget more than doubled the defence apportionment, to £60,000,000, a higher figure than that reached by South Africa in any year of the second world war. They know that they could defeat an invasion even by the combined forces of the independent African states, and they know that the independent Africa states are very far from combining. They recognize the dangers of internal disorder, but they and their predecessors have coped with such unrest since the races first encountered each other in the country. They know that they can still riots or shatter strikes with sufficient ruthlessness. The carefully segregated pattern of racial residence enables them to limit non-white disorders to the non-white areas, which can, when necessary, be bombed into submission. The millions of non-white workers live so close to starvation already that they cannot survive a withdrawal of wages for more than a short time. And the whites are sufficiently numerous to keep emergency services alive for themselves, even if – and this is itself improbable – every non-white in the country went on strike.

Mass civil disobedience could seriously embarrass the Nationalists only if they admitted any limits to their own reaction. The 1952–3 defiance campaign, jointly run by the African National Congress and South African Indian Congress, collapsed after some 8,000 arrests and the passing of the Criminal Laws Amendment Act, which made the breaking of a law as a political protest punishable by flogging and years of imprisonment. The 1962 General Law Amendment or 'Sabotage' Act indefinitely expands the legal interpretation of civil disobedience, provides for the death penalty and a minimum sentence of five years' imprisonment, and shifts the onus of proof from the prosecution to the accused.

21 (1) Subject to the provisions of sub-section (2), any person who commits any wrongful and wilful act whereby he injures, damages, destroys, renders useless or unserviceable, puts out of action, obstructs, tampers with, pollutes, contaminates or endangers

    (*a*) the health or safety of the public;

    (*b*) the maintenance of law and order;

    (*c*) any water supply;

    (*d*) the supply or distribution at any place of light, power, fuel, foodstuffs or water, or of sanitary, medical or fire extinguishing services;

    (*e*) any postal, telephone or telegraph services or installations, or radio transmitting, broadcasting or receiving services or installations;

    (*f*) the free movement of any traffic on land, at sea or in the air;

    (*g*) any property, whether movable or immovable, of any other person or of the State;

or who attempts to commit, or conspires with any other person to aid or procure the commission of or to commit, or incites, instigates, commands, aids, advises, encourages or procures any other person to commit, any such act, or who in contravention of any law possesses any explosives, fire-arm or weapon or enters or is upon any land or building or part of a building, shall be guilty of the offence of sabotage and liable on conviction to the penalties provided for by law for the offence of treason: Provided that, except where the death penalty is imposed, the imposition of a sentence of imprisonment for a period of not less than five years shall be compulsory, whether or not any other penalty is also imposed.

(2) No person shall be convicted of an offence under sub-section (1) if he proves that the commission of the alleged offence, objectively regarded, was not calculated and that such offence was not committed with intent to produce any of the following effects, namely

- (*a*) to cause or promote general dislocation, disturbance or disorder:
- (*b*) to cripple or seriously prejudice any industry or undertaking or industries or undertakings generally or the production or distribution of commodities or food-stuffs at any place:
- (*c*) to seriously hamper or to deter any person from assisting in the maintenance of law and order:
- (*d*) to cause, encourage or further an insurrection or forcible resistance to the Government:
- (*e*) to further or encourage the achievement of any political aim, including the bringing about of any social or economic change in the Republic:
- (*f*) to cause serious bodily injury to or seriously endanger the safety of any person:
- (*g*) to cause substantial financial loss to any person or to the State:
- (*h*) to cause, encourage or further feelings of hostility between different sections of the population of the Republic:
- (*i*) to seriously interrupt the supply or distribution at any place of light, power, fuel or water, or of sanitary, medical or fire extinguishing services:
- (*j*) to embarrass the administration of the affairs of the State.

A government which sharpens such blades is unlikely to let them rust when they are needed. And it is difficult to imagine large numbers of people effectively challenging the edges, even if they supposed that they would encounter no more summary an execution. The likelihood, however, is that any real defiance of the government's authority would be answered on the spot. Sixty-eight were killed and over two hundred wounded for peaceably protesting against the pass laws at Sharpeville on March 21st, 1960. Is there any reason to suppose that a government which killed sixty-eight at such little provocation, would stop, were its existence seriously threatened, at sixty-eight hundred, or sixty-eight thousand? Is it conceivable that any civil disobedience campaign would survive such slaughter?

For South Africa's 1,300,000 English-speaking whites, the world beyond signals an ultimate asylum. Equipped with their commercial experience, and the transferable capital of their language, they would be welcome enough in Britain, Canada, Australia or New Zealand. They have remained fundamentally a European people. But South Africa's 1,700,000 Afrikaners are different. They are essentially of Africa, their outlook, ideas and responses shaped by three hundred years of contact with the crags and plains, the hot clear skies and wandering horizons of the continent. Their language, religion and customs, like the Voortrekker fancy dress that they wear at their tribal festivals, distinguishes them, ludicrously and tragically, from the white world of the Midlands, the Canadian prairie or the Australian sheep-run. With them into the factories and mines and shops of the cities that they still see as foreign, they carry the traditions of a frontierless pastoral society, in constant migration from restraint, with survival the prize of perpetual war against the finally unvanquishable blacks. They believe that defeat must mean more than the surrender of privilege. It must mean their submergence by black Africa, or an anguished dispersion among the strange nations of men. Like the Jews, they intend to survive, but through the land rather than the law. A portion of Africa is theirs, by struggle, by possession, by achievement, and by love.

True, there are exceptions, who see survival in a shared South Africa. But they are more articulate than numerous. Even those – certainly many, perhaps most – who are careless of their culture and religion, who have lost in the cities even their sense of the land, have retained their sense of themselves as a lonely threatened people, relying on their own strength to secure them from the surge of colour everywhere around. For them, there is no flight. Where would they go? Who would accept, without requiring to absorb them? There is only victory or defeat. Such a people will surrender – they surrendered in the Boer War – but only once they have been beaten, inescapably, so that surrender is the sole alternative to suicide. It would be lunacy to expect them to retreat from their fastnesses of power before they are forced, or to refrain from using such force themselves as seems likely to secure their place. Their whole history proclaims a different pattern. There may be many who will wish to withdraw early from the struggle, as there were many – now despised – who surrendered in the early stages of the Boer War. But the extremists will retain the initiative – as they have done throughout the fluctuating advance of Afrikanerdom – and it is they who will fight their way to decisive defeat.

All resistance will be crushed, with a growing abandonment of scruples, while resistance itself is forced to take ever more costly forms. Those who promote passive resistance might do well to consider what the consequences would have been in Nazi-occupied Europe. Those who proclaim the power of a general strike might do worse than ask themselves how the Nazis would have reacted to any wide-scale industrial stoppage. And what, after all, makes South Africa so different? Except that the armies of intervention are not preparing for invasion, or a liberating air force flying overhead? True, the South African government has not shown itself as brutal, even to the blacks, as Nazism did to its captive peoples during the war. But has it been as seriously threatened? Have we any reason to suppose that a desperate Afrikanerdom would reveal more pressing moral qualms than the Nazism which South Africa's present Prime Minister and Minister of Justice both so passionately admired?

In any event, a significant section of the non-white resistance movement in South Africa has clearly come to the conclusion that violence alone is likely to achieve more than the pacific protests which bear similar penalties. On December 16th, 1961, the annual celebration of Afrikanerdom's victory over the Zulus in 1838 at the Battle of Blood River, four explosions in Johannesburg and five in Port Elizabeth heralded a new kind of struggle between the apostles and the antagonists of white supremacy.

Terrorism in South Africa would provide only emotional rewards. The bomb in the crowded café, the knife in the night, might exalt for a moment those to whom violence had become a sensation rather than an instrument. But it would do little damage to authority. Indeed, if Algeria is any parallel, it would simply stiffen reaction. Besides, violence must be considered an evil, even – or especially – by those who are at last compelled to employ it. It is wrong to kill another – for those who believe in God, because God has said so, for those who do not, because life itself is an irreplaceable value. Yet it is surely less wrong to shoot a homicidal maniac, if that seems the only way of arresting his activities, than to permit him the freedom of killing whomever he pleases. The morality of violence consists, accordingly, in limiting the cost of life to the effective minimum. Were it possible to produce a campaign of violence against property which would achieve the same objectives as a campaign of violence against people, the campaign against property would clearly be preferable.

Some such considerations were surely in the minds of those who resolved upon violence at all in resisting white supremacy. A highly developed and complex industrial society, South Africa is vulnerable, as few others, to the disruption of transport and the destruction of machinery. Between its two largest cities, Johannesburg and Cape Town, run 950 miles of railway track, across single bridges and vast stretches of barren deserted earth. Between the industrial core of the country in the Southern Transvaal and the nearest port of Durban, run some 450 miles of railway line. The unsuitability of the terrain for effective guerrilla warfare is its very suitability for industrial sabotage. It is difficult, accordingly, to believe that any campaign of violence will not be directed at industrial installations in the urban areas and along the lines of communication between them. It is equally difficult to believe that the South African government will not exact, for every act of effective sabotage, a terrible revenge. The present leaders of South African resistance, violent and non-violent alike, are already too well known to the government, to be of any long use. At them, inevitably, the government will fire the first shots. But, sooner or later, new leaders will arise in their stead, whose presence alone is discovered. And surrounded by such faceless antagonists, the government would soon enough be driven to the hostage form of retribution, the seizure of those, innocent themselves, whose lives would be forfeit at any further act of violence. Yet this would accomplish no more than it did in Algeria. Rather would it rally around the apostles of violence the same solidarity of suffering which resulted from the sweep of Algiers by the French paratroops in early 1957.

Short of international intervention, therefore, the prospect before South Africa is that of a constant internal haemorrhaging, ending only with the end of all civilized society. Those who cannot conceive of so massive a horror trust to the resignation of either black or white. And it is true that a people, prostrated by suffering and desperate of help, will often endure any humiliation for relief. Yet Afrikanerdom sees submission as a racial death, and it will struggle till struggle itself is no longer possible. And the Africans will not submit while Africa around them is free and the hope of help can survive.

Certainly, international action is improbable while the authority of the South African government remains unchallenged. As violence mounts, however, and the subjection of the non-white majority grows ever more savage, so the demands for intervention by the United Nations will increase throughout independent Africa. Such demands, the West is likely, with the most polite evasions, to resist. Not only is its own vast financial stake in South Africa safe and profitable enough under white supremacy – and who can assure the amenability of succession? – but the costs of intervention would be huge. Huge costs have, of course, been met before, but only in pursuit of a full-scale cold war campaign. Indeed, it would be surprising if the Soviet Union and the People's Republic of China did not recognize this as well.

One of the mysteries of post-war Soviet policy has been its silence over South Africa. As a consequence either of sheer political ineptitude, or a deferentially capitalist attitude to commerce, the Soviet Union has traded with South Africa in genial indifference to the character of the regime which its purchases have inevitably enriched. It has even surrendered disposal of its diamonds to the Diamond Corporation, controlled by Harry Oppenheimer and his South African company, De Beers. Associated communist states, like Czechoslovakia and East Germany, have dispatched special missions to promote trade with South Africa. Even the People's Republic of China, its revolutionary fervour less tempered by affluence than the Soviet Union's, buys millions of pounds worth of wool and maize each year from South Africa, and without the excuse of selling in return anything like the same worth of its own products. For its imports it pays almost entirely in cash, and so swells the resources with which white supremacy buys its Saracen armoured cars, its Sten-guns, its jets and its rockets.

South Africa is rich and getting richer. The *Sunday Times*, with other newspapers, published on June 3rd, 1962 an advertisement by the South African government. Entitled 'At the end of the first year ... ', it gave a singularly selective account of South Africa's first year as a republic outside the Commonwealth. Its statistics, however, were based less on fantasy than its political assessments.

'Apart from gold, exports increased by £32 million – or 7% – last year to £474 million. At present they are running at even higher levels. And gold production, which finances half the country's imports, reached the new record of £288 million. There is a surplus on current account of more than £100 million. Foreign exchange reserves have been nearly trebled in rather less than a year. The national income increased by more than 5%.'

An advertisement in the *Financial Times* of July 9th tabulated the economic accomplishments of Nationalist rule in South Africa.

	1949	1954	1960
Net National Income	£830,400,000	£1,405,000,000	£2,017,400,000
Value of Mineral Output	£151,386,000	£228,284,000	£414,650,000
Value of Agricultural Output	£184,042,000	£340,593,000	£389,536,000
Value of Manufacturing Output	£674,551,426	£1,229,753,000	£1,700,000,000
Foreign Trade: Imports	£313,100,000	£439,000,000	£555,500,000
Exports (inc. gold)	£266,600,000	£488,000,000	£724,500,000

These figures, of course, reflect a fixed price of $35 for an ounce of gold. Any rise in this dollar price, to $70 or even, as some newspapers speculate or propose, $100 an ounce, would provide South Africa with an unprecedented international subsidy for repression. The weakness of the dollar in the currency markets of Western Europe, the persistent loss of gold by the United States, and the growing portents of an economic recession in the West have given rise to increasing discussion on the necessity for raising the dollar price of gold. During 1962, South African gold shares have raced upward, with only brief pauses for breath, on the stock exchanges of the main Western capitals. Influential British newspapers – some of them with a record of unequivocal hostility towards the South African government – have demanded a rise in the price of gold to avert the spectre of a slump throughout the West, while providing the international liquidity for a vast increase in trade and a significant programme of aid to the underdeveloped states.

The moral argument is dismissed as irrelevant. The United States will raise the price of gold if economic circumstances demand it. That South Africa, as the world's largest gold producer, will be the principal beneficiary must be accounted a

distasteful but unavoidable side-effect. Indeed, it hardly matters. A rise in the price of gold would enormously swell the
resources of the South African government. But the resources
are, after all, adequate already. Whether the price of gold is
raised or not, the South African government will effectively be
able to contain the discontent of its non-white subjects.

The conclusion is inescapable. The South African government, left to itself, can pursue its frenzied career without fore-
seeable possibility of interruption. Yet few believe that white
supremacy can last for long. For few, least of all the governors
of the country, believe that South Africa will long be left to itself. Apartheid is a singular affront to the vast majority of the
world's population. Even the most conservative of Afro-Asian
leaders, with a rigid distrust of change, regard the policy of the
South African government as a personal insult, requiring a
rapid retribution. In Africa itself it is seen, by president and
populace alike, as a continental challenge which must successfully be answered if black dignity and independence are to be
secured.

Soon after my flight from South Africa, I was invited by Dr
Nkrumah to visit Accra and consult with members of his
government there. I was provided with voluptuous accommodation at the Ambassador Hotel and was waiting in the
lobby for collection by an official one morning when I caught
sight of a gorgeous gold-and-green kente cloth on display at a
souvenir kiosk. Behind the counter was a young and wide-
smiling Ghanaian girl, and we were soon in friendly dispute
over the price of the cloth. 'Where do you come from?' she
genially asked me. 'South Africa,' I said with a grin, assuming
that she would at once remember my photograph on the front
pages of the Ghanaian papers. 'You are shooting my people,'
she hissed at me. 'I'm not, you know,' I answered weakly. 'You
are killing my brothers and my sisters,' she cried, her voice
rising. I felt a hand on my shoulder, and jumped. It was the
government official appointed to collect me. 'Please explain to
this woman,' I almost whispered to him, 'that I am not shooting down her people.' He laughed hugely – he spent the rest of

the morning in inadequate attempts at polite self-control – and explained.

Both East and West may want to shelve the South African problem for motives of strategy or trade. But Africa will not let them. Indeed, for the world beyond, the distresses and allurements of apartheid are likely to lie more in the effects that the policy has on the rest of Africa than on South Africa itself. The governments of many independent African states have discovered that their electorates will not permit them to be prudent or casual in their attitude towards South Africa. And it is not inconceivable that, despite the almost certain failure of the attempt, such governments might under popular pressure be forced into mounting a military attack. The consequences of any defeat would rock them, and the political structures which engendered them, to their foundations. It is not enough to reply that this prospect would effectively inhibit action by such governments. A series of Sharpevilles in South Africa, set off perhaps by an act of spectacular sabotage, would inflame the whole continent to a degree where the rulers of no African state would be able easily to withstand the demands for intervention.

Of course, the African governments would first appeal for international action through the United Nations. But such an appeal might not receive the necessary support if it were directed solely at the liberation of South Africa's own subjugated non-white peoples. For it would raise distressing issues of interference in the affairs of an independent state.

This argument, of course, has little, if any, moral validity. There must be some limit to the authority exercised by any government over its subjects. As I wrote in an editorial for *Africa South in Exile*: 'Let us suppose that there exists a small republic somewhere in the Pacific, ruled by a religious fanatic and his followers. Let us suppose too that the ruler's peculiar fanaticism pivots upon the evils of this world and requires national salvation in the purity of death. Suppose then that, supported by his well-armed converts, he sets out assiduously to transport his subjects to heaven, by slaughtering them all.

Are we to accept that this is a "domestic affair"? Is the world idly to watch the final murder, before intervening to the extent of repeopling the cemetery? Let us suppose that the population of the republic does not share the fanaticism of its rulers, that it struggles with sticks against Sten guns to survive and so only accelerates the approach of its end. Suppose too that it cries out for help in order to survive, that it appeals to the United Nations, over the heads of its own legal government. Are the great powers to quote the Charter at each other, or threaten counter measures to any unilateral intervention, while the slaughter proceeds?'

Yet, international conduct, as every newspaper proclaims, is but distantly related to morality. And few governments in the unaligned world, let alone in the West or the East, are likely to watch, without some stirrings of disquiet, the setting of so troublesome a precedent. South Africa may possess the ugliest political organization in the world; but there are many ugly ones. A stage may well be reached in the repression of non-white resistance by the South African government which would compel even the risk of such a precedent. It is far more probable, however, that support for intervention would gather around the status of South West Africa.

For the status of South West Africa is everyone's concern. South Africa continues to control the international trust territory, in blatant disregard of all the objects for which it was first presented with the mandate, and in defiance of all United Nations demands for supervision. With its white settlers alone represented in the South African parliament, and its indigenous peoples governed directly by South Africa's Minister of Bantu Administration, South West Africa is less a mandate than an occupied country. And South Africa's continued administration, by gun and armoured car, or its overwhelmingly hostile African majority, may be held to constitute the aggression of one state against another, and so an open threat to world peace. A two-thirds majority of the United Nations General Assembly may very well coalesce around such a contention and produce an ultimatum to the South African government – either to yield South West Africa to international administration, or invite intervention.

It is improbable, of course, that the South African government would ever agree to retreat from its control over the territory. It recognizes, not unreasonably, that an independent South West Africa on its borders would soon enough endanger its domestic authority. Much of its strength lies precisely in the protection of its borders by societies practising a similar pattern of racial rule. Its refusal to risk its own security by withdrawing from South West would accordingly make sanctions unavoidable.

South Africa, it cannot too often be repeated, is a highly industrialized society dependent upon intensive mechanization. And for the survival of such a society, a constant supply of oil is imperative. Without it, communications, factories, and – of particular significance to South Africa – the mechanized instruments of defence, armoured cars and aeroplanes, would rust in their tracks. In 1960, South Africa imported 1,503,000 metric tons of crude oil and 3,670,000 metric tons of refined oil from abroad, most of it from Iran. For its own natural oil production is insignificant. It has developed an oil-from-coal extraction plant at Sasolburg in the Orange Free State, but this at present produces only 140,000 tons of petrol a year, and though it is expected to double its output by 1968, this would still constitute merely one sixth of the Republic's current annual demand for petrol, and less than 8% of its refined oil requirements. South Africa at present has facilities for storing only six or seven weeks' supply of oil, and though this figure may be raised under pressure of any embargo, nothing but a small increase seems probable. Such international action, combined with the internal upheaval which would accompany it, might well lead to the swift collapse of all government. It would, however, require the most detailed organization, to ensure that oil for South Africa was not illicitly channelled through Portuguese African ports or shipped into South Africa itself, with the connivance of the international oil companies, by South African or free-lance freighters. Inevitably, such an embargo would entail a close watch on South African and neighbouring ports, and this might soon enough lead to armed collision between South Africa and any supervisory forces of the United Nations.

A general embargo on all trade with South Africa would, of course, do the job of an oil embargo more rapidly and efficiently, especially if food-stuffs were included. Yet such an embargo would prove more prolonged and probably more costly of human life than armed intervention, which might shatter South African intransigence in a matter of days. But in order to escape the risk of fiasco, such action would have to be massive in extent, a more than manifest match for the forces of the South African government. It is improbable that anything short of a Korea-type intervention, with some if not all of the great powers operating under United Nations auspices, would succeed.

It is, of course, one thing for the General Assembly of the United Nations to institute action, and another for any of the dissenting member states to co-operate in implementing such a decision. The protracted crisis in the Congo Republic over the secession of Katanga has emphasized how ineffectual United Nations action can be when undermined by one of the great powers. And Britain's moral inhibitions against the use of force would doubtless be multiplied by the degree to which its investments in South Africa exceed those in the Congo. Any U.N. programme of economic sanctions or armed intervention against South Africa could in safety be ignored by the South African government unless all the great powers were prepared, at the very least, to connive at its performance. It is at this point, however, that the survival of the United Nations and the liberation of South West Africa from South African control might become inextricable. The League of Nations was killed, perhaps more than anything else, by the failure of sanctions against Italy over the invasion of Abyssinia. It seems doubtful that the United Nations Organization would survive – or be much worth preserving – if a massive attempt, by the overwhelming bulk of its members, to uphold its authority against a minor state like South Africa, were to be turned, through the efforts of one or more of the great powers, into fiasco.

This sort of speculation slights, of course, the mounting pressures of the cold war. True, the Soviet Union and the People's Republic of China seem to have ignored the political embarrassments of white South Africa in the past. But it would be surprising if they continued much longer to do so. They would lose little by cutting all trade with South Africa; the West would lose much if forced to follow their example. And far less slow and insidious courses may recommend themselves. For they must know that the West could never afford openly to assist the South African government in maintaining its authority.

I once asked a Scandinavian Prime Minister, during a discussion on South Africa, what he thought would happen if the Soviet government suddenly announced: 'We are losing patience with the cruelties of South Africa's rulers. And when we complain at the United Nations and call for action against them, the West approves and protects them. The suffering peoples of South Africa have appealed to the outside world for help. We offer it now. The criminal clique that controls South Africa must withdraw, or we will take such measures as are fit to force it to do so. We do not wish to govern South Africa ourselves. Why should we? We propose that a committee of African states should administer it, till its people themselves have freely chosen a government of their own.'

The Prime Minister looked at me with surprise. 'I'm sure they wouldn't,' he said. 'And if they tried, the United Nations, of course, would have to act before they did.' 'So in the end, it seems, the Africans must wait for a Soviet initiative?' I asked. 'What would you have us do?' he replied. 'The United Nations is no more than its member states. And if the great powers will not collaborate in sanctions, what will it serve the General Assembly to decide? I remember the League.' And he sighed. 'None of us can afford to send the United Nations the same way.'[1]

---

[1] This section was written several weeks before the General Assembly of the United Nations, on November the 6th, 1962, requested member governments, by a two-thirds majority, to take collective measures

In a crowded London street, I will see a coloured handkerchief wrapped round a head, or smell a pile of oranges on a
barrow, and my blood will bound. I do not know what will
happen in South Africa. For me and others in exile from themselves, what will happen must be felt immediately. We know
how the bushes clamber down to the beach, how the pine trees
gather in the dusk, how the bleached earth cracks in the Karroo
beneath the hot flat sky. South Africa remains our country,
whatever passports we carry, and wherever we live, we remain
– grudgingly or gladly, always helplessly – with its people. Yet
it is also everyone else's country and people. Can anyone, anywhere, any more separate himself?

---

against South Africa in an effort to persuade its government to abandon
apartheid. The resolution specifically recommended the rupture of all
diplomatic relations with South Africa, the closing of ports to all South
African ships, the refusal of landing and passage facilities to South
African aircraft, the enacting of legislation by individual states to ban
their ships from entry to South African ports, the boycott of all South
African goods, and an end to the export of goods, including all arms and
ammunition, to South Africa. If such sanctions failed, the General
Assembly recommended that the Security Council should take appropriate
measures, including, if necessary, the expulsion of South Africa from the
United Nations.

Voting for the resolution were 67 member states, comprising almost
the whole Afro-Asian bloc and the communist states. The Scandinavian,
and most of the Latin American, countries were among the 23 that
abstained. The 16 member states that voted against the resolution were
Australia, Britain, Belgium, Canada, France, Greece, Ireland, Japan,
Luxembourg, the Netherlands, New Zealand, Portugal, South Africa,
Spain, Turkey, and the United States. Four states were absent – the Central
African Republic, Ecuador, Gabon, and Paraguay.

Immediately after the vote, a British spokesman stated that, although
Britain abhorred apartheid like other member states, it could not comply
with the request to take sanctions against South Africa.